Monographien und Texte zur Nietzsche-Forschung

Monographien und Texte zur Nietzsche-Forschung

Herausgegeben von

Mazzino Montinari · Wolfgang Müller-Lauter
Heinz Wenzel

Band 4

1977

Walter de Gruyter · Berlin · New York

Nietzsche's
Theory of Knowledge

by

Ruediger Hermann Grimm

1977

Walter de Gruyter · Berlin · New York

Anschriften der Herausgeber:

Prof. Dr. Mazzino Montinari
via d'Annunzio 237, I-50135 Florenz

Prof. Dr. Wolfgang Müller-Lauter
Adolf-Martens-Straße 11, D-1000 Berlin 45

Prof. Dr. Heinz Wenzel
Harnackstraße 16, D-1000 Berlin 33

Library of Congress Cataloging in Publication Data

Grimm, Ruediger Hermann, 1947—
Nietzsche's theory of knowledge.
(Monographien und Texte zur Nietzsche-Forschung ; Band 4)
Bibliography: p.
Includes indexes.
1. Nietzsche, Friedrich Wilhelm, 1844-1900--
Knowledge, Theory of. I. Title. II. Series.
B3318.K7G74 121 76-51294
ISBN 3-11-006568-1

CIP-Kurztitelaufnahme der Deutschen Bibliothek

Grimm , Ruediger Hermann
Nietzsche's theory of knowledge. — Berlin, New York : de Gruy-
ter, 1977.
(Monographien und Texte zur Nietzsche-Forschung ; Band 4)
ISBN 3-11-006568-1

©

ACKNOWLEDGEMENTS

The author wishes to acknowledge his indebtedness to Le Moyne College, for a generous financial grant which was instrumental in the publication of this work; to The Bodley Head, for permission to quote from Erich Heller, *The Disinherited Mind*; to the Hutchinson Publishing Group Ltd., for permission to quote from H. W. Walsh, *Metaphysics*; to Princeton University Press, for permission to quote from *The Collected Works of C. G. Jung*, Bollingen Series xx; to W. H. Freeman and Company, for permission to quote from Robert Ornstein, *The Psychology of Consciousness* (copyright 1972 by W. H. Freeman and Co.); to Macmillan Publishing Co., Inc., for permission to quote from Arthur Danto, *Nietzsche as Philosopher* (copyright 1965 by Macmillan Publishing Co., Inc.). If the author has incurred debts other than these in writing this book, he is unaware of them.

PREFACE

If one were to choose that modern thinker who has been more misunderstood and maligned than any other, I have little doubt that a consensus of opinion would award that dubious honor to Friedrich Nietzsche. The name of Nietzsche has for years elicited a stream of invective from devout Christians (to name but one group), for whom Nietzsche took great pains to be as offensive as possible. I well remember my pious Bavarian grandfather muttering anathemas when that name was uttered by the careless student who was his grandson. And this is by no means simply the result of an innocent misunderstanding, for Nietzsche himself invited such abuse by his incendiary language and often lurid examples. Even in the intellectual world, the name of Nietzsche very often divides a group of scholars very neatly into two camps: those who make Nietzsche their patron antisaint and ape his healthy contempt for all that is mediocre (meaning anything which they happen to dislike),[1] or those who make Nietzsche their whipping boy for all the cultural ills of the modern world[2].

Unfortunately, Nietzsche has probably suffered more at the hands of his admirers than of his detractors. There is no shortage of learned works on Nietzsche's provocative and incendiary moral philosophy, his vicious attack on Christianity, his vague but intoxicating ideal of the *Übermensch*, and a never-ending flood of articles on what precisely Nietzsche might have meant by the "eternal recurrence of the same". On the other hand, there is a conspicuous lack of scholarship (particularly in English) which penetrates beneath the mask of Nietzsche's flamboyant and deliberately offensive examples, and seeks to come to grips with the philosophical substructure which supports these examples, and of which they are illustrations. Even an otherwise commendable work such as Arthur Danto's *Nietzsche as Philosopher* is symptomatic of this, because by its very title, this book suggests that there is something novel about regarding Nietzsche as a philosopher[3].

---

[1] E. g. H. L. Mencken, *The Philosophy of Friedrich Nietzsche* (Port Washington, N.Y., 1967).
[2] E. g. Frederick Copleston, S. J., *Friedrich Nietzsche, Philosopher of Culture* (London, 1942); Crane Brinton, *Nietzsche* (New York, 1965); Paul Elmer More, *Nietzsche* (Boston, 1912).
[3] Arthur C. Danto, *Nietzsche as Philosopher* (New York, 1965).

The often-treated themes of morality, *Übermensch*, the eternal recurrence, etc. are conspicuous in this work only by their absence. Themes such as these are, to be sure, important aspects of Nietzsche's thinking, and a full understanding of Nietzsche's work presupposes more than a casual acquaintance with them. Nevertheless, they are symptoms and illustrations which arise out of a much more profound philosophical problematic than most commentators have suspected exists in Nietzsche's writings. This work is therefore not concerned with Nietzsche's views on religion, morality, politics, women, etc. but with those profound depths to which his philosophical insight penetrated.

More specifically, we shall be concerned with Nietzsche's principle of the will to power as an epistemological paradigm, as a way of knowing. It might strike some readers as mildly incredible that Nietzsche incorporated in his writings anything as staid and proper as an ontology or an epistemology. This is but another instance of that prevalent unwillingness to take Nietzsche seriously, to regard him as a profound thinker in his own right, and to come to grips with that profound and enormously fruitful principle which forms the backbone of Nietzsche's thinking: the will to power. Without a grasp of how the will to power functions as a world-principle and without understanding that a remarkably original theory of knowledge is implicit within this principle one can at best only partially understand those more notorious of Nietzsche's utterances.

There has been practically no work done in the area of Nietzsche's theory of knowledge. Obviously, this is a critical area for the adequate understanding of any philosopher, and the lack of such research with regard to Nietzsche has led, I feel, to serious misunderstandings of how such notions as the *Übermensch*, the critique of Christianity, the "eternal recurrence", etc. are to be understood within the whole of his work. Thus, it is partially for therapeutic reasons that I have undertaken a work of this nature, to provide that context within which these notions acquire their authentic meaning and intent.

A term such as "epistemology", however, sounds very formidable, i. e. very systematic and scholarly, and this is precisely what Nietzsche wished to avoid. Nietzsche, of course, entertained only the liveliest horror with regard to "systems", and this may in part account for the fact that the more "systematic" portions of his own thinking have largely been ignored. Thus, my primary motive in undertaking this work was the isolation and elaboration of the Nietzschean theory of knowledge in its own right, as one of the most profound and fruitful treatments of the whole problematic of human knowing yet put forth. Nietzsche intends ". . . to construct a philosophy consistent with the extraordinary openness he felt was available to man, or

at least a philosophy that would entail this openness as one of its consequences"[4]. Nietzsche's treatment of the problem of knowledge demands a
radical rethinking of our traditional epistemological categories. One result
of this is that if we plunge immediately into Nietzsche's writings on knowledge *per se*, we are confronted with a whole host of alarming utterances,
to the effect that there is no truth, there are no facts, there is no knowledge,
etc. How, one may well ask, is one to construct a theory of knowledge
out of this conceptual chaos? That is the task we have set for ourselves.

In order to provide the proper context for an adequate discussion of
Nietzsche's theory of knowledge, it was found necessary to first discuss
the will to power in some detail as a world-principle, i. e., the will to power
qua being. Once this is established, the will to power as a way of knowing
can be more adequately discussed within its proper context. Even though
we are primarily concerned with knowledge here, the reader must bear in
mind that the will to power is an all-inclusive principle for Nietzsche, and
ultimately embraces all the traditional philosophical categories of ontology,
axiology, anthropology, as well as epistemology, and our discussion of
knowledge makes frequent reference to these other areas. We are taking
one of several valid approaches to that essential core which unifies all of
Nietzsche's thinking, an approach which in itself is no more or no less
valid than these other possible approaches. I have chosen the epistemological approach, however, because so few have done so before.

In the elaboration of Nietzsche's theory of knowledge I have purposely
concentrated on his later works and on the *Nachlass* of the 1880's, in which
the notion of the will to power achieved its mature formulation. I have
attempted, however, to show the origin of Nietzsche's mature epistemology
in his earliest works and its subsequent development, so that the reader
might become aware of the continuity and growth of Nietzsche's thinking,
and that the principles developed here apply to Nietzsche's thinking as an
organic whole. And if this is not the ultimate work on Nietzsche's theory
of knowledge, I believe it is the most definitive to date.

In conclusion, I should like to acknowledge my indebtedness to a
number of persons who at some point were instrumental to the conception
and execution of this work. It was Prof. Dr. Fritz Leist of the Universität
München who helped me to overcome my youthful infatuation with
Nietzsche, and armed me with the critical apparatus necessary for coming
to terms with this most enigmatic of thinkers. I would like to thank Dr.
Christoph Eykman who directed my doctoral dissertation on Nietzsche at

[4] Danto, p. 12 f.

Boston College, as well as Prof. Thomas J. Owens and Rev. Joseph
F. Flanagan, S. J. of that institution. I owe a debt of gratitude to my colle-
agues Dr. Charles Kelly and Dr. Robert Flower of Le Moyne College, in
discussion with whom many of the arguments in this book achieved what
I hope is an acceptable level of clarity and precision. I am grateful to
Le Moyne College for a financial grant which was instrumental in the
preparation of this work. Finally, I would like to express my appreciation
to Susan Armiger, who endured my company during the writing of this
work, and agreed to marry me in spite of that.

Syracuse, New York   Ruediger Hermann Grimm
November 11, 1975

CONTENTS

Dem Andenken meines Vaters gewidmet

RUDOLF GRIMM
1912—1974

CHAPTER ONE

THE WORLD AS WILL TO POWER

I. *What there is for Nietzsche*

Any philosophical system which claims to be at all comprehensive must answer, or at least presuppose an answer to, an apparently naive question: What is there? While seeming to be rather simplistic, this question is without doubt one of the fundamental and perennial questions with which philosophers have historically occupied themselves. In answer to the question: What is there?, a plethora of answers have been given. For example, for Democritus, all that existed was atoms and the void; for Plato, ideal forms and the inferior material world of becoming; for Aristotle, matter and form; for Hegel, "Geist," and for Schopenhauer, "Wille." If we ask this seemingly simple question of Nietzsche, the answer we receive is again deceptively simple. What there is is will to power: and nothing else. Very well, we say. But what is will to power?

> Und wisst ihr auch, was mir „die Welt" ist? Soll ich sie euch in meinem Spiegel zeigen? . . . Diese Welt ist der Wille zur Macht — und nichts ausserdem! Und auch ihr selber seid dieser Wille zur Macht — und nichts ausserdem![1]

It appears to be obvious that Nietzsche considers the whole of reality — being as such — to be will to power. It is an ultimate, all-inclusive principle, other than which there is simply — nothing. A more detailed explanation is certainly in order.

> Und wisst ihr auch, was mir „die Welt" ist? Soll ich sie euch in meinem Spiegel zeigen? Diese Welt: ein Ungeheuer von Kraft, ohne Anfang, ohne Ende, eine feste, eherne Grösse von Kraft, welche nicht grösser, nicht kleiner wird, die sich nicht verbraucht sondern nur verwandelt, als Ganzes unveränderlich gross, ein Haushalt ohne Ausgaben und Einbussen, aber ebenso ohne Zuwachs, ohne Einnahmen, vom „Nichts" umschlossen als von seiner Gränze, nichts Verschwimmendes, Verschwendetes, nichts Unendlich-Ausgedehntes, sondern als bestimmte Kraft einem bestimmten Raum eingelegt, und nicht einem Raume, der irgendwo „leer" wäre, vielmehr als Kraft

---

[1] Nachlass Juni-Juli 1885, 38 [12]; KGW VII 3, 338f.

überall, als Spiel von Kräften und Kraftwellen zugleich Eins und „Vieles“,
hier sich häufend und zugleich dort sich mindernd, ein Meer in sich selber
stürmender und fluthender Kräfte, ewig sich wandelnd, ewig zurücklaufend
... mit einer Ebbe und Fluth seiner Gestalten, aus den einfachsten in die
vielfältigsten hinaustreibend, aus dem Stillsten, Starrsten, Kältesten hinaus in
das Glühendste, Wildeste, Sich-selber-widersprechendste, und dann wieder
aus der Fülle heimkehrend zum Einfachen, aus dem Spiel der Widersprüche
zurück bis zur Lust des Einklangs ...[2]

Upon unraveling this apocalyptic vision, we learn that the will to power
is an enormous, though finite, quantity of energy or power. This power is
not to be thought of in terms of a smoothly unfolding world-substance,
evolving or exfoliating according to its own immutable internal laws.
On the contrary: the will to power is a grand and monumental chaos
which can only be characterized, insofar as it can be characterized at all, by
negative qualities. The will to power is ambiguity, contradiction, paradox,
mobility, and incessant change.

The history of metaphysics is certainly full of ultimate principles which,
upon first glance, would seem to bear a strong resemblance to the will to
power. It might seem that Nietzsche's concept of the will to power is very
similar to the *arche* of the Milesians, the Vedantic Brahman, the Prakriti of
Samkhya, Spinoza's God or Hegel's "Weltgeist." Such resemblances,
however, are largely accidental, and it would be misleading in the extreme
to regard Nietzsche as simply another figure within the tradition of German
Idealism. The world-principles or world-substances referred to above are
all more or less overtly metaphysical. But Nietzsche is not interested in
doing metaphysics, in constructing a merely speculative model of the
universe or any such thing, and heaps abuse upon those who make such
attempts. Nietzsche does not think in terms of substance and accidence,
or being and becoming. He is not interested in describing the universe
(although it might appear that he does precisely that) and uses the more
modest term "world" in the section quoted above, while addressing himself to "you and I." Even though it would seem that Nietzsche is claiming
a cosmic scope for the will to power, this must be seen as arising out of
his more immediate concerns. For the present, let it suffice to say that
Nietzsche does not intend to offer us a new metaphysical system — in the
traditional sense — at all. It should be mentioned, however, that he very
nearly does exactly that, as Martin Heidegger amply illustrates[3]. Yet to
persistently regard Nietzsche as a metaphysician, as I shall show, is to
misunderstand him rather badly.

[2] Ibid.
[3] Martin Heidegger, *Nietzsche*, 2 vols. (Pfullingen, 1961).

II. The Quantification of the Will to Power

One of the fundamental differences between the will to power and the unified, homogeneous, continuous world-substances of traditional metaphysics is the fact that the will to power is discontinuous. It consists of discrete, separate power-quanta which differ from one another only quantitatively (i. e. in degree of power), qualities being derivative of these quantitative differences. If were to use more traditional metaphysical terminology, we might say that while the will to power is formally one, it is specifically many[4].

> Meine Vorstellung ist, dass jeder spezifische Körper danach strebt, über den ganzen Raum Herr zu werden und seine Kraft auszudehnen (— sein Wille zur Macht:) und Alles das zurückzustossen, was seiner Ausdehnung widerstrebt. Aber er stösst fortwährend auf gleiche Bestrebungen anderer Körper und endet, sich mit denen zu arrangiren („vereinigen"), welche ihm verwandt genug sind: — so conspiriren sie dann zusammen zur Macht. Und der Prozess geht weiter . . .[5]

These quanta of will to power are not to be regarded as ultimate, irreducible entities in any sense whatever[6]. The term "quantum" is to be taken quite literally and quite ambiguously as meaning simply "amount," and nothing further. These quanta of will to power are in constant struggle with one another, each seeking to increase its own power at the expense of the others. This inner tension and mutual antagonism provides that dynamism which drives the will to power on toward incessant change and activity. The opposition which exists between power-quanta is not derivative of any absolute polarity or absolute contrariety existing in the nature of things, and Nietzsche denies the existence of any sort of absolute "opposites" ("Gegensätze"). Yet he does uphold an immanent contrariety existing between the quanta of the will to power, and it is this immanent contrariety which is the motive force back of all phenomena[7].

Each unit of the will to power, i. e. each power-quantum, has precisely one existential tendency or fundamental drive: to increase its own power by dominating or assimilating other power-quanta. More precisely, each

---

[4] Nachlass November 1887—März 1888, 11 [73]; KGW VIII 2, 278f., ". . . es giebt keinen Willen: es giebt Willens-Punktationen, die beständig ihre Macht mehren oder verlieren . . ."

[5] Nachlass Frühjahr 1888, 14 [186]; KGW VIII 3, 165f.

[6] Nachlass November 1887—März 1888, 11 [73]; KGW VIII 2, 278f.

[7] Cf. Wolfgang Müller-Lauter, *Nietzsche: Seine Philosophie der Gegensätze und die Gegensätze seiner Philosophie* (Berlin and New York, 1971), p. 30: "Die Wirklichkeit, auf die Nietzsches Philosophieren letztlich trifft, ist die in Gegensätzen auf einander bezogene und in solcher Beziehung die eine Welt bildende Vielheit von Willen zur Macht."

power-quantum *is* this drive toward domination and assimilation, since Nietzsche specifically rejects the distinction between action and actor ("Thun" and "Thäter")[8]. However, since every other power-quantum displays the same fundamental drive, power-quanta arrange themselves into groups or what Nietzsche calls power-constellations ("Machtkon-stellationen") in order to collectively increase their individual power. These power-constellations should not be thought of as necessarily constituting a new type of unified, homogeneous entity. The unity which these power-groups display is analogous to that of a political federation, in which each member is primarily concerned with furthering his own ends, but finds that his own ends are better accomplished by combining forces with others[9]. The passing reference in the paragraph quoted above to power-quanta which are "sufficiently related" so as to make an association possible should not be misconstrued to mean that there are different sorts of power-quanta. There are not. The only differences existing between power-quanta or power-constellations are differences of relative strength or energy, and the particular context in which this power is discharged. By anticipating our discussion of the will to power as life, an example may be furnished to clarify this point.

Let us regard a house cat as one power-constellation, and a phonograph as another. These two entities would normally be regarded as distinctly different from one another. For Nietzsche, however, the differences between the two would not be formal, logical, or substantial differences, but rather, a difference in quantity of power and the manner in which that power is discharged relative to me, who constitute yet another power-constellation. Even the distinction between organic and inorganic, or living and inert matter is treated as a difference of degree, not kind (and ultimately, is not treated as a difference at all, as we shall shortly see). Nonetheless, the manner in which a house cat discharges that quantity of power which it is (not has!) and the manner in which a phonograph does the same are far enough removed from one another that a conflict of interests or a power

Nachlass Frühjahr 1888, 14 [79]; KGW VIII 3, 49 ff.
This should not be construed to mean that individual quanta are inviolate or irreducible entities. Nietzsche sometimes speaks as though individual quanta could merge to form a single, greater quantum of power, or split apart into lesser quanta, and does this, no doubt, to preclude any misinterpretation of the will to power as some sort of rigid, mechanistic atomism. Nietzsche's account of the manner in which power-quanta combine, increase or decrease is purposely left ambiguous, so that the conceptual structure of the will to power can remain as elastic and fluid as that reality which it seeks to express. Cf. Nachlass Juni-Juli 1885, 36 [21]; KGW VII 3, 284. The will to power is "... zugleich Eins und 'Vieles' ..." Nachlass Juni-Juli 1885, 38 [12]; KGW VII 3, 338 f.

struggle simply does not arise. For purposes of increasing power, a cat and a phonograph are useless to one another and, relatively speaking, unrelated (although properly speaking, this is not the case: both are will to power). I, however, represent a much greater quantity of power than either of the two entities mentioned, and am capable of utilizing both of them for the enhancement and increase of my will to power. To put it quite simply, I can use the cat to catch mice for me, and the phonograph to make music for me, while neither of the two can use me (or one another) for anything.

III. Interactions of the Power-Quanta

The nature of the will to power as manifested in its quantified units might be made more understandable if we turn our attention, for the moment, away from objects and entities (as power-constellations) to the interactions and relationships prevailing between power-quanta and power-groups as such. The reader should bear in mind that the distinction between action and actor or subject and object should not be "read into" the following account, since Nietzsche rejects any such distinction.

The manner in which the will to power expresses itself is through resistance. Static, isolated, inactive power is inconceivable for Nietzsche. The will to power is, by its very nature, completely active, and can express or discharge itself only by meeting and overcoming resistance.

> Der Wille zur Macht kann sich nur an Widerständen äussern; er sucht nach dem, was ihm widersteht . . .[10]

All activity is conceived as the aggression and will-to-dominate and -assimilate which exists between individual quanta or groups of power-quanta:

> . . . es handelt sich um einen Kampf zweier an Macht ungleichen Elemente: es wird ein Neuarrangement der Kräfte erreicht, je nach dem Mass von Macht eines jeden. Der zweite Zustand ist etwas Grundverschiedenes vom ersten (nicht dessen „Wirkung"): das Wesentliche ist, dass die im Kampf befindlichen Faktoren mit anderen Machtquanten herauskommen[11].

All activity is a struggle for more power, the decisive factor in any such confrontation being simply the quantity of power involved and the rearrangement of power-quanta resulting from the confrontation.

[10] Nachlass Herbst 1887, 9 [151]; KGW VIII 2, 88.
[11] Nachlass Frühjahr 1888, 14 [95]; KGW VIII 3, 65.

> Der Grad von Widerstand und der Grad von Übermacht — darum handelt
> ⟨es⟩ sich bei allem Geschehen . . .[12]

Within this intensely dynamic framework, it would be a serious misunderstanding to regard power-quanta or power-constellations as things, as entities which possessed will to power or exercised will to power — indeed, to make any distinction whatever between the existence of a power-quantum and its activity. A power-quantum or -constellation *is* precisely what it *does*:

> Ein Machtquantum ist durch die Wirkung, die es übt und der es widerstrebt,
> bezeichnet . . .[13]

This equation of essence with activity is not univocal, for the simple reason that the same power-group or -quantum may act differently toward every other opposing power-group. Thus, any complete designation of any entity's essence is simply the sum total of all its effects on all other power-quanta or -constellations. As such complete knowledge of something's effects on everything else is methodologically impossible, the only meaningful question is: What is it for me?

> Kurz, das Wesen eines Dings ist auch nur eine Meinung über das „Ding".
> Oder vielmehr: das „es gilt" ist das eigentliche „das ist", das einzige „das
> ist"[14].

A consequence of this radical equation between a thing's essence and the sum total of its effects is that the same object (i. e. power-quantum or -constellation) might very well *be* something different for every other object upon which it exercises its will to power. The notion that the same object might appear different to different observers might not appear to be especially novel, but we must rememver that the object *is* the sum of its effects and does not exist apart from its effects. Entity exists only in relationship: there are no "things" apart from their relationships to, and effects upon, other "things[15]."

> Die Eigenschaften eines Dings sind Wirkungen auf andere „Dinge": denkt
> man andere „Dinge" weg, so hat ein Ding keine Eigenschaften d. h. es giebt
> kein Ding ohne andere Dinge d. h. es giebt kein „Ding an sich"[16].

[12] Nachlass Frühjahr 1888, 14 [79]; KGW VIII 3, 49ff.
[13] Ibid.
[14] Nachlass Herbst 1885—Herbst 1886, 2 [150]; KGW VIII 1, 138.
[15] Strictly speaking, a power-quantum is not a "thing": "thinghood" is an interpretation projected onto one particular power-configuration by another.
[16] Nachlass Herbst 1885—Herbst 1886, 2 [85]; KGW VIII 1, 102

The Kantian thing-in-itself is an absurdity for Nietzsche. If we abstract all "qualities" and "activities" away from a thing, we have, in the process, annihilated that thing. A thing, abstracted from all relationships would not only cease to be a thing — it would simply cease to be[17]. Ultimately, there are no entities at all. The power-quanta and power-constellations of which the world is constituted are not things or objects. If we were to characterize these units of the will to power in metaphysical terminology (which Nietzsche would not!), we would be forced to call them pure activity.

> Das „Ding an sich" widersinnig. Wenn ich alle Relationen, alle „Eigenschaf-
> ten", alle „Thätigkeiten" eines Dinges wegdenke, so bleibt nicht das Ding
> übrig: weil Dingheit erst von uns hinzufingirt ist, aus logischen Bedürfnissen,
> also zum Zweck der Bezeichnung, der Verständigung . . .[18]

The consequences of Nietzsche's equation of essence with activity is of greatest importance to an understanding of his theory of knowledge. I shall therefore postpone a more detailed analysis of this concept until later chapters, in order to avoid giving what at this point could only be an incomplete and misleading account of one of the major features of the epistemological function of the will to power.

IV. The Will to Power as Life

Life, as Nietzsche points out, is that form of the will to power with which we are most familiar[19]. But if we ask the question, What, for Nietzsche, is life?, our answer may at first appear paradoxical. The proper answer is that life, for Nietzsche, is nothing essentially different from anything else. It is a "particular form" of the will to power, and nothing else. Nietzsche's working hypothesis is that everything consists of power-quanta in various states of activity and in assorted combinations and configurations[20]. That which distinguishes life from what we refer to as inert, inorganic matter is its greater complexity, its greater diversity, and its greater ability to overpower, assimilate, and control other power-quanta. Human life is only an especially rich and complicated aggregation of power-quanta (e. g. drives, instincts, faculties, etc.) which, by joining forces, are better able to extend and express themselves[21]. Again, the difference between

---

[17] Nachlass Herbst 1887, 9 [40]; KGW VIII 2, 17.
[18] Nachlass Herbst 1887, 10 [202]; KGW VIII 2, 246.
[19] Nachlass Frühjahr 1888, 14 [82]; KGW VIII 3, 53f.
[20] Ibid.
[21] Nachlass August—September 1885, 40 [21]; KGW VII 3, 370f. Nachlass August—
September 1885, 40 [42]; KGW VII 3, 382.

human life and the simplest bit of "inorganic matter" is a difference of perspective and degree, not an essential or substantial difference. Both are simply manifestations of the fundamental will to power.

> ... das Leben als die uns bekannteste Form des Seins ist spezifisch ein Wille zur Accumulation der Kraft: alle Prozesse des Lebens haben hier ihren Hebel: nichts will sich erhalten, alles soll summirt und accumulirt werden ... [22]

In elaborating his notion of life, Nietzsche employs one of his favorite techniques, the juxtaposing of two apparent opposites and their subsequent reduction to a more fundamental unity[23]. In this instance, he takes the organic-inorganic (i. e. life and non-life) distinction and reduces it to will to power. This should mot be viewed as some perverse sort of mechanistic degradation of life at all. Rather, it is a profoundly original insight into the dynamic nature of what we are accustomed to calling inert, dead matter. For Nietzsche, everything is alive, everything is active and dynamic in the most fundamental sense, and everything is ultimately constituted out of the primal drive to increase power.

> Das Leben, als ein Einzelfall: Hypothese von da aus auf den Gesamtcharakter des Daseins.
> : strebt nach einem Maximal-Gefühl von Macht
> : ist essentiell ein Streben nach Mehr von Macht
> : Streben ist nichts anderes als Streben nach Macht
> : das Unterste und Innerste bleibt dieser Wille: Mechanik ist eine blosse Semiotik der Folgen[24].

Or more simply,

> Das „Sein" — wir haben keine andere Vorstellung davon als „leben". — Wie kann also etwas Todtes „sein"?[25]

If, as Nietzsche maintains, everything is will to power, it should surprise no one that life is also explicated on the model of the will to power and conceived as a particular form of the will to power.

> Eine Vielheit von Kräften, verbunden durch einen gemeinsamen Ernährungs-Vorgang, heissen wir „Leben". Zu diesem Ernährungs-Vorgang, als Mittel seiner Ermöglichung, gehört alles sogenannte Fühlen, Vorstellen, Denken,

---

[22] Nachlass Frühjahr 1888, 14 [82]; KGW VIII 3, 53f.
[23] This is what Arthur Danto refers to as Nietzsche's "methodological monism." See Arthur C. Danto, *Nietzsche as Philosopher* (New York, 1965), pp. 216—218. Nietzsche's linguistic techniques will be more fully discussed in Chapter V.
[24] Nachlass Frühjahr 1888, 14 [82]; KGW VIII 3, 53f.
[25] Nachlass Herbst 1885—Herbst 1886, 2 [172]; KGW VIII 1, 151.

d. h. 1. ein Widerstreben gegen alle anderen Kräfte; 2. ein Zurechtmachen derselben nach Gestalt und Rhythmus; 3. ein Abschätzen in bezug auf Einver-
leibung oder Abscheidung[26].

Life is not to be thought of as a particular mode of existence which is
peculiar to organic entities. For Nietzsche, there is no such thing, ultimately,
as dead matter which might serve as a species of being overagainst which
"living" beings might be defined. Even a crystal displays an organizational
power, a power to assimilate surrounding matter and utilize it for growth.
Furthermore, it is capable of organizing and giving a distinct form to that
which it assimilates. Even chemicals in a test tube display similar characteristics. An acid will "attack" a metal, and seek to appropriate its
constituents for the enhancement of its own "growth." Nietzsche does not
consider such an act of aggression committed within the narrow confines
of a test tube to be essentially different from aggression among animals,
human individuals, or whole nations. The difference is one of degree, not
kind: the same fundamental force — the will to power — is operative
everywhere.

> Der Wille zur Accumulation von Kraft als spezifisch für das Phänomen des
> Lebens, für Ernährung, Zeugung, Vererbung, für Gesellschaft, Staat, Sitte,
> Autorität: sollten wir diesen Willen nicht als bewegende Ursache auch in der
> Chemie annehmen dürfen? und in der kosmischen Ordnung? nicht bloss
> Constanz der Energie: sondern Maximal-Ökonomie des Verbrauchs: so dass
> das Stärker-werden-wollen von jedem Kraftcentrum aus die einzige Realität
> ist, — nicht Selbstbewahrung, sondern Aneignung, Herr-werden-, Mehr-
> werden-, Stärker-werden-wollen[27].

That which we call a human being is nothing less than a particular
plurality of power-quanta (or a power-constellation), which are united and
organized by a common drive to extend and increase their power. This
holds true for any higher organism: it is "higher" (i. e. more powerful)
because it is a complex, a federation of separate and ultimately antagonistic
forces which exploit this association as a means to an end, the end being, as
always, an increase of power. It would thus be a mistake to think of a
human individual as a unity, as a substance, or any such thing. We are
composed of more primitive, simpler drives and instincts which are organized, perhaps tyrannized, by one dominating force. In most of us, this
dominant force might be called intelligence, reason, conscience, or
something similar. It might equally be the sex drive, the appetite for
food or drink, love of learning, a passion for athletics, etc. While the

[26] GA XVI, 117.
[27] Nachlass Frühjahr 1888, 14 [81]; KGW VIII 3, 52ff.

dominant power-quantum or force might be viewed as organizing the other power-quanta in its particular constellation into a particular configuration and giving its own characteristics to the whole (e. g. a scholar, a drunkard, an athlete), we should not mistake the part for the whole. The domination and organization of a power-constellation by a particular power-quantum serves the function of keeping the individual constituents of the constellation from encroaching upon one another and directing their collective energies more efficaciously. In anthropological terms, we might say that the "ruling passion" keeps the personality intact, and prevents the various drives, urges, instincts, etc. which comprise a human being from fragmenting and disrupting the whole. Indeed, such a fragmentation or disruption might occur, in which case we would have a situation very much like the clinical definition of neurosis, viz. the fragmentation of the personality structure, so that a destructive tension or conflict may arise between these fragmented elements. In psychological terms, examples of such a fragmentation might be hysteria, hypochondriasis, neurasthenia, or any other such disturbance resulting from the disruption and disorganization of that power-complex which we call the personality[28]. In a note from the *Nachlass* of 1888 in which Nietzsche specifically discusses the will to power as the elemental and unifying factor back of all psychological phenomena, he maintains

> Dass der Wille zur Macht die primitive Affekt-Form ist, dass alle anderen Affekte nur seine Ausgestaltungen sind ... Dass alle treibende Kraft Wille zur Macht ist, das es keine physische, dynamische oder psychische Kraft ausserdem giebt ...[29]

Of course, Nietzsche does not regard intelligence, mind, spirit, etc. as man's highest faculties in the traditional sense at all. In terms of human chronology, these features are rather late developments, and have no privileged status within that power-complex which we call a human person.

---

[28] Nietzsche's model of power-complexes has found a number of echos in the psychoanalytic tradition. There is a striking similarity between Nietzsche's power-based psychology and the individual psychology of Alfred Adler, and Nietzsche's influence upon Adler is unquestionable. Cf. Carl G. Jung, *Two Essays on Analytical Psychology* in *The Collected Works of C. G. Jung*, trans. by R. F. C. Hull (New York, 1953), vol. 7, p. 39: "It is unquestionable that the urge to power plays an extraordinarily important part. It is correct that neurotic symptoms and complexes are also elaborate 'arrangements' which inexorably pursue their aims, with incredible obstinacy and cunning. Neurosis is teleologically oriented. In establishing this, Adler has won for himself no small credit." For an account of Nietzsche's influence upon the psychoanalytic movement see Henri Ellenberger, *The Discovery of the Unconscious* (New York, 1970).

[29] Nachlass Frühjahr 1888, 14 [121]; KGW VIII 3, 92f.

Nietzsche singles out a "common mode of nutrition" as being the unifying factor in a "living" organism. This is not to be thought of as a biological banality. Nietzsche is not concerned here with hunger or with replenishing what the body has lost through elimination. Hunger, he says, is only derivative of the more fundamental drive for increased power. Similarly, Nietzsche does not consider the pleasure-pain principle or the drive for self-preservation to be basic features of life. These also are superficial, human interpretations of our basic — indeed, our only — drive, to increase our power. Nietzsche would certainly not deny that human life exhibits those features which we ordinarily refer to as the pursuit of pleasure and the avoidance of pain, as well as the instinct of self-preservation. What he does deny is that the two drives just mentioned are in any way fundamental or irreducible to something more basic. And he does, in fact, regard them as epiphenomena of the basic life force, as narrow, perspectival interpretations of something much more basic. Pleasure, for example, is a function of increasing power: we do not do something because we find it pleasant; rather, we find it pleasant because we derive a feeling of increased power from it.

> Lust und Unlust sind Nebensachen, keine Ursachen; es sind Werthurtheile zweiten Ranges, die sich erst ableiten von einem regierenden Werth; ein in Form des Gefühls redendes „nützlich" „schädlich", und folglich absolut flüchtig und abhängig. Denn bei jedem „nützlich" „schädlich" sind immer noch hundert verschiedene Wozu? zu fragen[30].

Pleasure is only a secondary and derivative phenomenon associated with an increase of power. If we relate this to the pleasure-pain principle, it becomes apparent that what the individual organism really seeks is "pain" rather than "pleasure." Why is this the case?

> Die Unlust, als Hemmung seines Willens zur Macht, ist also ein normales Faktum, das normale Ingredienz jedes organischen Geschehens, der Mensch weicht ihr nicht aus, er hat sie vielmehr fortwährend nöthig: jeder Sieg, jedes Lustgefühl, jedes Geschehen setzt einen überwundenen Widerstand voraus[31].

It will be recalled that the will to power expresses itself only through resistance; a particular power-quantum or power-constellation expresses itself and grows by means of overcoming and assimilating other power-

---

[30] Nachlass November 1887—März 1888, 11 [61]; KGW VIII 2, 272. Nietzsche's definition of value, here as well as elsewhere, is this: "Werth ... Das höchste Quantum Macht, das der Mensch sich einzuverleiben vermag ... der Mensch, nicht die Menschheit..." Nachlass Frühjahr 1888, 14 [8]; KGW VIII 3, 152f.

[31] Nachlass Frühjahr 1888, 14 [174]; KGW VIII 3, 152f.

groups. These other power-groups, of course, display the same fundamental drive themselves, and oppose any and all efforts to overcome them. Thus, in order to express itself and to discharge that energy which it is, a power-quantum or -constellation must constantly seek out resistance and opposition, which it must then overcome in order to grow. Any force which opposes or resists our will to power, or attempts to assimilate it for its own growth, would certainly be regarded as inimical to our interests and existential tendencies. In psychological terms we would call this pain or displeasure, but we see how a power-constellation seeks out this sort of "pain" in order to overcome it. "Pain" is the stimulant of life, it is the essential ingredient in all vital activity, and rather than be avoided, Nietzsche maintains that it is sought out.

> Die Unlust hat also so wenig nothwendig eine Verminderung unseres Macht-gefühl zur Folge, dass, in durchschnittlichen Fällen, sie gerade als Reiz auf dieses Machtgefühl wirkt, — das Hemmnis ist der Stimulus dieses Willens zur Macht[32].

Naturally, this principle is operative on all levels. Even an amoeba when it stretches out a pseudopod in search of something edible, does not do so out of hunger, but rather, out of will to power. Even a relatively simple organism such as an amoeba seeks out creatures similar to itself in order to overcome, appropriate, and assimilate them. The amoeba, according to Nietzsche, is not primarily seeking to nourish itself, but to become stronger. Nutrition happens to be one of the consequences of this increase in power[33].

Nietzsche's treatment of the pleasure-pain principle should not be confused with the scholastic notion of irascible appetition (or the subsequent psychological formulations of Alfred Adler) simply because of the pre-dominance in it of what we would ordinarily call pain or displeasure. The whole thrust of Nietzsche's treatment of this principle is to demonstrate that pleasure and pain are simply secondary and derivative phenomena of an infinitely more basic life-drive: the will to power. Thus, any explication of life which revolves around the pleasure-pain principle, any hedonistic ethics or utilitarian social theory, simply does not seek a sufficiently radical point of departure; it mistakes the part for the whole, the epiphenomena for the authentic phenomena. Nietzsche certainly makes no secret of his scorn for hedonism, utilitarianism, etc., but his point is that such "ism's" presuppose an understanding of life which is wholly inadequate. They

[32] Ibid.
[33] Ibid.

are inadequate not only in psychological, sociological, or biological terms — their very ontology is wrong.

V. The Two Types of "Displeasure"

We have seen that "pleasure" is a function of increased power. It would seem to follow that "displeasure" must be associated with a decrease of power, or a thwarting of the drive to increase power. In order to clarify this point, we must examine what Nietzsche means by "displeasure" ("Unlust").

Nietzsche recognizes basically two forms of displeasure, and deplores the fact that the two have practically always been confused. The first type of displeasure, let us call it the positive type, is what a strong, dynamic will to power experiences when it meets opposition and resistance, when it is somehow constrained. Naturally, this sort of displeasure acts as a stimulus to the will to power to overcome whatever happens to be resisting it. It represents an occasion for the will to power to express itself, discharge its accumulated force, and grow. This positive type of displeasure is the leavening for any and all growth, and is the necessary precondition for growth.

The second and negative type of displeasure is a result of exhaustion. Exhaustion is the inability to overcome or even to withstand resistance and opposition. It signifies a weakened or disrupted will to power, and is a symptom of decline in any power-constellation. Pleasure in the first instance is the overcoming of resistance, triumph, and growth. In the second instance, it is the avoidance of any conflict or opposition, e. g. peace, rest, quietude, etc.

> Die grosse Verwechslung der Psychologen bestand darin, dass sie diese beiden Lustarten die des Einschlafens und die des Sieges nicht auseinanderhielten.
> die Erschöpften wollen Ruhe, Gliederausstrecken, Frieden, Stille — es ist das Glück der nihilistischen Religionen und Philosophien die Reichen und Lebendigen wollen Sieg, überwundene Gegner, Überströmen des Machtgefühls über weitere Bereiche als bisher: alle gesunden Funktionen des Organismus haben dies Bedürfniss, — und der ganze Organismus, bis zum Alter der Pubertät, ist ein solcher nach Wachsthum von Machtgefühlen ringender Complex von Systemen . . .[34].

Nietzsche's treatment of the pleasure-pain principle ultimately rests upon the relationship existing between relative quantities of power, and

[34] Ibid.

whether these quantities are increasing or decreasing. This leads to the further qualification that a strong and vital power-constellation (e. g. a person) will have totally different pleasures (and pains) than a weak and exhausted power-constellation. As a result of this, the very terms "pleasure" and "pain" lose their applicability, since Nietzsche demonstrates that both are derivative of a much more fundamental principle — the will to power —, and whether in any particular constellation it is increasing or decreasing. Thus, the pleasure-pain principle is invalidated, at least as the fundamental motive principle for all life.

VI. Self-Preservation as Derivative

Similarly, Nietzsche does away with the principle of self-preservation as the basic drive of all vital activity. Self-preservation, seen as an end in itself, is regarded by Nietzsche as an entirely negative affair. To simply exist, i. e. to maintain a constant level of power, is without value. Vital qualities and values come about only when an individual struggles to increase his power and enhance his vital forces. Thus, we do not struggle in order to exist: we exist in order to struggle[35].

The reader will recall that for Nietzsche, the basic drive of all life is will to power. More specifically, it is the will to increase power. Within this context, Nietzsche recognizes only two fundamental types of change: a power-constellation can either increase its power and grow, or it can fail increase to its power and decline. There is no middle stage. To stand still, to maintain a *status quo*, is already to be in decline. Mere self-preservation is a symptom of weakness and decline. Just as an organism with vital and exuberant will to power seeks out obstacles and opposition (i. e. "displeasure") in order to assert itself and grow, it also seeks out situations which might very well destroy it. Opposition, resistance, even danger, are to be regarded as stimulants to life because, as Nietzsche says, „Was mich nicht umbringt, macht mich stärker"[36]. This is also the meaning of Nietzsche's injunction to "live dangerously[37]." Those who would posit self-preservation as the fundamental life-drive are once more guilty of confusing effects with causes[38]. The fundamental drive of life is to grow and

---

[35] FW 349; KGW V 2, 267f.
[36] GD I 8; KGW VI 3, 54.
[37] FW 283; KGW V 2, 206f.
[38] Nietzsche also rejects the traditional view of the cause-effect relationship, and such terminology must be viewed as metaphorical. Nietzsche's view of causality will be discussed in Chapter IV.

increase in power, and this may very well result in an organism's putting itself into peril. Self-preservation is only a consequence of this and is not the end in view.

> Die Physiologen sollten sich besinnen, den Selbsterhaltungstrieb als kardinalen Trieb eines Wesens anzusetzen. Vor allem will etwas Lebendiges seine Kraft auslassen — Leben selbst ist Wille zur Macht —: die Selbsterhaltung ist nur eine der indirekten und häufigsten Folgen davon[39].

What Nietzsche does here is considerably more than simply to take two fairly common, traditional views on the nature of life and, out of sheer perversity, confute them. What he does show is the total inadequacy of such views for grasping the intensely dynamic, exuberant reality which is life. Nietzsche's investigation proceeds on a much deeper level than hedonism or self-preservation, deeper to such an extent that the pleasure-pain principle and the drive for self-preservation are seen to be mere surface appearances. Furthermore, Nietzsche demonstrates that even if we are to talk in terms of pleasure and pain and self-preservation, the two principles in question are simply mistaken: an organism displaying the healthy, exuberant sort of vitality which Nietzsche has in mind will be seen to (a) seek "pain" rather than pleasure, and (b) will behave in a manner which might appear to be highly inimical to its own self-preservation. The point is that, in the context which Nietzsche develops, self-preservation, pleasure and pain, and other similar notions simply do not apply. By locating the point of departure for his analysis of life on what he considers to be the most fundamental level, Nietzsche shows all other interpretations of life to be inadequate. More precisely, they are interpretations of life based on the mistaken notion that a secondary phenomenon of life (e. g. pleasure, self-preservation) is the key to understanding life *in toto*. Such interpretations are narrow, perspectival, anthropocentric constructs, laden with unexamined value judgements, which simply remain ignorant of their own presuppositions. By taking such a fundamentally radical point of departure, Nietzsche is able to unify the whole biosphere, and show that all living organisms display the same fundamental drive — the will to increase their power. But Nietzsche does even more than this. By pointing out similarities in what we have heretofore called "inorganic" or dead matter and living beings, he has shown them to be fundamentally similar, differing only in degree of complexity and quantity of power. Ultimately, everything is grounded in the sole, underlying reality: the will to power.

[39] JGB 13; KGW VI 2, 21 f.

VII. *Summary and Conclusion*

We began this chapter by asking a (seemingly) naive question: what is there? Our answer? There is will to power — and nothing else. We are now in a somewhat better position to draw some preliminary conclusions which will be necessary for understanding the remainder of our discussion.

For Nietzsche, all that exists is the will to power. All phenomena are explainable in terms of the will to power and its internal operations. The will to power itself, however, is not a unified, homogeneous world-substance, *arche*, or anything remotely similar to such metaphysical world principles. It is unnecessary to repeat here what has been said earlier about the discontinuous nature of the will to power, power-quanta and power-constellations, etc. What is important, however, is the fact that for Nietzsche, all phenomena, all entities with all their varied qualities and characteristics are reducible to will to power. Everything is to be explained in terms of the quantity of power of a particular power-group, and whether that power-group is increasing or decreasing. All entities are to be thought of as power-constellations; all qualities are reducible to perspectival interpretations of quantitative power differences; all action is a struggle for more power. Even life conforms exactly to these principles since it, too, is a form of the will to power, like everything else.

Yet, in spite of what may very well appear to be a rather simple-minded, mechanistic reduction of the world to a single, robot-like principle, nothing could be further from Nietzsche's intentions. Nietzsche's "reductionism" has the net effect of showing us infinitely more variety, complexity, ambiguity, and — freedom — than we may have been capable of realizing before. By "reducing" the world to a single principle, Nietzsche cannot very well be said to be "simplifying" the world: indeed, by "reducing" all qualities to quantities of power, by "reducing" all differences to power differences, by "reducing" all action to a single drive, Nietzsche succeeds in making the world infinitely more complex than it appeared to be.

We have now given a sketch of the will to power as Nietzsche's model of reality; we have explicated this model on the basis of that form of the will to power which is most easily identifiable, viz. life itself. The task still remaining before us is to show how Nietzsche achieves a "logos", a mode of expression and a theory of knowledge adequate to a reality which is characterized by ceaseless change, contrariety, paradox, and contradiction. We turn, therefore, to an examination of how Nietzsche's concept of truth is itself an outgrowth of the will to power.

CHAPTER TWO

NIETZSCHE'S CONCEPT OF TRUTH

I. Nietzsche's Criterion for Truth

Since the turn of the last century, many writers who have concerned themselves with Nietzsche's works have gleefully pointed out what they regarded as gross logical blunders in his thinking[1]. Even commentators who are favorably disposed toward Nietzsche have resorted to embarrassed and apologetic logical sleights-of-hand, in order to rescue their idol from the damning charge of logical inconsistency[2]. Certainly the best known example of this is the alleged mutual exclusiveness existing between the notions of the will to power and the eternal recurrence of the same. Both notions, of course, loom large on the popular table of Nietzschean "doctrines." Unfortunately, such alleged "inconsistencies" or "contradictions" have led some writers to conclude that Nietzsche is simply not to be taken seriously as a thinker. Of course, anyone reaching such a conclusion is not only being unfair — he has not read Nietzsche closely enough[3]. If one accepts Nietzsche's own criterion for "truth," the problem of contradiction does not even arise. This is not to say that contradictions do not arise: they do, and Nietzsche fully intends that they should. What, then, is Nietzsche's criterion for truth?

Traditionally, truth has been inextricably bound up with the notion of a stable world order. Change and truth have generally been held to exclude one another. Plato, for example, held that the material world was constantly changing (i. e. "becoming" what it previously was not)[4]. This

---

[1] Cf. R. H. Grützmacher, *Nietzsche* (Leipzig, 1917); Alois Riehl, *Friedrich Nietzsche, Der Künstler und der Denker* (Stuttgart, 1923); Wilhelm Windelband, *Lehrbuch der Geschichte der Philosophie*, ed. by H. Heimsoeth (Tübingen, 1957); Paul Elmer More, *Nietzsche* (Boston, 1912) et al. Cf. also Müller-Lauter, op. cit., pp. 2—4.

[2] Cf. Hans Vaihinger, *Nietzsche als Philosoph* (Berlin, 1916); Alfred Baeumler, *Nietzsche, der Philosoph und Politiker* (Leipzig, 1931); Georg Simmel, *Schopenhauer und Nietzsche* (Leipzig, 1907).

[3] E. g. Frederick Copleston, S.J., *Friedrich Nietzsche: Philosopher of Culture* (London, 1942), p. 209: "Philosophy was no game for Nietzsche, but an earnest and passionate struggle, motivated by the firm resolve to shut his eyes to the truth."

[4] Cf. Plato, *Theatetus, Statesman, Phaedo, Philebus*.

apparently led him to the conclusion that, since the truer an idea is, the less subject to change it is, ultimate truth and reality are to be found only in the hyperouranian realm of the eternal, immutable, ideal forms[5]. Further examples of thinkers who equated truth, more or less, with immutability or permanence (or the adequate correspondence of statements and ideas to fixed, eternal verities) would be Parmenides, Aristotle[6], Thomas Aquinas[7], Augustine[8], Descartes[9], and the list could be easily lengthened. The whole history of Western, Christian metaphysics, if we are to believe Martin Heidegger, has regarded being or reality (both of which could be said to be "true": truth is *of* them) as constant presence or eternal changelessness[10]. Clearly Nietzsche is out of place within this tradition.

As we saw earlier, for Nietzsche there is no such thing as a stable reality or an unchanging world order, of which it would simply be our task to gain "knowledge", this knowledge being "true" knowledge insofar as it accurately represents such a state of affairs. Nietzsche says again and again that there are no such things as "facts." There are only changing perspectives on an ever-flowing, ever-changing, chaotic "reality." "Reality" or "being" for Nietzsche consists of nothing less than a vast (though finite) number of power-quanta, which differ among themselves only quantitatively. By their very "nature" these power-quanta are constantly changing: indeed, the only constant which might be predicated of them is "constant" change! The phenomena which we experience are the result of the interplay of these "Machtquanten," the increase in power and growth of one particular constellation of power-quanta, the decrease in power and decline of another. It scarcely need be said that truth, as traditionally conceived, has no place within such a context[11]. Where is truth to be found within the chaos with which Nietzsche presents us? How are we to judge truth if we find it?

Nietzsche's answer to these questions springs directly from the ontology of power-quanta described earlier:

Das Kriterium der Wahrheit liegt in der Steigerung des Machtgefühls[12].

---

[5] Exactly what Plato might have meant by this is the subject of a good deal of scholarly debate. See W. Windelband, op. cit., pp. 98—113.

[6] Cf. Aristotle, *De Anima* III, Metaphysics I, IV, V, VII, XII, XIII.

[7] Cf. St. Thomas Aquinas, *Truth*, trans by R. W. Mulligan, Vol. I (Chicago, 1954).

[8] Cf. St. Augustine, *Soliloquies.*

[9] Cf. Rene Descartes, *Meditations, Principles of Philosophy*, Part I.

[10] Cf. Martin Heidegger, *Sein und Zeit* (Tübingen, 1967).

[11] An extended analysis of Nietzsche's critique of the correspondence theory of truth will be given in Chapter III. Cf. Danto, pp. 33, 72, 80—88, 130, 193.

[12] GA XVI, 45.

Truth, like everything else, is a function of power. I call something "true" if it increases my will to power, my "Machtgefühl." Conversely, something is "false" if it decreases my will to power. Let us assume for the moment that this principle applies to all cases. It nevertheless remains a "subjective" truth criterion because the same thing or proposition might be either true or false, depending on the perspective from which this judgement is made and the power-play involved. An example is in order.

An idea or concept, according to the criterion given above, would be true if it increased my will to power, false if it decreased it[13]. Let us take, as an appropriate example, the old rubric "Might makes right." Now, if by employing this dictum in my behavior I am invigorated, if my personal power is in some way increased, if my vital forces are enhanced, if this dictum functions in any positive fashion for me, it is true. On the other hand, if the same dictum depresses me, makes me somehow less capable of coping with or mastering my environment, if I feel that this principle is somehow "wrong" and this feeling hampers me, then the principle is false. Naturally, two different individuals (or the same individual at different times) could respond in such a way that the dictum "Might makes right" could be true for one of them, and false for the other. The case in point is this: Nietzsche's criterion for truth is not concerned at all with the logical content of the proposition. The content, in fact, is largely irrelevant. Its truth or falsity lies in the degree of efficacity, in the degree of power increase or decrease, with which the proposition functions when I employ it in my behavior.

This criterion is not to be taken as a symptom of that shallow, mindless sort of relativism which holds that "anybody's opinion is as good as anybody else's." Nothing could be further from Nietzsche's intentions. Nietzsche is not attempting to construct a new sort of modal or multi-valued logic, and he is not trying to proselytize a new method for solving logical quibbles. In fact, Nietzsche's criterion for truth is not intended to constitute a new logical *modus operandi* at all, and applying it to logical propositions is something like swatting gnats with a pile-driver. Since the world, for Nietzsche, is dynamic and active in the most radical sense, his notion of truth clearly reflects this. Truth is not a property of statements, but a function of activity; more specifically, individual activity.

> Der Intellekt setzt sein freiestes und stärkstes Vermögen und Können als Kriterium des Wertvollsten, folglich Wahren ...
> „Wahr": von seiten des Gefühls aus —: was das Gefühl am stärksten erregt („Ich");

---

[13] Literally, increased or decreased *me*, since I *am* will to power.

von seiten des Denkens aus —: was dem Denken das grösste Gefühl von Kraft
gibt;
von seiten des Tastens, Sehens, Hörens aus —: wobei am stärksten Widerstand zu leisten ist.
Also die höchsten Grade in der Leistung erwecken für das Objekt den Glauben an dessen „Wahrheit", das heisst Wirklichkeit. Das Gefühl der Kraft,
des Kampfes, des Widerstandes überredet dazu, dass es etwas gibt, dem hier
widerstanden wird[14].

We saw earlier that the will to power expresses or discharges itself by
acting upon or overcoming a resistance, resistance being simply the same
basic drive directed against the power-quantum in question[15]. This is the
case whether the activity in question is "mental" or "physical[16]."

An idea, concept, or mode of intellection which stimulates my intellect
or otherwise increases its power is, *ipso facto*, a true idea. This does not
mean that by thinking pleasant, edifying, titillating, or otherwise "stimulating" (in the usual sense) thoughts, I am thereby increasing my will to
power. A more accurate interpretation would be, that by thinking difficult,
problematic, frightening, or paradoxical thoughts, I am straining my intellect, pushing it beyond its previous limits, overcoming resistance and
thereby growing in (intellectual) power. Certainly we are more likely to
consider strong emotions "true" than weaker ones, about which we remain
indifferent, although ordinarily this judgement is reversed, so that we
appear to be emotionally vehement about "the truth." Anyone who has
ever undergone the agonies of adolescent love can verify this, as well as
the subsequent, rueful truth with which this emotional aberration acquaints
us — that strong, emotional counter-reaction which states that "love is
blind."

Physical objects and our relationships with them represent simply an
extension of this principle. An object is "real" (or a "true" object) because
it resists me, because it does not conform to my every whim. I know that
the wall is real because I cannot walk through it: it resists my passage.
Something which offers no resistance has no objective reality. While I am
sitting at my typewriter I am conscious of the words which I am typing,
and little else. Yet, should my typewriter fail to function properly, the

---

[14] GA XVI, 45.

[15] Nachlass Mai—Juli 1885, 35 [15]; KGW VII 3, 235f. Nachlass Herbst 1885—Herbst
1886, 2 [76]; KGW VIII 1, 94f. Nachlass Herbst 1887, 9 [151]; KGW 2, 88. Nachlass
November 1887—März 1888, 11 [114]; KGW VIII 2, 296.

[16] As might be expected, Nietzsche also abolishes this distinction. For a clarification of
these terms, see the following: Nachlass Juni—Juli 1885, 36 [35, 36]; KGW VII 3,
289f. Nachlass November 1887—März 1888, 11 [83]; KGW VIII 2, 282f. GA XVI,
128f.

keys jam, the ribbon run out, etc., it immediately becomes an object of active, conscious thought. It has resisted me, and I must overcome that resistance. Of course, once I have dealt with the typewriter's mechanical recalcitrance, it fades once more from my objective field of consciousness. I must overcome objects which resist me, and my strength, my will to power, lies in the fact that I can manipulate many objects and utilize them for my own advantage. The more an object resists me, the more I must exert myself to gain control of it, and such an object is, at any given instant, more real than an object which is conveniently at my disposal, and which I scarcely think about. Furthermore, my increased power is proportional to the amount of resistance which I have overcome. The whole notion of objectivity or "thinghood," in the sense in which Nietz-sche intends it, is perhaps best expressed by the German word "Gegen-stand," which literally implies resistance[17].

II. Revaluation of the Disjunction True—False

At this point it has undoubtedly become obvious that the traditional concept of truth and falsity scarcely applies anymore to this context of resistance and power differences[18]. If we regard truth as an objective (in the traditional sense), unchanging standard which is applied like a yard-stick to any given situation, we see that Nietzsche is not interested in giving us any such standard. It might be objected that the criterion for truth given earlier is precisely such a standard, but this must now be shown to be inaccurate.

The criterion for truth which pervades all of Nietzsche's later writings is the one quoted earlier:

Das Kriterium der Wahrheit liegt in der Steigerung des Machtgefühls[19].

Nietzsche does not say anything to the effect that the increase of the feeling of power is true, or that truth increases my will to power, or any such thing. What he says is that the criterion for truth, the very basis upon which notions such as truth or falsity can even arise, is a function of the increase of will to power. The case in point is this: the primary factum,

---

[17] Of course, a consideration of the Latin roots of the English word "object" would lead to the same conclusion: *ob-jactum* (Med. Lat. *objectum*).

[18] But cf. Copleston, p. 207: "Nietzsche tends to make his observations and assertions in function of a preconceived ideal which he generally disdains to support by any attempt at scientific proof."

[19] GA XVI, 45.

the sole significant factor within this context is the increase of power. That is the important thing — indeed, the only thing with which Nietzsche is concerned. The whole notion of truth and falsity is grounded in and derivative of this more fundamental state of affairs. When we call something true, what we are actually saying, according to Nietzsche, is that we experience some increase or enhancement of our will to power. This is the sole criterion for truth, but as we have seen, terms such as truth or falsity, laden as they are with millenia of logical and metaphysical presuppositions, are simply not adequate to the task of expressing that which Nietzsche seeks to express. Ultimately, we must say that the will to power is simply beyond the conventional categories of truth and falsity.

III. Karl Jaspers' Criterion of Communicability

Truth has been traditionally held to be universally valid, i. e. truth, in order to deserve that appellation, must be true for everyone and in all cases. If this is the case, truth will certainly be communicable, since there will be only one general or universal truth about any given case, which must then be valid for everyone. One might even raise the question of what Nietzsche's purpose in writing might have been if he did not believe in "the truth" or the communicability thereof. Karl Jaspers maintains that Nietzsche did in fact have a second criterion for truth:

> Lebensverbindende Wahrheit muss mitteilbar sein. Der Satz: „Es gibt viele Augen... und folglich gibt es vielerlei Wahrheiten" ... findet seine Grenze an dem, was Gemeinschaft möglich macht. Für diese und damit für den Menschen, der in ihr lebt, ist wahr allein, was mitteilbar ist; die allgemeine Mitteilbarkeit ist daher unbewußt die Quelle und das Kriterium der durch Gemeinschaft lebensfördernder Wahrheit[20].

Jaspers goes on to state that Nietzsche recognized certain limits for his thinking, beyond which he would have been unable to communicate his thoughts, or have them understood and acknowledged, thus tacitly accepting and employing a canon of communicability within his thinking. This begs the much larger question of how Nietzsche viewed the truth or falsity of his own untterances. We will deal with this problem in subsequent chapters. For the moment we must ascertain whether or not Nietzsche did accept or employ a second criterion for truth other than

---

[20] Karl Jaspers, *Nietzsche: Einführung in das Verständnis seines Philosophierens* (Berlin, 1950), p. 187. The passage Jaspers cites from Nietzsche is to be found at Nachlass April—Juni 1885, 34 [230]; KGW VII 3, 218.

the one indicated earlier. Upon examination, we find that Jaspers' alleged criterion of communicability is untenable for three major reasons: (1) Nietzsche's unconscious thoughts or motives are (to this writer at least) inaccessible. The introduction by Jaspers of an unconscious criterion on the part of Nietzsche is simply unacceptable. (2) Jaspers does not support his contention with any relevant passages from Nietzsche. This is not surprising, however, as there are none. (3) There are, however, a number of passages which argue persuasively that Nietzsche did not consider communicability a criterion for anything (other than perhaps communicability itself)[21]. In some passages, Nietzsche seems practically to despair of ever adequately communicating his thoughts:

> Wie ist es möglich, sich mitzuteilen? Wie kann man gehört werden? Wann komme ich aus der Höhle ins Freie? Ich bin der Versteckteste aller Versteckten[22].

Nietzsche is profoundly suspicious of "popular truths," and sometimes seems to indicate what amounts to an inverse relationship existing between "truth" and "communicability," e. g.

> Die Wahrnehmung, dass ich mit anderen übereinstimme, macht mich leicht misstrauisch gegen das, worüber wir übereinstimmen[23].

But Nietzsche's irony goes much further than this, not only in denying any relationship between communicability and "truth," but in even questioning the desirability of communication:

> Fortwährend scheidet jeder Körper aus, er sezerniert das ihm nicht Brauchbare an den assimilierten Wesen: das, was der Mensch verachtet, wovor er Ekel hat, was er böse nennt, sind die Excremente. Aber seine unwissende „Vernunft" bezeichnet ihm oft als böse, was ihm not macht, unbequem ist, den Feind, er verwechselt das Unbrauchbare und das Schwer-zuerwerbende, Schwer-zu-besiegende, Schwer-einzuverleibende. Wenn er „mittheilt" an andere, „uneigennützig" ist — so ist dies vielleicht nur die Ausscheidung seiner unbrauchbaren faeces, die er aus sich wegschaffen muss, um nicht daran zu leiden. Er weiss, dass dieser Dünger dem fremden Felde nützt und macht sich eine Tugend aus seiner „Freigebigkeit"[24].

Nietzsche was an elitist to the core and, odd as it might appear to those of democratic persuasions, apparently took some care to prevent his ideas

[21] Cf. Nachlass Herbst 1887, 9 [106]; KGW VIII 2, 59f. Nachlass Mai—Juni 1888, 17 [3]; KGW VIII 3, 318ff. GA XVI, 365. GA XII, 334. GA XIII, 253f.
[22] GA XII, 257.
[23] GA XII, 258.
[24] GA XII, 103f.

from becoming too accessible to *hoi polloi*. This is made clear in a letter to Overbeck from the fall of 1886, in which Nietzsche writes (referring to the just published *Jenseits von Gut und Böse*), "Meine Angst war gross geworden gerade in der umgekehrten Richtung, nämlich dass ich diesmal etwas zu deutlich gewesen sei und 'mich' schon zu früh verrathen habe."[25] Such passages are by no means unique, and should be sufficient to demonstrate that communicability is not a criterion of truth for Nietzsche[26].

IV. The Second Sense of Truth for Nietzsche

Those passages in which Nietzsche is concerned with "truth" fall generally into two categories: (1) those in which the whole concept of "truth" is shown to be derivative of a much more fundamental process of increasing will to power; (2) those in which the existence of "truth" at all is denied. We shall now examine this second category.

A consequence of the first position is that the same thing may be both true and false, depending upon whether it occurs in an ascending or descending mode of the will to power. "Dasselbe Quantum Energie

[25] This letter is cited by Eckhard Heftrich, *Nietzsches Philosophie: Identität von Welt und Nichts* (Frankfurt a. M., 1962), p. 157.

[26] This does not mean that Nietzsche denies the possibility of communication at all, even though he does raise serious questions as to its ultimate value. In all fairness to Jaspers, however, we might address the much larger and more difficult question of what Nietzsche's purpose in writing might have been if he seriously doubted the ability of ordinary language to communicate his ideas. Nietzsche often points to the uselessness of a fixed, static medium of communication such as language to express the dynamic and paradoxical nature of the world as he envisions it (cf. Nachlass November 1887—März 1888, 11 [73]; KGW VIII 2, 278f.), but is forced to do this in terms of the very language whose suitability for the task he specifically denies. Superficially, this might seem to indicate that Nietzsche, by his own admission, is uttering nonsense, but this is not the case. Nietzsche uses his terms and concepts as signs, as metaphors, as indicators of a realm of meaning which is inaccessible to ordinary language. As he is forced to use ordinary language, however, Nietzsche purposely creates such paradoxes and such a high degree of conceptual tension within the structure of the language he uses, that the normal limits of communicability and intelligibility are ruptured and a breakthrough to a new level of meaning is achieved. Nietzsche's scheme of communication is more closely allied to the entire realm of the aesthetic and the non-rational, than to the logical, linguistic realm in which philosophical discourse normally takes place. This does not mean that Nietzsche's thought lacks rigor or precision: on the contrary, Nietzsche's overcoming of the normal limits of communicability imparts to his language a profundity and a rigor of which ordinary language is incapable (cf. Aristotle, *De Interpretatione* II. 17a 1—8) and which might best be compared to that level of meaning on which a work of art such as classical Greek tragedy communicates. Cf. Jaspers, pp. 16—21, 399—409. Cf. also Heftrich, p. 74ff. Nietzsche's linguistic paradigm and the enormous difficulties with which it confronts us will be the subject of Chapter V.

bedeutet auf den verschiedenen Stufen der Entwicklung Verschiedenes . . . ."[27] Nietzsche exploits this ambiguity to the utmost in his attempt to shatter the conventional notion of absolute, unchanging truth. He wishes to do away, once and for all, with the notion that truth is simply "there," simply given, waiting to be discovered by us. "Truth," for Nietzsche, is a function of activity: it is something we *do*, not something we discover or possess. This leads Nietzsche to make a number of highly provocative statements about "truth," to the effect that there is no "truth" at all.

> Es giebt vielerlei Augen. Auch die Sphinx hat Augen: und folglich giebt es vielerlei „Wahrheiten", und folglich giebt es keine Wahrheit[28].

Each power-constellation, each organism is its own standard for determining the "truth," i. e. the growth or increase of its power. In the midst of this logician's nightmare, the traditional valid-in-all-cases concept of truth is simply dissolved. Truth is a function of individual will to power, and on this basis Nietzsche can claim, quite simply, ". . . es giebt keine 'Wahrheit'."[29] But does this mean that everyone is equally right at all times? Or perhaps equally in error?

> „Wahrheit": das bezeichnet innerhalb meiner Denkweise nicht nothwendig einen Gegensatz zum Irrthum, sondern in den grundsätzlichsten Fällen nur eine Stellung verschiedener Irrthümer zu einander . . .[30].

In the absence of any immutable, eternal standard for truth, it would seem to make no difference whether we were "right" all the time or "wrong." But perhaps Nietzsche wishes to emphasize the absence of any truth at all, in the traditional sense, by referring to "truth" as the interrelationship of various errors. By denying the existence of truth, what Nietzsche wishes to do is rid us once and for all of the need to employ an inapplicable standard in determining the value of our own existence. Since life is will to power, it is a dynamic, ever-changing reality. A standard of truth which purports to be immutable and eternal is inimical to that reality which is life (and will to power). An unchanging, rigid standard such as the traditional concept of truth constrains life, hampers it from fully expressing its ownmost possibilities. Someone who is convinced that he has "the truth" feels no need to look any further, thereby arresting his own development and failing to realize his own potentialities. By employing Nietzsche's own criterion for "truth," i. e. "die Steigerung des Machtgefühls", we

---

[27] Nachlass Herbst 1887, 10 [138]; KGW VIII 2, 201f.
[28] Nachlass April—Juni 1885, 34 [230]; KGW VII 3, 218.
[29] Nachlass Herbst 1885—Herbst 1886, 2 [108]; KGW VIII 1, 112.
[30] Nachlass Juni—Juli 1885, 38 [4]; KGW VII 3, 326.

might even venture to say that truth, as traditionally conceived, is false
because it is inimical to the growth of the will to power.

> Was ist Wahrheit? (inertia, die Hypothese, bei der Befriedigung entsteht,
> geringster Verbrauch von geistiger Kraft usw.)[31].

Only a conception of truth grounded in the ever-changing reality of the
will to power is of any use at all. Of course, such a "truth" is itself a
function of incessant change and for this reason, no truth at all according
to traditional standards. But this demonstrates nothing but the total
inadequacy of static concepts of truth, and I think that Nietzsche's motives
for discarding the conventional concept of truth have been sufficiently
made clear.

V. The Paradoxes of Nietzsche's Notion of Truth

Now that we have dealt with Nietzsche's notion of truth in some
detail, a legitimate question, certainly, is this: Is what Nietzsche tells us
"true"? Does Nietzsche's criterion for truth, which he uses to great effect
to puncture commonly held, popular "truths," apply equally to his own
philosophy? If this were not the case, if Nietzsche's thoughts were not
internally consistent, there would certainly be grounds for maintaining
that he is merely indulging in extravagant rhetoric and not to be taken
seriously. Such a view, however, would be gravely mistaken. Nietzsche's
philosophy — I purposely refrain from calling it a system — is rigorously
consistent within the guidelines of its own, internally established criteria[32].
The alleged contradictions which we mentioned at the beginning of this
chapter arise only if one applies an inappropriate standard (viz. the traditional, static, correspondence theory standard) to Nietzsche's writings, a
standard which he himself has overcome.

Nietzsche tells us again and again that there is no truth. But by claiming that there is no truth, is he not in fact offering us another truth? Is he
not claiming, in effect, that the statement "there is no truth" is a true
statement? And, if so, is this not a flagrant self-contradiction? It takes
no great amount of philosophical acumen to point out this superficial

---

[31] Nachlass Herbst—1885 Herbst 1886, 2 [126]; KGW VIII 1, 122f. There are numerous
passages throughout Nietzsche's works in which he attacks, denies, or otherwise
impugns the notion of "truth." It is impossible to give more than a few representative
examples here. For a comprehensive listing of where such passages are to be located,
see Richard Oehler's index to the "Grossoktavausgabe" (GA XX). This index is also
reprinted as Vol. XII of the *Sämtliche Werke in zwölf Bänden* (Stuttgart, 1965), the
so-called "Dünndruckausgabe," although in slightly altered form.
[32] Cf. Heftrich, p. 20.

paradox, but the "paradox" arises only if one applies the traditional, static standard of truth to what Nietzsche tells us, a standard to which he specifically denies any validity. Martin Heidegger points out, and rightly so, that to seize upon this so-called paradox and imagine that one has thereby discredited Nietzsche is rather too facile: such a procedure is indicative of nothing other than a failure to have understood what Nietzsche means when he says that there is no truth. To claim that a statement of this sort must purport to be a true statement (and thereby contradict itself) is ultimately not even an interesting objection[33].

What Nietzsche means when he says " . . . es giebt keine 'Wahrheit'" is this: there exists no ultimate, immutable, eternal standard for truth. The quanta of the will to power (i. e. "reality") are constantly shifting, realigning themselves, overcoming or being overcome. A never-changing standard of truth simply does not apply, for it presupposes a totally inadequate understanding of being. Reality is constantly changing, constantly in flux, and a concept of truth which remains ignorant of this is imply irrelevant. Now, Nietzsche denies that there is "truth" such that it is eternal and immutable, but as we have seen, he does give us a criterion for "truth" viz. "die Steigerung des Machtgefühls." He does not mean by this that an increase of power is "true," thereby setting up another inflexible standard, the possibility of which he has already denied. What he means is that an increase in will to power is the primordial experience, the brute fact, which is the condition for the possibility of even forming a concept of truth in the first place. When we normally make a statement about truth, this "truth" is derivative of a more fundamental increase in power. Therefore, Nietzsche's own criterion for "truth" does not claim to be an inflexible, universally valid criterion: Nietzsche offers it to us as an "illusion," as a "useful fiction" which, if implemented in our own sphere of activity, will lead to an increase in will to power. *That is to say, if I believe that whatever increases my will to power is true, this belief will serve to increase my will to power.* Similarly, if this belief somehow weakens me, it is false. Nietzsche fully intended that this and other related notions of his should serve as stimulants for a strong, vigorous will to power, and have a destructive effect on a weak will to power. Thus we see that in either case, Nietzsche's criterion for "truth" is self-verifying (or self-referentially consistent): it is "true" for those capable of implementing it successfully, false for those incapable of doing this. In both cases, Nietzsche's principle is rigorously consistent. Nietzsche's criterion for truth can, according to its own internal sliding scale, be both "true" and "false" at the same time.

[33] Martin Heidegger, *Nietzsche* I, pp. 501—502 and ff.

We are now in a better position to ask the larger question: is what Nietzsche is telling us true? Is there "truly" only will to power — and nothing else? We are here confronted with a problem similar to the one previously discussed. If there is no "truth" in any ultimate, objective sense, then Nietzsche's philosophy must be as "false" as any of those which he attacks, or so it would seem. If Nietzsche were simply substituting one static, inflexible world-view for another, certainly his criticisms would apply as much to his own philosophy as to any other. But again we find that this is not the case. Nietzsche is not saying that his conception of the world (i. e., the will to power) is the only possible correct one (correct here referring to the traditional correspondence theory of truth). What he is saying, given his criterion for truth, is that if I believe that the world is will to power — and nothing else — and implement this belief in my own behavior, it will serve to enhance my vital powers, my growth, and stimulate me to realize (and exceed) my own potentialities, in short, to increase my will to power[34]. The will to power is itself another "illusion" or "useful fiction" which is "true" for those who can utilize it to grow and increase their power, false for those who cannot. Certainly Nietzsche would insist that his own world-view was more authentic and efficacious than any other, but by the same token he would have to allow that another world-view which promoted the growth and enhancement of power even more than his own would be preferable, indeed, "more true." Even if the notion of the will to power were to be flatly contradicted by another world-view which proved even more conducive to the growth and enhancement of power, Nietzsche's basic position would nonetheless be upheld: the only applicable standard for anything is the increase or decrease of power. Nietzsche's position is once again seen to be self-verifying.

The apparent inconsistencies and contradictions to be found in Nietzsche's statements about truth arise to a very large degree out of the extraordinarily difficult problem of linguistic formulation. Nietzsche wishes to deny that there exists any absolute, unchanging standard for truth, but the language in which he is forced to express such an idea is already based upon the tacit metaphysical assumption that such a standard exists. Language, as Martin Heidegger has pointed out, always contains an implicit metaphysics[35]. Obviously, using language to deny something which that

---

[34] Cf. Carl G. Jung, "The Transcendent Function," *Collected Works of C. G. Jung*, trans. by R. F. C. Hull (Princeton, 1969), Vol. 8, p. 73: "Man needs difficulties; they are necessary for health."

[35] See Martin Heidegger, *Sein und Zeit, Unterwegs zur Sprache* (Pfullingen, 1959), *Einführung in die Metaphysik* (Tübingen, 1966).

language one is using already presupposes is a proceeding fraught with difficulties, and Nietzsche is very much aware of this:

> Mag nämlich auch die Sprache, hier wie anderwärts, nicht über ihre Plump-
> heit hinauskönnen und fortfahren, von Gegensätzen zu reden, wo es nur Gra-
> de und mancherlei Feinheiten der Stufen giebt . . .[36]

> . . . — die Ausdrucksmittel der Sprache sind unbrauchbar, um das Werden
> auszudrücken, es gehört zu unserem unablöslichen Bedürfniss der Erhaltung,
> beständig die eine gröbere Welt von Bleibend ⟨em⟩, von „Dingen" usw. zu
> setzen[37].

Nietzsche attempts to solve this problem by a skillful juxtaposing of concepts which, according to the traditional concept of truth, are mutually exclusive. The case in point here is Nietzsche's use of the term "truth" in two very different senses: on the one hand, Nietzsche gives us a criterion for "truth" which is quite consistent with his ontology of power-quanta, but on the other hand he denies that there is any such thing as "truth" at all. By skillfully interweaving passages which affirm truth of a sort, and then deny truth of any sort, Nietzsche gradually wears away the logical septum dividing his two uses of the term "truth[38]." The result is a gradual destruction of the traditionally static concepts of truth and falsity, and a breakthrough to a totally new and completely flexible standard for "truth." Nietzsche purposely creates a paradoxical situation, purposely strains the traditional strictures of linguistic usage past their breaking point, and uses the conceptual tension thereby created as the driving force of his argument. In this manner, the traditional concept of truth is dissolved. Yet in spite of this, there remains an additional, perhaps unavoidable, difficulty: Nietz- sche is still forced to use terms such as "truth" and "falsity" simply because there are no others available to him, and the resulting ambiguity demands that Nietzsche's readers be fully aware of the context in which he uses a particular term. Nietzsche's generous use of quotation marks and other qualifying punctuation is a constant reminder that he is using his terms to indicate something quite different from their lexical meanings, and this often gives his writings the appearance of a "Philosophie der Gänsefüsschen[39]."

---

[36] JGB 24; KGW VI 2, 37.
[37] Nachlass November 1887—März 1888, 11 [73]; KGW VIII 2, 278f.
[38] Naturally, the degree of success with which Nietzsche overcomes these linguistic obstacles is open to question. See Chapter V. Cf. Muller-Lauter, esp. Chapters I and II.
[39] Cf. Heftrich, p. 74.

VI. Logical "Truths" as Value Judgements

Western logic and metaphysics have been traditionally founded upon a handful of principles which were regarded as being self-evidently true, and therefore neither requiring nor admitting of any further proof[40]. One of these principles we have already dealt with at some length, the notion that truth must be unchanging. Rather than further belabor the whole question of truth, we shall now turn to Nietzsche's analysis of why it is that truth should be regarded as necessarily unchanging in the first place.

Nietzsche's view of reality (the will to power) is such that all that exists is an ever-changing chaos of power-quanta, continually struggling with one another for hegemony. Nothing remains the same from one instant to the next. Consequently there are no stable objects, no "identical cases," no facts, and no order. Whatever order we see in the world, we ourselves have projected into it. By itself, the world has no order: there is no intrinsically stable "world order," no "nature." Yet metaphysics, logic, and language — indeed, our whole conceptual scheme — is grounded in the assumption that there is such a stable order. Why?

> ... die Annahme des seienden ist nöthig, um denken und schliessen zu können: die Logik handhabt nur Formeln für Gleichbleibendes
> deshalb wäre diese Annahme noch ohne Beweiskraft für die Realität: „das Seiende" gehört zu unserer Optik[46].

This can perhaps be best clarified by anticipating our discussion of Nietzsche's perspectivism.

Even if reality is a chaos of power-quanta, about which any statement is already an interpretation and "falsification," we nevertheless must assume some sort of order and continuity in order to function at all. But the assumption of order and continuity — even if it is a necessary assumption — is certainly not any sort of proof. We ourselves, as will to power, gain control over our environment by "interpreting" it, by simplifying and adapting it to our requirements. Life itself is an ongoing process of interpretation, a process of imposing a superficial order upon a chaotic reality.

---

[40] I use the termini "logic" and "metaphysics" here in a very broad and general sense to indicate the general features of Western thought, as well as those specialized disciplines which they have become. See Chapter VI. Cf. Martin Heidegger, *Sein und Zeit*, and *Vom Wesen der Wahrheit* (Frankfurt a. M., 1961).
[41] Nachlass Herbst 1887, 9 [60]; KGW VIII 2, 28 ff.

In Wahrheit ist Interpretation ein Mittel selbst, um Herr über etwas zu werden. (Der organische Prozess setzt fortwährendes *Interpretieren* voraus[42].

Thus we create for ourselves a world in which we can live and function and further enhance and increase our will to power. Even our perceptual apparatus is not geared to gleaning "truth" from the objects of our experience. Rather, it arranges, structures, and interprets these objects so that we can gain control over them and utilize them for our own ends. The "truth" about things is something we ourselves have projected onto them purely for the purpose of furthering our own power. Thus Nietzsche can say

Wahrheit ist die Art von Irrthum, ohne welche eine bestimmte Art von lebendigen Wesen nicht leben könnte. Der Werth für das Leben entscheidet zuletzt[43].

Thus the "truth" about reality is simply a variety of error, a convenient fiction which is nevertheless necessary for our maintenance. In the last analysis it is not a question of "truth" at all, but rather, a matter of which "fiction," which interpretation of reality best enables me to survive and increase my power.

In an absolute sense, the traditional standard of unchanging truth is no more true or false than Nietzsche's own. But on the basis of Nietzsche's criterion for truth we can make a vital distinction. All statements about the truth or falsity of our experiential world are functions of the will to power, and in this sense, all equally true (or false). The difference lies in the degree to which any particular interpretation increases or decreases our power. The notion that truth is unchanging is the interpretation of a comparatively weak will to power, which demands that the world be simple, reliable, predictable, i. e. "true." Constant change, ambiguity, contradiction, paradox, etc. are much more difficult to cope with, and require a comparatively high degree of will to power to be organized (i. e. interpreted) into a manageable environment. The ambiguous and contradictory — the unknown — is frightening and threatening. Therefore we have constructed for ourselves a model of reality which is eminently "knowable," and consequently subject to our control. Pain and suffering have traditionally been held to stem from "ignorance" about the way the world "really" is: the more predictable and reliable the world is, the less our chances are of suffering through error, of being unpleasantly surprised.

[42] Nachlaß Herbst 1885—Herbst 1886, 2 [148]; KGW VIII 1, 137f. The emphasis and missing parenthesis are Nietzsche's.
[43] Nachlaß April—Juni 1885, 34 [253]; KGW VII 3, 226.

However, " ... darin drückt sich eine gedrückte Seele aus, voller Miß-
trauen und schlimmer Erfahrung ... [44]."

The demand that reality and truth be stable, reliable, predictable, and
conveniently at our disposal is a symptom of weakness. The glossing over
of the chaotic, contradictory, changing aspect of reality is the sign of a
will to power which must reduce the conflict and competition in the world
to a minimum. Yet resistance and competition are the very factors which
enable any particular power-constellation to express itself and grow in
power. As we saw earlier, the will to power can only express itself by
meeting resistance, and any interpretation of reality which attempts to
minimize these factors is profoundly anti-life (since life is will to power).
Furthermore, a person embodying a strong and vigorous will to power
will "interpret" the "threatening" aspect of the world — the chaos, ambiguity, contradiction, danger, etc. — as stimuli, which continually offer him
a high degree of resistance which he must meet and overcome if he is to
survive and grow. Rather than negate change and make the world predictable, a "strong" person would, according to Nietzsche, welcome the
threat and challenge of a constantly changing world. Referring to those
who require a world as changeless as possible in order to survive, Nietzsche says

> ... (eine umgekehrte Art Mensch würde diesen Wechsel zum Reiz rechnen)
> Eine mit Kraft überladene und spielende Art Wesen würde gerade die Affekte,
> die Unvernunft und den Wechsel in eudämonistischem Sinne *gutheissen*,
> sammt ihren Consequenzen, Gefahr, Contrast, Zu-Grunde-gehn usw[45].

A large part of the intellectual energy of the West has been spent in
trying to discover "facts," "laws of nature," etc., all of which are conceived
to be "truths" and which, therefore, do not change. For Nietzsche, this
conceptualization of our experience is tantamount to a "mummification":
when an experience is conceptualized, it is wrenched from the ever-
changing stream of becoming which is the world. By turning our experiences into facts, concepts, truths, statistics, etc. we "kill" them, rob them
of their immediacy and vitality and embalm them, thus transforming them
into the convenient bits of knowledge which furnish our comfortable,
predictable, smug existences[46].

> Der Mensch sucht „die Wahrheit": eine Welt, die nicht sich widerspricht,
> nicht täuscht, nicht wechselt, eine wahre Welt, — eine Welt, in der man nicht
> leidet: Widerspruch, Täuschung, Wechsel — Ursachen des Leidens![47]

[44] Nachlass Juli—August 1888, 18 [16]; KGW VIII 3, 336f.
[45] Ibid. Nietzsche's emphasis.
[46] JGB I.; KGW VI 2, 9—33.
[47] Nachlass Herbst 1887, 9 [60]; KGW VIII 2, 28ff.

For Nietzsche, this whole tendency to negate change which is so intimately connected with the presupposition that "truth" always means "unchanging, eternal truth," is a symptom of decadence, a symptom of the weakening and disruption of the will to power. This outlook says, in effect, "This far shall you go, and this much shall you learn, but no more than this . . . ."

In the absence of any fixed and ultimate standard for truth, of course, this outlook is no more true or false than Nietzsche's own. Yet it is not a question here of rightness or wrongness, but a question of power. More specifically, it is a matter of vital power. "Der Werth für das Leben entscheidet zuletzt[48]." Nietzsche's conclusion is that this static world-interpretation has a negative, depressing effect on a person's vital energies (will to power). It constricts growth, it sets limits and hampers the self-assertion of the will to power. The strong individual, whom Nietzsche so much admires, flourishes only in an environment of change, ambiguity, contradiction, and — danger. The chaotic and threatening aspect of the world is a stimulus for such individuals, demanding that they constantly grow and increase their power, or perish[49]. It demands that they constantly exceed their previous limits, realize their creative potential and surpass it, become more than they were. In the absence of any stability in the world, the strong individual who can flourish in such an environment is radically free from any constraint, radically free to create. It need scarcely be said that this world-interpretation is immeasurably more conducive to the growth and enhancement of the will to power than the static world-view. And the increase of will to power is Nietzsche's only criterion:

> Alles Geschehen, alle Bewegung, alles Werden als ein Feststellen von Grad- und Kraftverhältnissen, als ein Kampf . . .[50]

VII. The "Real" World and the "Apparent" World

The static view of truth and reality, which Nietzsche sees as totally antithetical to his own, is certainly not regarded by its adherents as simply one possible interpretation of the world among a host of other possible interpretations. Understandably, this traditional outlook claims for itself absolute versimilitude within the boundaries of its own presuppositions. Historically, the conflict which arises when those who claim that truth is by its very nature unchanging, while living in a world where change

---

[48] Nachlass April—Juni 1885, 34 [253]; KGW VII 3, 226.
[49] "Aus der Kriegsschule des Lebens — Was mich nicht umbringt, macht mich stärker." GD I.8; KGW VI 3, 54.
[50] Nachlass Herbst 1887, 9 [91]; KGW VIII 2, 49.

is everywhere apparent, has led to the somewhat perverse denial of the
truth and reality of the physical world. The chief offenders in perpetrating
this decadent and reprehensible notion are, according to Nietzsche, Plato
(more properly, Platonism) and Christianity (". . . denn Christenthum ist
Platonismus für's Volk' . . ."[51]). The ontological dualism in question
here between the "real" world and the world of "mere appearances"
(i. e. the "unreal" world) might be paraphrased like this: the physical world
in which we normally think of ourselves as living is a world of constant
change, a world full of contradictions and paradoxes, of pain and suffering,
all of these things being undesirable. Reason and revelation, however,
reveal to us the existence of a stable and unchanging (and therefore
"true") order transcending the changing, material order of things. All true
knowledge and true values are to be found in this transcendent, unchanging, immaterial realm of pure intelligibility or spirituality. Christianity goes one step further and reduces the status of the present, corporeal
life to a sort of trial period which, if successfully undergone, entitles one
to an existence of undiminished bliss in the transcendental "real" world,
or heaven.

Plato and the majority of subsequent adherents of some sort of philosophical idealism were not so much concerned with demonstrations of a
beatific afterlife, but rather with the problem of true and objective knowledge. Plato's approach to the problem was basically this: since knowledge,
if it is to be valid, objective and universal, must be eternally valid and therefore unchanging, it cannot be derived from the material world. The material
world i. e., the world of becoming, is in a state of continual flux and
offers nothing constant in which to ground true knowledge. Since we
obviously do have knowledge, however, we must have gotten it from
somewhere, and this somewhere must necessarily be somewhere other
than the fluctuating, transitory realm of corporeal existence. This subsequently led Plato to the development of his theory of ideal forms, of
which the soul already has prior knowledge before it is born into the body.
Knowing therefore is simply a process of recollection (anamnesis) of the
soul's prior knowledge, which we mistakenly think to be derived from the
flux of material events[52]. It is not difficult to see how this inductive process
is capable of being transformed into a proof for the immortality of the
soul or the existence of an ultramundane realm of pure reality (e. g. the
notion of heaven and the afterlife)[53]. After Plato, the notion that truth

[51] JGB Vorrede; KGW VI 2, 4.
[52] See Plato, *Phaedo, Phaedrus, Meno, Theatetus.*
[53] Cf. Plato, *Phaedo.* Cf. also St. Augustine, *The City of God.*

presupposes stability, reliability, predictability — in short, permanence — became firmly entrenched in Western thought.

Parallel with this identification of truth with permanence was the transferral of all value to the transcendent, non-physical world of permanent reality. Just as truth must be unchanging if it is to be valid, it was thought, so must value be unchanging if it is to be genuinely valuable. It will be remembered that for Plato, the supreme reality was the "Good" which had "truth" (as well as beauty) as one of its essential attributes[54]. The same is true for Augustine, who gave this concept a theistic interpretation[55]. This was subsequently converted by the Neoplatonists and early Christian church fathers to mean that value (as the basis of morality) as well as truth must be unchanging, and be ultimately derived from the unchanging, transcendental realm of true being. This outlook had far-reaching results, such as the subsequent glorification of the soul or mind (at the expense of the body) as that organ or faculty which enables us to grasp eternal truth and value, the moral superiority of an ascetic or "otherworldly" life-style, the superiority of the church over the state, and so on[56].

An obvious presupposition of this way of thinking is the equation of truth and value. If we expand this equation, we find that permanence = truth = value. Phrased somewhat differently, this equation would state that goodness (i. e. value) and truth are necessarily interconnected, and both are eternal and unchanging. Truth, as has been sufficiently pointed out, must be eternal. But now the value judgement is made that truth, and therefore permanence, is "good". This is the point which Nietzsche seizes upon to begin his critique of Western Christian-Platonic dualism, and all that it implies.

To begin with, the shift from truth to permanence to value clearly makes the value judgement that whatever is unchanging is "better" than something transitory. But why should this be so? We must keep in mind that ultimately all judgements are value judgements for Nietzsche. All judgements are interpretations, and all interpretations are made solely for the purpose of increasing and enhancing our vital powers. Thus all values are vital values: our only standard (sic) for judging them is the extent to which they increase or decrease our will to power. With this in mind, let us follow Nietzsche's inquiry into precisely why that particular value judgement was made, viz. that value is a function of permanence or that truth, which is timeless, is good.

---

[54] Plato, *Republic* VI.
[55] St. Augustine, *De Trinitate* XIV, XV.
[56] See Windelband, pp. 235—246.

> . . . „die wahre und die scheinbare Welt" — dieser Gegensatz wird von mir zurückgeführt auf Werthverhältnisse
> wir haben unsere Erhaltungs-Bedingungen projicirt als Prädikate des Seins überhaupt
> dass wir in unserm Glauben stabil sein müssen, um zu gedeihen, daraus haben wir gemacht, dass die „wahre" Welt keine wandelbare und werdende, sondern eine seiende ist[57].

Furthermore, all value judgements are symptoms of the relative strength or weakness of whomever is making the judgement.

> Alle Werthschätzungen sind Resultate von bestimmten Kraftmengen und dem Grad Bewusstsein davon . . .[58]

Thus Nietzsche concludes that the value judgement in question is symptomatic of a weak, sick, decadent will to power which negates the changing, enigmatic character of the world to the greatest possible degree in order to survive at all. A strong, vigorous person will welcome change, contradiction, and suffering as stimulants which force him to grow in strength. A weaker individual would be crushed by this situation and is forced by his inferior degree of power to interpret the world in the manner most conductive to his continued existence, i. e., by denying the "reality" of change, contradiction, etc. All change and unpredictability, everything which cannot be "counted upon," thus becomes "evil."

> Die Verachtung, der Hass gegen Alles, was vergeht, wechselt, wandelt: — woher diese Werthung des Bleibenden?
> Ersichtlich ist hier der Wille zur Wahrheit bloss das Verlangen in eine Welt des Bleibenden.
> Die Sinne täuschen, die Vernunft corrigirt die Irrthümer: folglich, schloss man, ist die Vernunft der Weg zu dem Bleibenden; die unsinnlichsten Ideen müssen der „wahren Welt" am nächsten sein. — Von den Sinnen her kommen die meisten Unglücksschläge — sie sind Betrüger, Bethörer, Vernichter . . .[59]

This sort of evaluation and interpretation could only be carried out by a will which is weakened, decadent, sick in the extreme, which is simply incapable of coping with the world as, according to Nietzsche, it is.

> Was für eine Art Menschen reflektirt so? Eine unproduktive leidende Art; eine lebensmüde Art. Dächten wir uns die entgegengesetzte Art Mensch, so hätte sie den Glauben an das Seiende nicht nöthig: mehr noch, sie würde es verachten, als todt, langweilig, indifferent . . .[60]

[57] Nachlass Herbst 1887, 9 [38]; KGW VIII 2, 16f.
[58] GA XIII, 256.
[59] Nachlass Herbst 1887, 9 [60]; KGW VIII 2, 28f.
[60] Ibid., p. 29.

The weaklings and decadents who think in this manner, however, have apparently constituted an historical majority, because the consequences of this manner of reasoning are at the root of our whole cultural tradition: the reality and value of the world we live in are denied, in favor of a transcendent and immaterial world of eternal truth and value. Certainly Nietzsche regards this conclusion with the liveliest horror, as a monstrous perversion of all natural instincts. This is the origin of the historical distinction, so prevalent in Western philosophical and religious thought, between the "real" world, and the world of becoming, the world of "mere appearances."

This attempt to distinguish between "appearance" and "reality" — indeed, this whole conceptual structure — is most unpalatable to Nietzsche, who regards the value judgement upon which it is based as irreconcilably hostile to the fundamental reality of life, the will to power. The only world is the one in which we are living, here and now, with all its change, paradox, and impermanence. The "other world" is a fiction, an illusion, which has no existence outside the sick imaginations of decadents and intellectual cripples.

> Es ist von kardinaler Wichtigkeit, dass man die wahre Welt abschafft. Sie ist die grosse Anzweiflerin und Werthverminderung der Welt, die wir sind: Sie war bisher unser gefährlichstes Attentat auf das Leben . . .[61].

The "true" world of this passage is, of course, the "real" (i. e., permanent, transcendent, immaterial, etc.) world of the Platonic-Christian tradition. Its reality is only the result of denying that of the actual world of lived experience, that world *which we are*.

> Die „wahre Welt", wie immer auch man sie bisher concipirt hat, — sie war immer die scheinbare Welt noch einmal[62].
> Kritik des Begriffs „wahre und scheinbare Welt"
> von diesen ist die erste eine blosse Fiktion, aus lauter fingirten Dingen gebildet . . .[63].
>
> Der Gegensatz der scheinbaren Welt und der wahren Welt reduzirt sich auf den Gegensatz „Welt" und „Nichts" — . . .[64]

Nietzsche's intent is, I think, obvious enough. Still, there remain a number of difficulties with Nietzsche's own position which must be dealt with, beyond the perplexing tangle of the terms "true", "real," "false,"

---

[61] Nachlass Frühjahr 1888, 14 [103]; KGW VIII 3, 73.
[62] Nachlass November 1887—März 1888, 11 [50]; KGW VIII 2, 266.
[63] Nachlass Frühjahr 1888, 14 [93]; KGW VIII 3, 62.
[64] Nachlass Frühjahr 1888, 14 [184]; KGW VIII 3, 163.

etc. For one thing, Nietzsche hasn't the least right to call his "world" any more "real" than the statically, immaterially perfect world of Platonism and Christianity. If Nietzsche were to contend that he is concerned with the "real" world, while the weaklings and decadents (i. e., Christians and Platonists) are talking only about a "false," imaginary world, this would certainly seem to presuppose an objective standard for truth and reality. Nietzsche often makes the point himself that to call something either true or false, in the absolute sense of the traditional correspondence theory, requires knowledge of what is actually and unchangingly true. But there is no such thing as truth, no such thing as a fact, no stable world order which could function as a basis for immutable and objective truth. Nietzsche denies all these things, because ". . . es giebt keine 'Wahrheit'[65]." Thus, one cannot maintain either a) that the metaphysical world is false; b) that the changing world of vital activity is true; or c) the converse. Nietzsche has denied the very presuppositions necessary for making any apodictic statements about truth or falsity. It would appear that Nietzsche has painted himself into an epistomological corner. Martin Heidegger maintains in his Nietzsche lectures that what Nietzsche has done is simply to reverse the metaphysical tradition, to reverse Platonism, and exchange one "real" world for another, thereby not overcoming the traditional metaphysical presuppositions at all and, by reversing them, entrenching them all the more firmly[66]. This would be a correct observation if Nietzsche were thinking in traditional conceptual terms and merely replacing an outmoded concept of static truth with a new but equally static concept. But this is not the case: Nietzsche does not simply negate or reverse traditional categories — he attempts to overcome them.

We must always bear in mind that Nietzsche is not using the terms "true" and "false" in their traditional sense. He is aware that such a usage implies a static type of knowledge, of which he denies the very possibility. If we keep in mind that Nietzsche's sole criterion for what has heretofore been called "truth" or "falsity" is ". . . die Steigerung des Machtgefühls", the apparent inconsistency is resolved. Truth is a function of the increase of power, and this is the only "standard" for judging the "truth" or the vital value of anything. Furthermore, Nietzsche's criterion for truth is entirely consistent, because *it can be applied to itself*, and this is a very great advantage over the traditional correspondence theory of truth.

The world for Nietzsche, as we have seen, is the vital, dynamic, world of lived experience with all its change and contradiction. Not only do we

---

[65] Nachlass Herbst 1885—Herbst 1886, 2 [108]; KGW VIII 1, 112.
[66] Martin Heidegger, *Nietzsche* II.

live "in" this world, *we live this world itself* [67]. We, as active centers of force, constitute and structure our world through active interpretation and projection of vital values (i. e., provisional "truths" which serve to increase will to power, i. e. life). "World" and "being" and life itself are all will to power for Nietzsche. Each center of force or power structures and projects (i. e. "lives") its own world, and this world might in each case be different.

> . . . jedes Kraftcentrum hat für den ganzen Rest seine Perspektive d. h. seine ganz bestimmte Werthung, seine Aktions-Art, seine Widerstandsart
> Die „scheinbare Welt" reduzirt sich als ⟨o⟩ auf eine spezifische Art von Aktion auf die Welt, ausgehend von einem Centrum
> Nun giebt es gar keine andere Art Aktion: und die „Welt" ist nur ein Wort für das Gesammtspiel dieser Aktionen
> Die Realität besteht exakt in dieser Partikulär-Aktion jedes Einzelnen gegen das Ganze . . . [68]

Since the concept of an "unreal world" (i. e., a world of change and "mere" appearances) presupposes knowledge of the existence of an unchanging world of absolutely valid truth and value, and since Nietzsche has demonstrated the untenability of such a view, the whole notion of an "apparent world" loses its meaning. Appearance can exist only as one component of the traditional appearance-reality dichotomy and, since Nietzsche has negated the "reality" half of the dichotomy, the "appearance" half also becomes meaningless.

> Es bleibt kein Schatten von Recht mehr übrig, hier von Schein zu reden . . .
> Die spezifische Art zu reagiren ist die einzige Art des Reagirens: wir wissen nicht wie viele und was für Arten es Alles giebt.
> Aber es giebt kein „anderes", kein „wahres", kein wesentliches Sein — damit würde eine Welt ohne Aktion und Reaktion ausgedrückt sein . . . [69]

Furthermore,

> . . . die „Scheinbarkeit" gehört selbst zur Realität: sie ist eine Form ihres Seins d. h.
> in einer Welt, wo es kein Sein giebt, muss durch den Schein erst eine gewisse berechenbare Welt identischer Fälle geschaffen werden . . . [70]

Nietzsche thus completely dissolves the traditional religious-philosophical scheme. Instead of a changeless world of absolute, static truth and value,

---

[67] Nachlass Frühjahr 1888, 14 [103]; KGW VIII 3, 73.
[68] Nachlass Frühjahr 1888, 14 [184]; KGW VIII 3, 163.
[69] Ibid.
[70] Nachlass Frühjahr 1888, 14 [93]; KGW VIII 3, 63.

we get a constantly changing world of relative truth and vital value. Each individual creates his own world, which is essentially different from that of any other individual. The world

> ... ist essentiell Relations-Welt: sie hat, unter Umständen, von jedem Punkt aus ihr verschiedenes Gesicht: ihr Sein ist essentiell an jedem Punkt anders: sie drückt auf jeden Punkt, es widersteht ihr jeder Punkt — und diese Summirungen sind in jedem Falle incongruent.
> Das Mass von Macht bestimmt, welches Wesen das andre Mass von Macht hat: unter welcher Form, Gewalt, Nöthigung es wirkt oder widersteht ...[71]

Thus far it might appear that Heidegger's point is well taken, viz. that Nietzsche simply reverses Platonism or stands metaphysics on its head. But if we apply Nietzsche's sole criterion for anything — the increase or decrease of power — to this scheme, we find that such is not so: Nietzsche is very literal and very specific when he says

> Das Mass von Macht bestimmt, welches Wesen das andere Mass von Macht hat: unter welcher Form, Gewalt, Nöthigung es wirkt oder widersteht ...[72]

Thus we see a strict consistency between a) the flux ontology of power-quanta outlined in Chapter I.; b) Nietzsche's criterion for truth; and c) the destruction of the dichotomy between the "real" world and the "apparent" world on the basis of a) and b). Some further clarification is in order.

We might be tempted to say that Nietzsche is wrong in maintaining that the metaphysical world is "false" and that the transitory, material world is "true," but this is not really his intention. His critique of what has traditionally been regarded as the "real" world is not that it is necessarily and demonstrably false in the apodictic sense of traditional logic (for the changing, physical, life-world is just as false in this sense), but rather, that it is of inferior value according to the scale of vital values — the will to power *qua* life. It is basically a question of values here, ultimately of vital values which, in turn, are power values, and not a question of logic or metaphysics. The metaphysical world is just as true or false as the world in which we live. Both are creations or products of a particular will to power. The difference is that the spiritual, metaphysical world was created or projected out of weakness, out of "Lebensmüdigkeit," out of what Nietzsche calls a "hangman's metaphysics." People have traditionally

[71] Ibid.
[72] Ibid.
[73] GD VI.7; KGW VI 3, 89f.

regarded reason (and perhaps religious faith) as ultimate standards, and it is this which Nietzsche calls into question, showing that such a judgement includes or is based upon a value judgement of an inferior order.

> Die Moralischen Werthe in der Theorie der Erkenntniss Selbst
> das Vertrauen zur Vernunft — warum nicht Misstrauen?
> die „wahre Welt" soll die gute sein — warum? die Scheinbarkeit, der Wechsel, der Widerspruch,
> der Kampf als unmoralisch abgeschätzt: Verlangen in eine Welt, wo dies Alles fehlt[74].

The desire to create a changeless world of timeless truths is itself a sign of weakness. „Was Halt macht (bei einer angeblichen causa prima, bei einem Unbedingten usw.) ist die Faulheit, die Ermüdung —"[75]. Both worlds have the same truth value, which is to say, no truth at all in the traditional, apodictic sense. They do, however, have vastly different power values. One is the product of a weak, sick will to power; the other, the product of a vigorous and growing will to power. Nietzsche's paradigm is the strong, creative, productive individual who is continuously increasing his power, creating and projecting new values, new conditions, thereby enhancing his existence and making it stronger, richer, and more sublime. Such an individual would be, as one might expect, contemptuous of any static truth or value which would restrict his growth and self-expression:

> Insgleichen der *Wechsel*, die *Vergänglichkeit* gefürchtet: darin drückt sich eine gedrückte Seele aus, voller Misstrauen und schlimmer Erfahrung (Fall Spinoza: eine umgekehrte Art Mensch würde diesen Wechsel zum Reiz rechnen) Eine mit Kraft überladene und spielende Art Wesen würde gerade die Affekte, die Unvernunft und den Wechsel in eudämonistischem Sinne *gutheissen*, sammt ihren Consequenzen, Gefahr, Contrast, Zu-Grunde-gehn usw.[76].

The conclusion we must reach is this, that the whole contrast between a true world and a false one is simply meaningless. A better (though still inadequate) contrast might be between strong and weak world interpretations, or superior and inferior world interpretations. The point is basically this: the metaphysical world which Nietzsche deprecates cannot really be called false; neither can the life-world be called true. Such distinctions are meaningless. What Nietzsche attempts to demonstrate is that the whole metaphysical framework, in which this distinction is couched, rests upon inferior vital values and an inferior interpretation of life and world.

---

[74] Nachlass Herbst 1887, 9 [160]; KGW VIII 2, 94.
[75] Nachlass Herbst 1885—Herbst 1886, 2 [132]; KGW VIII 1, 131.
[76] Nachlass Juli—August 1888, 18 [16]; KGW VIII, 337.

Naturally, there is a good bit of confusion in Nietzsche's often reckless juxtaposing of the terms "true" and "false." Certainly he capitalizes upon the irony created by calling the "true world" of the metaphysical tradition a "false world," and even reverses this contrast on occasion, calling the "false world" of tradition (i. e. the physical world of "mere appearances") the "true world[77]." There is no absolute "truth" or "falsity"; there are only superior and inferior degrees of will to power. Thus, any "world" (in the absence of a fixed standard for comparison) is an individual creation with no claim whatsoever to universal validity.

> Die wahre Welt haben wir abgeschafft: welche Welt blieb übrig? die schein-
> bare vielleicht? ... Aber Nein! mit der wahren Welt haben wir auch die
> scheinbare abgeschafft![78]

[77] JGB 34—36, KGW VI 2, 48—51; GA XIV, 326; GA XIII, 50f.; Ecce Homo, Vorwort 2, KGW VI 3. 255f.
[78] GD IV.6; KGW VI, 75.

CHAPTER THREE

NIETZSCHE'S CRITIQUE OF THE CORRESPONDENCE THEORY

We have already seen some of Nietzsche's more notorious utterances upon "truth," to the effect that there is no truth, that truth is nothing more than a variety of error, that the world in which we live is a "false" world, etc. Statements of this sort are not at all uncommon in Nietzsche's writings, and his attack upon "truth" may be traced from his very earliest works through the *Nachlass* of his last productive period. Utterances of this sort have led some to regard Nietzsche as the "enfant terrible" of modern philosophy and to dismiss his views on "truth" as paradoxical and stimulating, perhaps, but ultimately meaningless. It will be our purpose in this chapter to show that this is not at all the case.

Upon closer examination it shall become obvious that what Nietzsche is really attacking is the correspondence theory of truth in its very broadest outlines. There are, of course, a number of other theories about what truth "is" or "means" such as the coherence theory, the pragmatic theory, the performative theory, et al. These, however, are relatively late developments for the most part, of little interest to anyone outside of academic philosophy, and it would be anachronistic to chide Nietzsche for focussing his attacks upon only one particular theory of truth. The correspondence theory (*adequatio intellectu et rei*) holds a privileged position within the history of Western thought: it is fundamental to what we have come to regard as rational thinking, and in attacking it Nietzsche is not engaging in a mere logical dispute — he is attempting to overthrow an entire mode of perceiving reality i. e., an entire cognitive paradigm.

The notion that the truth of our ideas or statements is a function of the accuracy of their correspondence to external objects or eternal verities is to be found throughout the Western intellectual tradition in one form or another. Needless to say, it has not always appeared as a strictly logical, formal tool. Associated with that mode of thinking, that cognitive paradigm, which is grounded in a correspondence theory are such derivative ideas as the distinction between appearance and reality, being and becoming, the "true" (i. e. ideal, spiritual, eternal) world and the "false" (i. e. material, temporal, changing) world, to name only a few. Nietzsche's attacks upon the moral and religious notions which presuppose a correspondence theory are too well known to require further elaboration here. Nevertheless, it is of fundamental importance to realize that Nietzsche is not only attacking symptoms or outgrowths of a particular view of truth and reality: he is attacking that fundamental viewpoint itself, and attempts to show that the correspondence view of truth and reality is simply incommensurate with, and inadequate for coming to grips with, that world which is the case.

The correspondence theory has taken a multitude of forms and received myriad applications within our tradition. For this reason, Nietzsche's critique of this theory has also taken a variety of forms, which require individual attention. Therefore, we shall first examine the formal incompatability of the correspondence theory with Nietzsche's own view of reality as will to power. I stress the formal nature of this initial investigation, because questions concerning the "correctness" or "incorrectness" of Nietzsche's own position will be suspended. After this we shall examine Nietzsche's charge that the correspondence theory is self-contradictory and useless even on its own criteria, particularly as this theory is presupposed by Kant in the *Kritik der reinen Vernunft*. We shall subsequently examine some of the difficulties inherent in Nietzsche's own position with regard to truth.

I. Truth as the Correspondence of "Thoughts" and "Things"

There can be no relevant theory of truth which does not rest upon some theory of reality, whether implicitly or explicitly. One of Nietzsche's major contributions to critical philosophy was his demonstration that many traditional philosophical positions were inconsistent with their very presuppositions. It is, I believe, sufficiently accurate to claim that any theory of truth which is not completely vacuous must be grounded within a particular view of reality, whether this takes the form of the naive realism of the natural attitude, or an elaborate ontology and epistemology. Having made this claim, I feel it necessary to briefly review some of the points made in Chapter I regarding Nietzsche's model of reality before we can profitably discuss his critique of the correspondence theory.

Nietzsche's term for being — or, to borrow a phrase from Wittgenstein, that world which is the case — is will to power, and nothing else. The will to power is an all-inclusive "principle," but must not be regarded as a homogeneous world-substance (like the *arche* of the Milesians, or Hegel's "Geist") which smoothly exfoliates according to its own internal principles. The will to power is neither homogeneous nor continuous. It is comprised of a vast (though finite) number of power-quanta which do not possess but *are* this will to ever-increased power. Viewed *in toto*, the will to power is comprised of these discrete quanta, which might be regarded as specific instances or particular cases of the will to power. The quanta are not inviolate, ultimate entities (i. e. they are not monads, nor are they necessarily synonymous with the atoms of physics), but may merge to form a new, single quantum, or may be split into separate quanta[1]. Yet Nietzsche equally cautions against regarding the will to power as an all-embracing, organic, collective entity: „. . . es giebt keinen Willen: es giebt Willens-Punktationen, die beständig ihre Macht mehren oder verlieren . . ."[2] These power-quanta do not have will to power — they *are* will to power, i. e. they are identical with their activity. All activity — indeed, that entire process which is the world — is conceived as the aggression and will-to-dominate and -assimilate which prevails between individual power-quanta or groups of quanta ("Machtkonstellationen"). Thus, reality for Nietzsche is a continually changing flux of mutually antagonistic power-quanta which ceaselessly struggle against one another, align and realign themselves to ever increase that power which they are. As might be expected, all the traditional philosophical categories such as value, knowledge, being, and of course, truth, are reinterpreted in terms of degree of power.

What Nietzsche is denying is pretty clearly the correspondence theory of truth in its very broadest outlines. Nietzsche regards this view of truth in all its various forms and with all its myriad presuppositions as having been paradigmatic for the vast majority of Western thinkers. If, as in the correspondence theory of truth, we were to measure truth according to how perfectly our ideas represented external objects, or how accurately our statements mirrored facts, in Nietzsche's flux ontology of power-quanta there is simply nothing which could correspond to anything else. One of the presuppositions of the correspondence view of truth is that there are stable entities which exist independently of the cognitive processes of the perceiver. This is a *sine qua non*, without which there would be nothing for our ideas, concepts, or statements to correspond to. In addition to existing separately from consciousness, these entities must also exhibit a certain degree of stability and self-sameness. Were this not the case, our ideas and concepts would lack that general applicability which is regarded as a necessary condition for rational thought and communication. Indeed, if we could be not reasonably certain that the objects of our experience would remain relatively stable and predictable, then we could no longer be

[1] Nachlass November 1887—März 1888, 11 [73]; KGW VIII 2, 278f.
  Nachlass Herbst 1887, 9 [151]; KGW VIII 2, 88.
[2] Nachlass November 1887—März 1888, 11 [73]; KGW VIII 2, 278f.

sure that our thoughts and statements did in fact correspond *to* something, and the basis for this relationship of correspondence between thought and thing would be destroyed. If, for example, birds suddenly began to bear fur and teeth, our entire system of concepts relating to the class *Aves* would no longer correspond to anything, and therefore become meaningless. Nietzsche leaves none of these presuppositions unchallenged.

The correspondence theory must presuppose a world of (relatively) stable objects and facts about which we make statements or form ideas, and to which these statements and ideas must adequately correspond if they are to be "true." But Nietzsche's model of reality is such that it is in constant, turbulent change, and therefore admits of neither stable objects nor facts[3]. Facticity and objectivity are interpretations from the perspective of any given power-center and are completely relative or, as Nietzsche has it, "perspectival."

> Gegen den Positivismus, welcher bei dem Phänomen stehen bleibt „es giebt nur Thatsachen", würde ich sagen: nein, gerade Thatsachen giebt es nicht, nur Interpretationen. Wir können kein Factum „an sich" feststellen: vielleicht ist es ein Unsinn, so etwas zu wollen[4].

Facts and objects are our interpretations, subject to constant reinterpretation, of the flux of power-quanta.

> Der interpretative Charakter alles Geschehens.
> Es giebt kein Ereigniss an sich. Was geschieht ist eine Gruppe von Erscheinungen ausgelesen und zusammengefasst von einem interpretirenden Wesen[5].

Since what there is is will to power, and since the will to power is in constant, turbulent flux, there exists nothing stable to which our statements or concepts could be meaningfully said to apply. Since within this scheme there can be no substances, entities, things, facts, objects, etc. (except in a completely relative sense, which is still sufficient to compromise the correspondence theory), there is nothing which could ground that relationship of intentionality, i. e. the subject-object relationship, which must be valid if our ideas and statements are to correspond *to* anything else. Facts and objects are idiosyncrasies of our "optics," not independently existing "things." Nietzsche makes this quite explicit in a note from the *Nachlass* of 1887:

---

[3] Nachlass Herbst 1885—Herbst 1886, 2 [85]; KGW VIII 1, 102.
   Nachlass Frühjahr 1888, 14 [184]; KGW VIII 3, 162f.
   Nachlass Herbst 1887, 9 [106]; KGW VIII 2, 59f.
   Nachlass Frühjahr 1888, 14 [103]; KGW VIII 3, 72—74.
[4] Nachlass Ende 1886—1887, 7 [60]; KGW VIII 1, 323.
[5] Nachlass Herbst 1885—Frühjahr 1886, 1 [115]; KGW VIII 1, 34.

... die Annahme des Seienden ist nöthig, um denken und schliessen zu können: die Logik handhabt nur Formeln für Gleichbleibendes
deshalb wäre diese Annahme noch ohne Beweiskraft für die Realität: „das
Seiende" gehört zu unserer Optik.
die fingirte Welt von Subjekt, Substanz, „Vernunft" usw. ist nöthig —: eine
ordnende, vereinfachende, fälschende Macht ist in uns. „Wahrheit" — Wille,
Herr zu werden über das Vielerlei der Sensationen.
— die Phänomene aufreihen auf bestimmte Kategorien
— hierbei gehen wir vom Glauben an das „An sich" der Dinge aus (wir
nehmen die Phänomene als wirklich)
Der Charakter der werdenden Welt als unformulirbar, als „falsch", als „sich-
widersprechend"
Erkenntniss und Werden schliesst sich aus.
Folglich muss „Erkenntniss" etwas anderes sein: es muss ein Wille zum
Erkennbar-machen vorangehn, eine Art Werden selbst muss die Täuschung
des Seienden Schaffen[6].

There are a number of important ideas in this passage, some of which have
already been dealt with at some length, others of which shall be examined
in subsequent chapters. For the present, however, I would like to make the
following observations.

With regard to the mutual exclusivity of being and becoming, Nietzsche
quite emphatically decides in favor of becoming, and regards being (by
which he always means static being) as simply a perspectival interpretation
or falsification on our part. „Man muss das Sein leugnen[7]." He can thus
characterize the world of becoming as "false" because, if one accepts the
criterion of correspondence as paradigmatic for determining truth, that
world which is the case does not correspond at all to our ideas and statements: reality flows and changes, while our ideas and concepts stand still
and give us the "illusion" that they refer to an equally unchanging state of
affairs.

There is, however, another and probably more telling criticism of the
correspondence theory implicit to the critique just given. Nietzsche also
rejects the subject-object distinction, i. e. that distinction which we
customarily make between doer and deed, actor and act, thinker and
thought, etc. This distinction, as I have stated, is a necessary presupposition
of the correspondence theory of truth. If this distinction is illusory, if it
is simply a perspectival falsification, then the correspondence theory is
once again discredited.

Within a typical act such as the act of thinking or cognizing, we may
distinguish three moments: the thinker, his activity of thinking, and the

---

[6] Nachlass Herbst 1887, 9 [89]; KGW VIII 2, 46.
[7] Nachlass Frühjahr 1884, 25 [513]; KGW VII 2, 143.

object of his thought. Nietzsche identifies all three of these moments in the most radical sense. Within his ontology of power-quanta, there exist no things which may either act or not act. Everything is active and dynamic in the most fundamental sense: a thing *is* precisely what it *does*, i. e. the usual distinction we make between subject and object is simply a logical quirk, a perspectival idiosyncrasy, and no reflection upon the way things "really are." Naturally Nietzsche also discards the Kantian "Ding an sich" as an absurdity, and maintains that if we were to abstract a "thing" from its activities and relationships to other "things," this would be tantamount to negating that thing[8].

If we apply this reasoning to the activity of thinking itself, we see that thinker, thought, and the object of thought are identical. Nietzsche seems to envision the cognitive act as a continuum of interpretive activity which constitutes thinghood, objectivity, facticity, etc. out of that matrix of interlocking power relationships which is the world. To oversimplify this somewhat, we might say that the thinker *is* the thinking which, in turn, is the object of thought. This is not the same as the traditional idealist stance, which would maintain that things and thoughts are identical, because Nietzsche includes the thinker within this active continuum. Obviously, within this context of identity, it makes little sense anymore to speak of the correspondence of thought to thing, because the thought, as well as the thinker, *is* the thing[9].

> Dass die Dinge eine Beschaffenheit an sich haben, ganz abgesehen von der Interpretation und Subjektivität, ist eine ganz müssige Hypothese: es würde voraussetzen, dass das Interpretiren und Subjektivsein nicht wesentlich sei, dass ein Ding aus allen Relationen gelöst noch Ding sei. Umgekehrt: der anscheinende objektive Charakter der Dinge: könnte er nicht bloss auf eine Graddifferenz innerhalb des Subjektiven hinauslaufen? — dass etwa das Langsam-Wechselnde uns als „objektiv" dauernd, seiend, „an sich" sich herausstellte
> — dass das Objektive nur ein falscher Artbegriff und Gegensatz wäre innerhalb des Subjektiven?
>
> Der Begriff „Wahrheit" ist widersinnig ... das ganze Reich von „wahr" „falsch" bezieht sich nur auf Relationen zwischen Wesen, nicht auf das „An sich" ... Unsinn: es giebt kein „Wesen an sich", die Relationen constituiren erst Wesen, so wenig es eine „Erkenntnis an sich" geben kann ...[11]

I should point out once again that the kind of truth which Nietzsche dismisses as "widersinnig" is the correspondence variety. I should further

---

[8] Nachlass Herbst 1885—Herbst 1886, 2 [85]; KGW VIII 1, 102.
[9] See Chapters VI and VII.
[10] Nachlass Herbst 1887, 9 [40]; KGW VIII 2, 17.
[11] Nachlass Frühjahr 1888, 14 [122]; KGW VIII 3, 94.

like to point out that Nietzsche's identification of thought, thinker, and thing within one active continuum should not be regarded as an idealistic, solipsistic ego as with, for example, Fichte. The unity of this continuum, embracing the three moments we have distinguished, is a unity of organization, a unity of function[12]: it is itself perspectival, and out of its perspective, i. e. the sum of its power-relationships with other power-configurations, it interprets those elements which we simplistically and erroneously regard as being substantially different. The unity of thinker, thinking, and object of thought is analogous to the unity of chemical forces which constitute a cell, or of the cells which constitute a body, of those bodies which constitute a political federation[13].

> Diese Scheidung des Thuns und des Thuenden, des Thuns und des Leidens, des Seins und des Werdens, der Ursache und der Wirkung
> schon der Glaube an die Veränderung setzt den Glauben an etwas voraus, das „sich ändert".
> die Vernunft ist die Philosophie des Augenscheins . . .[14]

The unity of thinker, thought, and thing will be elaborated in greater detail in subsequent chapters. For present purposes the point I would like to make is this: on the basis of this identity, there is nothing which could conceivably stand in a relationship of correspondence to anything else. Thus, within this context, correspondence is simply useless as a criterion for "truth."

II. The Formal Inconsistency of the Correspondence Theory

Up to this point, we have done nothing more than demonstrate that, within the Nietzschean model of reality, the traditional correspondence view of truth and reality loses all meaning and applicability. It goes without saying that if one does not accept Nietzsche's scheme of things, one will not accept his destruction of correspondence as a truth-criterion as it has thus far been elaborated. Certainly one does not "disprove" a point simply

---

[12] „Alle Einheit ist nur als Organisation und Zusammenspiel Einheit: nicht anders als wie ein menschliches Gemeinwesen eine Einheit ist: also Gegensatz der atomistischen Anarchie; somit ein Herrschafts-Gebilde, das Eins bedeutet, aber nicht eins ist . . . wenn alle Einheit nur als Organisation Einheit ist? aber das 'Ding', an das wir glauben, ist nur als Ferment zu verschiedenen Prädikaten hinzuerfunden. Wenn das Ding 'wirkt', so heisst das: wir fassen alle übrigen Eigenschaften, die sonst noch hier vorhanden sind und momentan latent sind, als Ursache, dass jetzt eine einzelne Eigenschaft hervortritt: d. h. wir nehmen die Summe seiner Eigenschaften — x als *Ursache* der Eigenschaft x: was doch ganz dumm und verrückt ist!" Nachlass Herbst 1885—Herbst 1886, 2 [87]; KGW VIII 1, 102f.
[13] Nachlass Herbst 1885—Herbst 1886, 2 [87]; KGW VIII 1, 102f.
[14] Nachlass Herbst 1885—Herbst 1886, 2 [141]; KGW VIII 1, 134f.

by making contrary assertions. There does emerge from Nietzsche's notes, however, a critique of the correspondence theory which states that this view is self-contradictory and inconsistent with itself, a critique which is essentially similar to Wittgenstein's critique of the same notion. Both Nietzsche and Wittgenstein recognized that the thinker cannot step outside his cognitive faculties and observe to what extent his ideas represent or correspond to an independent, external reality. Both realized that the correspondence theory purports to verify facts or statements on the basis of a principle which does not itself admit of such verification. A principle which analyzes facts or statements, but which is itself exempt from such scrutiny, can have no higher logical status than that of an axiom or assumption. Nietzsche makes an analogous observation about the intellect, viz. that the intellect cannot transcend itself to observe and comment upon its operations or its relationships with external reality. But as we have seen, Nietzsche's identification of thinker, thinking, and thing makes this both unnecessary and impossible. Nietzsche asks, „. . . ist es wahrscheinlich, dass ein Werkzeug seine eigene Tauglichkeit kritisiren kann[15]??" Consider the following passage from the Nachlass of 1886—1887:

> Der Intellekt kann sich nicht selbst kritisiren, eben weil er nicht zu vergleichen ist mit andersgearteten Intellekten und weil sein Vermögen zu erkennen erst Angesichts der „wahren Wirklichkeit" zu Tage treten würde d. h. weil, um den Intellekt zu kritisiren, wir ein höheres Wesen mit „absoluter Erkenntniss" sein müssten. Dies setzte schon voraus, dass es, abseits von allen perspektivischen Arten der Betrachtung und sinnlich-geistiger Aneignung, etwas gäbe, ein „An-sich" — Aber die psychologische Ableitung des Glaubens verbietet uns von „Dingen an sich" zu reden[16].

Nietzsche makes explicit here some of the difficulties encountered in a theory of knowledge which is grounded in a correspondence theory of truth. If one were to assert that "truth" lay in the adequate correspondence of thoughts with things, this assertion presupposes that one has an extra-cognitive (or supra-human) vantage from which to compare the cognitive act and the object of cognition, and comment upon the adequacy of their correspondence to one another. That such an extra-cognitive vantage is not given us goes without saying, and we see that in order to uphold its own validity, the correspondence theory must have recourse to a type of knowledge which, simply by definition, is inaccessible.

In objection to Nietzsche's criticism one might assert that — even granting this inconsistency, the correspondence theory must claim

---

[15] Nachlass Herbst 1885—Herbst 1886, 2 [161]; KGW VIII 1, 141f.
[16] Nachlass Sommer 1886—Herbst 1887, 5 [11]; KGW VIII 1, 192.

exemption from its own criteria of verification — this does not suffice to invalidate it, and that it is still a theoretical possibility that truth may, in fact, reside within such a relationship of correspondence. To this we might reply that it is indeed an odd sort of truth criterion which — granting its validity — this validity can never be established without violating the very principle which it seeks to verify. This is to say that, if the correspondence theory is valid, we are prevented by this very theory from ever ascertaining that fact; if, on the other hand, reasons can be brought forth in support of this theory, they must by their very nature be violations of that theory. It is impossible to maintain that the correspondence theory accurately "corresponds" to the real nature of the world without invoking that very principle and becoming involved in an obvious *petitio principii*. Again, if it were possible to somehow transcend the relationship of correspondence in order to gather evidence for the validity of that relationship as constitutive of truth, one would have violated the same principle that one was attempting to verify: one would have gained "true knowledge" which transcended (and therefore discredited) the correspondence criterion.

I have maintained that one of the consequences (or assumptions) of the correspondence theory is that sort of epistemological dualism which distinguishes between things as they really are in themselves, and their appearance to an observer. With regard to this distinction Nietzsche says

> Um eine solche Unterscheidung machen zu können, müsste man sich unsern Intellekt mit einem widerspruchsvollen Charakter behaftet denken: einmal, eingerichtet auf das perspektivische sehen, wie dies noth thut, damit gerade Wesen unserer Art sich im Dasein Erhalten können, andrerseits zugleich mit einem Vermögen, eben dieses perspektivische Sehen als perspektivisches, die Erscheinung als Erscheinung zu begreifen. Das will sagen: ausgestattet mit einem Glauben an die „Realität", wie als ob sie die einzige wäre, und wiederum auch mit der Einsicht über diesen Glauben, dass er nämlich nur eine perspektivische Beschränktheit sei in Hinsicht auf eine wahre Realität. Ein Glaube aber, mit dieser Einsicht angeschaut, ist nicht mehr Glaube, ist als Glaube aufgelöst. Kurz, wir dürfen uns unsern Intellekt nicht dergestalt widerspruchsvoll denken, dass er ein Glaube ist und zugleich ein Wissen um diesen Glauben. Schaffen wir das „Ding an sich" ab und, mit ihm, einen der unklarsten Begriffe, den der „Erscheinung"! Dieser ganze Gegensatz ist, wie jener ältere von „Materie und Geist" als unbrauchbar bewiesen . . .[17]

Nietzsche's charge that the correspondence theory is inconsistent with itself (if not manifestly self-contradictory) given in this passage is clear enough from the foregoing discussion to require no further belaboring

---

[17] Nachlass Sommer 1886—Frühjahr 1887, 6 [23]; KGW VIII 1, 246ff.

here. I should only like to add that a number of thinkers since Nietzsche
have repeated and further elaborated what is substantially the same criticism
of the correspondence theory, and that we might claim a sort of nominal
priority for Nietzsche in this regard[18].

III. Kant and Correspondence

I have already stated and shall state once more that Nietzsche's destruction of the correspondence theory of truth represents a frontal attack
upon the dominant cognitive paradigm of our intellectual tradition i. e.,
an entire mode of viewing reality, and not simply a formal, logical critique
of a formal, logical tool. Closely associated with this mode of viewing
reality are, of course, the correspondence notion of truth and its derivative
notions, e. g. the subject-object and appearance-reality distinctions. The
thrust of Nietzsche's attack is to show that this cognitive paradigm is self-
defeating, i. e. untenable even on grounds of its own internal criteria. In
its broadest form, this inconsistent or self-contradictory nature of our
cognitive paradigm appears as the phenomenon of nihilism. And while
we cannot concern ourselves with cultural criticism, morality, etc. in a book
of this nature, I think it would be correct to claim that what we are dealing
with here is itself a form of that nihilism which Nietzsche so incisively
described in other areas, nihilism on the level of logic and epistemology.

A major figure, not only with regard to the critical elaboration of this
cognitive paradigm but of Western thought as a whole, was Immanuel
Kant. Now, if Nietzsche's critique of the correspondence theory is sound,
and if such a view of truth and reality is implicit to Kant's critical philosophy, we may then demonstrate that even in so sophisticated a version as
the *Kritik der reinen Vernunft*, the correspondence theory leads either to
self-contradictory or to otherwise unacceptable results. I have chosen to
focus upon Kant here for two reasons: a) Nietzsche specifically confronts
Kant with that criticism which is the subject of this chapter; b) Kant's
influence in Western thought is so far-reaching that if Nietzsche's attempt
to undermine Kant's critical theory is successful, the reader may himself
anticipate a similar undermining of the views of those other thinkers who
(whether implicitly or explicitly) concur with the essential features of
Kant's critical theory.

---

[18] See J. O. Urmson, *Philosophical Analysis: Its Development Between the Two Wars*
(Oxford, 1956), pp. 50—53; A. D. Woozley, *Theory of Knowledge* (London, 1949),
pp. 29—34; L. Wittgenstein, *Tractatus Logico-Philosophicus* (London, 1961).

As is the case in his relationship with so many other important thinkers, Nietzsche's relationship to Kant is decidedly ambivalent. In one of Nietzsche's earliest works, he speaks — and not without admiration — of a similar intellectual greatness in both Parmenides and Kant[19]. His own view that the human mind bestows order and meaning upon an otherwise chaotic reality bears more than a superficial resemblance to Kant's views[20]. Even the stridency of Nietzsche's attacks upon Kant might be viewed as a tacit admission on Nietzsche's part of Kant's intellectual prowess. And yet, Nietzsche's rejection of Kantian philosophy becomes so strong in his later works that there is no mistaking his intent. Indeed, one of the longest and clearest notes from the *Nachlass* of the 1880's is a succinct summation of Nietzsche's critique of Kant, and it is with this fragment that we shall initially concern ourselves.

It might appear odd or questionable to mention Kant in this context as having embraced some type of correspondence theory. For the most part one usually tends to regard Kant as having once and for all laid to rest the naively realistic sort of epistemological dualism with which the correspondence theory is generally associated. Yet Nietzsche's point is that, in spite of his critical stance, Kant nevertheless assumed a type of knowledge for which the correspondence theory is axiomatic, and that the internal inconsistencies of this view led to inconsistencies on Kant's part. Nietzsche rejects Kant's critical philosophy on basically three grounds: 1) he accuses Kant of a *petitio principii* in asking not "Is there knowledge?", but rather, simply assuming that there is and asking the begged question "What are the conditions under which knowledge is possible?", thereby restricting his analysis to the conventional, paradigmatic view of knowledge; 2) he accuses Kant of a *contradictio in adjecto* with regard to the noumenon-phenomenon distinction; 3) he accuses Kant of moral prejudice in insisting upon the noumenon-phenomenon distinction and exploiting that mode of cognition proper only to intelligible objects as a justification of conventional religious morality. This might be regarded as an error of category. In all of these criticism we may detect the strong influence of Schopenhauer[22].

---

[19] "Die Philosophie im Tragischen Zeitalter der Griechen" 15; KGW III 2, 351.
[20] See Hans Vaihinger, "Nietzsches Philosophie des Bewussten Gewollt-Seins" in *Die Philosophie des Als-Ob* (Leipzig, 1911), p. 771 ff.
[21] Nachlass Ende 1886—Frühjahr 1887, 7 [4]; KGW VIII 1, 272.
[22] Cf. Arthur Schopenhauer, "Anhang: Kritik der Kantischen Philosophie" in *Die Welt als Wille und Vorstellung, Schopenhauers Sämmtliche Werke*, ed. by E. Griesbach (Leipzig, 1890), Vol. I, pp. 529—677. Cf. also the "Kritik des von Kant der Ethik gegebenen Fundaments," Vol. III, pp. 497—565.

The first of these points is dealt with in the *Nachlass* passage referred to above:

> Das πρῶτον ψεῦδος: wie ist die Thatsache der Erkenntnis möglich?
> ist die Erkenntniss überhaupt eine Thatsache?
> Was ist Erkenntniss: Wenn wir nicht wissen, was Erkenntniss ist, können wir unmöglich die Frage beantworten, ob es Erkenntniss giebt. Sehr schön! Aber wenn ich nicht schon „weiss", ob es Erkenntniss giebt, geben kann, kann ich die Frage „was ist Erkenntniss" gar nicht vernünftigerweise stellen. Kant glaubt an die Thatsache der Erkenntniss: es ist eine Naivetät, was er will: die Erkenntniss der Erkenntniss!
> „Erkenntniss ist Urtheil!" Aber Urtheil ist ein Glaube, dass etwas so und so ist! Und nicht Erkenntniss![23]

In this passage Nietzsche quite clearly feels that the very point of departure of the *Kritik der reinen Vernunft* begs the question: Kant assumes a particular type of knowledge (viz. a correspondence view of knowledge, which I claim is paradigmatic to Western thought as a whole), and then seeks to elaborate the conditions under which this presupposed type of knowledge is possible. It is this presupposition which Nietzsche challenges.

It might be held that the very asking of the question of how knowledge is possible itself stands as evidence of the fact that there is knowledge. If we had no knowledge at all, if knowledge were not possible, it does not seem likely that we could even raise such a question. Yet Nietzsche feels that the variety of knowledge which Kant attempted to explicate still rested upon the naive, correspondence theory assumption that there is a world independent of our experience, that thoughts and things are in fact distinct, and that our knowledge is in some manner "of" or "about" this external, independent world. Naturally, this independent, external world was not itself a possible object of experience for Kant, but he nonetheless insisted upon it as a necessary feature of the *Kritik der reinen Vernunft*. In the preface to the second edition (B: 1787) of the *Kritik* we read:

> Gleichwohl wird, welches wohl gemerkt werden muss, doch dabei immer vor-behalten, dass wir ebendieselben Gegenstände auch als Dinge an sich selbst, wenngleich nicht erkennen, doch wenigstens müssen denken können. *Denn sonst würde der ungereimte Satz daraus folgen, dass Erscheinungen ohne etwas wäre, was da erscheint*[24].

In fairness to Kant it must be added that in the same preface (B xvi), he specifically states that all attempts to construct a theory of knowledge

---

[23] Nachlass Ende 1886—Frühjahr 1887, 7 [4]; KGW VIII 1, 272.
[24] Immanuel Kant, "Vorrede zur zweiten Auflage", *Kritik der reinen Vernunft*, ed. by A. Görland in *Immanuel Kants Werke* (Berlin, 1922), Vol. III, p. 23 (B xxvi). All subsequent references to Kant are to this edition.

which assumed that knowledge must correspond to objects were doomed to failure. But, we must ask, is anything essentially altered if we merely reverse this situation and make objects conform to our cognitive faculties i. e., to our knowledge? In either case, the distinction between thought and thing, phenomenon and noumenon, subject and object etc. is upheld, and it is this point which Nietzsche seizes upon.

Nietzsche is obviously suspicious of the attempt to gain knowledge about knowledge, which he sees as Kant's task in the *Kritik der reinen Vernunft*. Briefly, Nietzsche views this attempt as embodying the same inconsistencies which we have already pointed out as inherent to the correspondence theory. The attempt to gain knowledge about knowledge already presupposes that which it seeks, and therefore begs the entire question. According to Nietzsche, Kant's view of the nature of knowledge is possible only within that relationship assumed to exist between subject and object or thinker and thing (or thing-in-itself). In order to gain knowledge about knowledge, given this relationship, we are forced to posit knowledge as an additional something with which we can then enter into a cognitive relationship. But in Kantian terminology, this can yield only an analytic proposition about our initial assumption, and not any synthetic proposition or new knowledge, and this is far from proving anything at all. Again, if we take the phrase "knowledge about knowledge" in the sense in which I think it is intended, there is the implication of a second-order sort of knowledge, i. e. a variety of knowledge above and beyond the usual variety. This in turn seems clearly to imply that we must step outside the normal boundaries within which knowledge is supposedly possible (and which Kant so painstakingly elaborates) in order to become capable of ascertaining whether or not we do have knowledge. This involves either 1) an illegitimate suspension of the conditions under which knowledge is possible (and this obviously would defeat Kant's entire purpose), or 2) involves us in an infinite regress (i. e. a third order of knowledge to verify the second, and so on). A third alternative is that knowledge about knowledge, given that there is such a thing, is entirely vacuous, and there is considerable evidence that Nietzsche regarded Kant's *a priori* principles as precisely that — vacuous[25].

— Die grösste Fabelei ist die von der Erkenntniss. Man möchte wissen, wie die Dinge an sich beschaffen sind: aber siehe da, es giebt keine Dinge an sich! Gesetzt aber sogar, es gäbe ein Ansich-, ein Unbedingtes, so könnte es eben darum nicht erkannt werden! Etwas Unbedingtes kann nicht erkannt werden: sonst wäre es eben nicht unbedingt! Erkennen ist aber immer „sich-irgend-

---

[25] JGB 11; KGW VI 2, 18ff. GM III 12; KGW VI 2, 381ff. Nachlass Herbst 1887, 10 [205]; KGW VIII 2, 248.

wozu-in-Bedingung-setzen" —; ein solcher „Erkennender" will, dass das, was er erkennen will, ihn nichts angeht: wobei erstlich ein Widerspruch gegeben ist, im Erkennen-Wollen und dem Verlangen, dass es ihn nichts angehen soll (wozu doch dann Erkennen!) und zweitens, weil etwas, das Niemanden nichts angeht, gar nicht ist, also auch nicht erkannt werden kann[26].

IV. The "Thing-in-Itself"

The precise role of the noumenon, the thing-in-itself, in Kant's *Kritik der reinen Vernunft* has long been an object of scholarly dispute. It can be persuasively argued that the concept of the thing-in-itself is really quite dispensible to Kant's project in the *Kritik*; this, of course, would make Kant's position that of a transcendental idealist. Yet Kant, to all appearances, tenaciously clings to the concept of the noumenon, even to the point of introducing what certainly look like inconsistencies into his critical theory. Nietzsche's rejection of Kant, as I have been representing it, grows out of his observation that Kant presupposed a form of the correspondence theory (especially obvious in the noumenon-phenomenon distinction), and therefore fell victim to the inherent inconsistencies of this view.

Nietzsche is quite clearly at loggerheads with Kant on the issue of the thing-in-itself, and his formal grounds for the rejection of this concept were already elaborated in Chapter I. Nietzsche's understanding of the concept is this: the noumenon, for Kant, is the thing as it exists in itself, independent of its phenomenal representation for any agent. The noumenon is an intelligible object i. e., it is not a possible object of experience. The concept of the noumenon thus represents an object which cannot exist in any sort of cognitional or otherwise ascertainable relationship with regard to human cognition: the most we can know about the noumenon is that we can know nothing about it. Nietzsche rejects this outright as a blatant *contradictio in adjecto*.

Given this reading of the concept of the thing-in-itself, and given Nietzsche's flux ontology, the reasons for his rejection are not difficult to see: thinghood, for Nietzsche, is not a property of substantial, perduring, self-identical entities. Thinghood is a perspectival interpretation of an opposing power-complex ("Machtkonstellation," "Machtwille") carried out within that matrix of interlocking power relationships which is the world, and for the sole purpose of enhancing and increasing that will-to-power which the interpreting "agent" is. If, as Nietzsche claims, thinghood is an interpretation of dynamic relationships, then a thing-in-itself i. e.

[26] Nachlass Herbst 1885—Herbst 1886, 2 [154]; KGW VIII 1, 139 f.

a thing outside of any relationships is both an impossibility and a contradiction in terms.

> Die Eigenschaften eines Dings sind Wirkungen auf andere „Dinge": denkt man andere „Dinge" weg, so hat ein Ding keine Eigenschaften d. h. es giebt kein Ding ohne andere Dinge d. h. es giebt kein „Ding an sich"[27].

> Dass die Dinge eine Beschaffenheit an sich haben, ganz abgesehen von der Interpretation und Subjektivität, ist eine ganz müssige Hypothese: es würde voraussetzen, dass das Interpretiren nicht wesentlich sei, dass ein Ding aus allen Relationen gelöst noch Ding sei. Umgekehrt: der anscheinende objektive Charakter der Dinge: könnte er nicht bloss auf eine Graddifferenz innerhalb des Subjektiven hinauslaufen? — dass etwa das Langsam-Wechselnde uns als „objektiv" dauernd, seiend, „an sich" herausstellte
> — dass das Objektive nur ein falscher Artbegriff und Gegensatz wäre innerhalb des Subjektiven?[28]

This is *prima facie* not an especially devastating argument against Kant's position, for it does appear that the noumenon which Nietzsche rejects as an absurdity is something of an oversimplification and not entirely representative of Kant's position. In the "Transcendentale Analytik" Kant is painstakingly precise in elaborating exactly how the concept of the thing-in-itself is to be understood: it is a "Grenzbegriff," an empty concept of pure reason to which no possible object of experience can correspond, and which functions negatively as an indicator of those limits beyond which human understanding may not venture. An intellect capable of experiencing things-in-themselves would represent a mode of cognition entirely unavailable to man, and this would be a positive application of the concept "noumenon" which Kant rules out[29]. Indeed, when Nietzsche suggests "... dass das Objektive nur ein falscher Artbegriff und Gegensatz wäre innerhalb des Subjektiven ...," this seems to be rather in keeping with Kant's position. But Nietzsche is decisively aware of Kant's anomalous position in this regard viz., that he appears to have a great deal to say about that concerning which nothing can be said (unless it be that very fact). Kant does not wish to claim positive knowledge about things-in-themselves, as this would be idle metaphysical speculation of the sort which he rejected. Yet Kant is equally anxious to avoid the charge of subjective or solipsistic idealism, and states that it would be absurd to speak of appearances while denying that there is something which appears[30].

[27] Nachlass Herbst 1885—Herbst 1886, 2 [85]; KGW VIII 1, 102.
[28] Nachlass Herbst 1887, 9 [40]; KGW VIII 2, 17.
[29] See Immanuel Kant, "Vom dem Grunde der Unterscheidung aller Gegenstände überhaupt in Phaenomena und Noumena," *Kritik der reinen Vernunft, Werke*, Vol. III, pp. 212—224 (B 294—315).
[30] See footnote 24 above.

It is entirely conceivable that the concept of the noumenon could be deleted from the *Kritik der reinen Vernunft* without affecting Kant's thesis in any significant fashion. Yet Kant adamantly refuses to take this step, and Nietzsche attributes this unwillingness to drop that extraneous concept to moral prejudice. But rather than being merely an argument *ad hominem* or illegitimate psychologizing on Nietzsche's part, this charge represents a profound insight into some of the real difficulties with Kant's position.

Nietzsche asserts that the thing-in-itself is an impossibility. We have further argued that this concept is not really essential to Kant's critical theory of knowledge. Yet it does play a vital role in Kant's moral philosophy, and this is the meaning of Nietzsche's charge of moral prejudice. Kant's justification of the categorical imperative and the formula of autonomy rests upon the concept of freedom. The justification of the concept of freedom itself, however, is a most percarious undertaking. In order to resolve the antinomy existing between (natural) necessity and (intelligible) freedom, Kant is forced to fall back upon the noumenon-phenomenon distinction in this fashion: insofar as he is a sensible being within the realm of nature, man necessarily thinks of himself as a causally determined, natural creature. His self-knowledge in this regard can only be phenomenal, and therefore subject to the categories of the understanding, e. g. causality. Insofar as he is capable of pure reason independent of sensation, however, man can and must think of himself as an intelligible being who is not bound by laws of natural necessity and can, therefore, be free. In other words, man may think of himself as phenomenally determined, but can without contradiction regard himself as noumenally free[31].

This argument is initially introduced as a mere possibility, but as Kant develops it, it becomes increasingly evident that he must make positive assertions about man as noumenon in order to justify the moral law. Neither may we attribute this significant inconsistency to an oversight on Kant's part, for the same point is made even more strongly in the *Kritik der Praktischen Vernunft*[32]. The obligatory character of the moral law, for

---

[31] Cf. Immanuel Kant, *Grundlegung zur Metaphysik der Sitten, Werke*, Vol. 4, pp. 241—324, especially section III (pp. 305—324).

[32] The following passage from the *Kritik der Praktischen Vernunft* is most illuminating in this regard: "Die Bestimmung der Kausalität der Wesen in der Sinnenwelt als einer solchen konnte niemals unbedingt sein, und dennoch muss es zu aller Reihe der Bedingungen notwendig etwas Unbedingtes, mithin auch eine sich gänzlich von sich selbst bestimmende Kausalität geben. Daher war die Idee der Freiheit als eines Vermögens absoluter Spontaneität nicht ein Bedürfnis, sondern, was deren Möglichkeit betrifft, ein analytischer Grundsatz der reinen spekulativen Vernunft. Allein da es schlechterdings unmöglich ist, ihr gemäss ein Beispiel in irgend einer Erfahrung zu geben, weil unter den Ursachen der Dinge als Erscheinungen keine Bestimmung der Kausalität, die schlechterdings unbedingt wäre, angetroffen werden kann, so konnten

Kant, stands or falls with the concept of freedom. Since Kant is most emphatic about the bindingness of the moral law, he must be equally emphatic about man's freedom. But Kant demonstrates conclusively that man — insofar as he is an object of experience for himself — experiences himself as a causally determined natural being. Therefore freedom can be predicated only of man's noumenal character. But since man's noumenal character is — like all other noumena — utterly unknowable, Kant is put into the awkward position of claiming to know something about noumena after having denied that anything can be known about them.

What this represents is an illegitimate, positive application of the concept of the thing-in-itself, an application which is at odds with Kant's earlier claims in the *Kritik der reinen Vernunft*. Even though Kant had insisted in that work that a positive use of the thing-in-itself is admissable, he nevertheless does use the concept of the noumenon in a positive fashion to support his ethical views. And this approach is subject to the same refutation as the correspondence theory proper i. e., it presupposes a knowledge of ethical matters which is invalid on the basis of its epistomological presuppositions. We may not consistently claim to have knowledge of

wir nur den Gedanken von einer freihandelnden Ursache, wenn wir diesen auf ein Wesen in der Sinnenwelt, sofern es andererseits auch als Noumenon betrachtet wird, anwenden, verteidigen, indem wir zeigten, dass es sich nicht widerspreche, alle seine Handlungen als physisch bedingt, sofern sie Erscheinungen sind, und doch zugleich die Kausalität derselben, sofern das handelnde Wesen ein Verstandeswesen ist, als physisch unbedingt anzusehen und so den Begriff der Freiheit zum regulativen Prinzip der Vernunft zu machen, wodurch ich zwar den Gegenstand, dem dergleichen Kausalität beigelegt wird, gar nicht erkenne, was er sei, aber doch das Hindernis wegnehme, indem ich einerseits in der Erklärung der Weltbegebenheiten, mithin auch der Handlungen vernünftiger Wesen, dem Mechanismus der Naturnotwendigkeit, vom Bedingten zur Bedingung ins Unendliche zurückzugehen, Gerechtigkeit widerfahren lasse, andererseits aber der spekulativen Vernunft den für sie leeren Platz offen erhalte, nämlich das Intelligibele, um das Unbedingte dahin zu versetzen. Ich konnte aber diesen Gedanken nicht realisieren, d. i. ihn nicht in Erkenntnis eines so handelnden Wesens auch nur bloss seiner Möglichkeit nach verwandeln. Diesen leeren Platz füllt nun reine praktische Vernunft durch ein bestimmtes Gesetz der Kausalität in einer intelligiblen Welt (durch Freiheit), nämlich das moralische Gesetz, aus. Hierdurch wächst nun zwar der spekulativen Vernunft in Ansehung ihrer Einsicht nichts zu, aber doch in Ansehung der Sicherung ihres problematischen Begriffs der Freiheit, welchem hier objektive und, obgleich nur praktische, dennoch unbezweifelte Realität verschafft wird." Immanuel Kant, *Kritik der Praktischen Vernunft*, ed. by O. Buek, *Werke*, Vol. 5, p. 54f. Kant's reference to freedom as a regulative principle bears some resemblance to Nietzsche's notion of perspectival interpretation or "useful fictions," which resemblance Vaihinger (op. cit.) is quick to point out. When we become aware of Kant's insistence upon the *necessity* of adhering to a regulative principle, however, the apparent similarity is dissipated. Nietzsche denies the necessity of *any* regulative principle, interpretation, etc. in any ultimate sense, and thus his cognitive paradigm is far more flexible than Kant's, and avoids Kant's inconsistency.

things which we have defined as lying outside the scope of our cognitive faculties. And Nietzsche sees Kant as having done precisely that. Notions such as the kingdom of ends-in-themselves, the intelligible world, etc. appear to Nietzsche to be thinly disguised remnants of the traditional, dualistic sort of metaphysics with rests upon a correspondence view of truth and reality.

> Selbst noch in dem Kantischen Begriff „intelligibler Charakter der Dinge" ist etwas von dieser lüsternen Asketen-Zwiespältigkeit rückständig, welche Vernunft gegen Vernunft zu kehren liebt: „intelligibler Charakter" bedeutet nämlich bei Kant eine Art Beschaffenheit der Dinge, von der der Intellekt gerade so viel begreift, dass sie für Intellekt — ganz und gar unbegreiflich ist[33].

And thus, Nietzsche's charge of moral prejudice in Kant's critical theory takes on a much greater significance when seen in the light of our present discussion of the correspondence theory. Nietzsche views Kant as having shared that traditional, Western intellectual paradigm which we have broadly characterized as the correspondence view. Nietzsche finds evidence of this in Kant's refusal to abandon the noumenon-phenomenon distinction which, even if one regards the noumenon negatively as a "Grenzbegriff," nevertheless implies the existence of an objective realm which is the necessary condition for the possibility of experience. The subsequent positive use of this concept in Kant's ethical writings is regarded by Nietzsche as a further demonstration that Kant was still thinking in terms of the traditional religious "Zweiweltenlehre," and that he was still doing metaphysics implicitly, if not explicitly.

> Das Dasein im Ganzen von Dingen zu behaupten, von denen wir gar nichts wissen, exakt weil ein Vortheil darin liegt, nichts von ihnen wissen zu können, war eine Naivetät Kants, Folge eines Nachschlags von Bedürfnissen, namentlich moralisch-metaphysischen . . .[34]

All of these difficulties emerge organically out of that correspondence view of truth and reality which introduces illegitimate distinctions into the continuum of man's experience, which splits his experience into fragments such as knower and known, subject and object, phenomenon and noumenon, and in so doing depriving itself of the means either to justify this procedure, or to legitimately bridge the gap between these world-fragments it has created.

> Man müsste wissen, was Sein ist, um zu entscheiden, ob dies und jenes real ist (z. B. „die Thatsachen des Bewusstseins"); ebenso was Gewissheit ist, was

---

[33] GM III 12; KGW VI 2, 382.
[34] Nachlass Herbst 1887, 10 [205]; KGW VIII 2. 248. Cf. also AC 10; KGW VI 3, 174f.

Erkenntniss ist und dergleichen. — Da wir das aber nicht wissen, so ist eine Kritik des Erkenntnissvermögens unsinnig: wie sollte das Werkzeug sich selber kritisiren können, wenn es eben nur sich zur Kritik gebrauchen kann? Es kann nicht einmal sich selbst definiren![35]
Ein Erkenntniss-Apparat, der sich selber erkennen will!! Man sollte doch über diese Absurdität der Aufgabe hinaus sein! (Der Magen, der sich selber aufzehrt! —)[36]

V. Does Nietzsche Presuppose the Correspondence Theory?

Nietzsche's own position within his attack upon the correspondence theory of truth is not without some difficulties of its own. Having dealt with Nietzsche's flux ontology, his characterization of life as will to power, his notion of truth etc. in the preceding chapters, the following questions pose themselves as serious problems: Insofar as Nietzsche characterizes reality at all, insofar as he seeks to derive from his model of reality a consistent theory of truth and a perspectival epistemology, is he not still operating within that paradigm which we have characterized as the correspondence theory? Is he not making positive assertions about reality as such, above and beyond any "perspectival interpretation" of it? And is he not claiming, tacitly or otherwise, that his doctrine of the will to power "corresponds" to reality more adequately than any previous doctrine or view?

Martin Heidegger makes this point in his Nietzsche lectures[37]. In a discussion of Nietzsche's view of truth, Heidegger points out that the kind of truth which Nietzsche so vigorously rejects is the traditional correspondence-adequation variety. This "erroneous" sort of truth is rejected because it attempts to fix reality, to make the dynamic world of becoming into a static world of facts and objects, and because it is unaware of its own perspectival nature. The view of truth which Nietzsche does embrace, Heidegger states, is of an aesthetic sort which is aware of the perspectival nature of its propositions within a chaotic reality, and is therefore in "agreement" ("Einstimmigkeit") with that reality, which may not be said of the former type of truth. If we regard "Einstimmigkeit" as basically similar to the notion of correspondence, we might then say that Nietzsche has not overcome the traditional correspondence paradigm at all and is, in fact, merely claiming that his views correspond to reality more adequately than any previous views.

---

[35] Nachlass Herbst 1885—Herbst 1886, 2 [87]; KGW VIII 1, 102f.
[37] Martin Heidegger, Nietzsche I, p. 620f.

Karl Jaspers expresses a similar view in his book on Nietzsche[38]. Jaspers accuses Nietzsche of dogmatism in claiming absolute versimilitude for his notion of the will to power. Jaspers sees a formal similarity between Nietzsche's approach in this regard and the great dogmatic metaphysical systems of the seventeenth century. Jaspers views Nietzsche as having absolutized a specific interpretation of reality (viz. the will to power) and thereby sharing rather than overcoming the narrow dogmatism of his predecessors. Indeed, the implication in Jasper's charge is that 1) Nietzsche uses the same dogmatic approach which he finds so objectionable in his predecessors, and 2) claiming for his own views precisely that kind of correspondence to reality which he denies to his predecessors.

For purposes of the present discussion, we may simplify the views of both Heidegger and Jaspers on this matter into the assertion that Nietzsche himself still thought in terms of a correspondence theory of truth. The implication of this would be that Nietzsche claimed illegitimate knowledge of an essentially unknowable reality, and subsequently regarded his own views as representing the most adequate formulation yet of an ultimately unknowable world. And while this may at first appear to be a very tempting refutation of Nietzsche's enterprise, or at very least an embarassing inconsistency, this is an untenable position because objections of this sort rest upon a serious misunderstanding of Nietzsche.

Heidegger's contention that Nietzsche claims "Einstimmigkeit" with reality for his views rests upon the assumption that Nietzsche regarded the will to power as an *ens metaphysicum* to which ontological propositions could, in at least some sense, meaningfully correspond. But this is an untenable position: the will to power is not be regarded as an *ens metaphysicum* if we are to authentically grasp Nietzsche's meaning. Nietzsche goes out of his way to show that the will to power is not simply another world-principle, not simply another collection of ultimate entities or monads such as we find in the metaphysical tradition. His own characterization of the will to power — which ironically bears some resemblance to Kant's negative characterization of the thing-in-itself — is such that *no* characterization, *no* interpretation of that world which is the case can be any more than a perspectival interpretation. No theory, no ontological or metaphysical proposition is capable of adequately expressing the ultimate nature of that world which is the case, *including Nietzsche's own*. The reason for this is not far to seek: Nietzsche denies that it is meaningful to speak of an "ultimate nature of things": this is most often expressed in Nietzsche's

---

[38] Karl Jaspers, *Nietzsche*, p. 309 ff.

writings as an assertion to the effect that there *is* no ultimate nature of things, and this might be construed as a claim to have positive knowledge of a metaphysical nature. This is to say that Nietzsche's assertion that there is no ultimate nature of things might be construed as tacitly claiming a correspondence to some ultimate but unknowable state of affairs. This, however, is a problem of language rather than an inconsistency on Nietzsche's part. Heidegger himself has amply demonstrated that ordinary language itself contains an implicit metaphysics (which notion he may very well have derived from Nietzsche). The problem we face here is the problem of attempting to express the untenability of certain views, but do this in a language which is grounded in those very views which one seeks to overthrow. Nietzsche attempts to invalidate the correspondence theory of truth, but is forced to do this within a language which presupposes that very theory. This is the reason that Nietzsche may appear to be claiming a type of knowledge, the possibility of which he seeks to deny. And this, as I have maintained, is basically nothing more than a linguistic problem, and will be further examined in Chapter V. For the present, this brief explanation must suffice.

Nietzsche is well aware of the implications which all of this has for the status of his own pronouncements. No philosophical position can be anything more than a perspectival interpretation, and Nietzsche must admit that his views are not more true (in the correspondence sense) than those of his predecessors — they are preferable because they are aware of their own perspectival nature. Nietzsche does not claim to have a more adequate understanding of the ultimate nature of reality, on the basis of which he could then dismiss the views of his predecessors as incorrect. There is no ultimate nature of reality to which his or anyone else's views could correspond or, at very least, it is meaningless and inconsistent to make such an assumption. Nietzsche's ultimate objection to other philosophies is not that they fail to correspond to reality, but that they assume such a correspondence to be possible in the first place. This is itself a self-defeating position, as we have seen. The views of Plato, Descartes, Leibniz, Kant, et al. are not less true — in the correspondence sense — than Nietzsche's own: they are objectionable because they insist too strongly upon their own versimilitude, and do this in an inconsistent, self-defeating manner. Nietzsche's real objection to such views is not that they are false (for his own are equally false), but that they rob their adherents of their inherent possibilities, they preclude the possibility of any new and more useful interpretations of the world, they restrict that drive to overcome, rearrange, and assimilate *which we are*: they do nothing for "... [die] Steigerung des Machtgefühls," except perhaps to impede it.

Thus the correspondence theory is not false in any ultimate (and therefore meaningless) sense: it is simply useless.

One seriously misunderstands Nietzsche if one regards him as proclaiming a new model of reality which accurately corresponds to the true nature of things. Nietzsche rejects entirely that whole paradigm in which such a correspondence is even conceivable. One can hold a view such as Heidegger's only if one presupposes the correspondence theory one's self, or is determined to interpret Nietzsche in light of it. I believe the latter to be the case with Heidegger. Within his destruction of the Western metaphysical tradition, Heidegger regards Nietzsche as the last major figure *within* this tradition, who certainly attempted to overthrow it, but who nevertheless remained firmly within the mainstream of Western metaphysics as its last great proponent. If we regard Nietzsche as a metaphysician, and if we regard the correspondence theory (as I have characterized it) as an essential feature of this tradition, then it follows that Nietzsche must have shared the correspondence view in at least some sense. Yet this is a serious misunderstanding of Nietzsche, in whose writings the striving to overcome this tradition and its inherent limitations is everywhere apparent. Whether or not Nietzsche entirely succeeded in overcoming the metaphysical tradition and the paradigm of correspondence is perhaps still an open question, but I hope to have demonstrated that he did (or very nearly did) exactly that. To assert that Nietzsche was engaged in metaphysics and claimed a correspondence to (or "Einstimmigkeit" with) ultimate reality for his own views is to seriously miss Nietzsche's major point. Such charges either presuppose a correspondence criterion themselves (which Nietzsche emphatically does not), or they claim to have discovered in Nietzsche a correspondence view which they themselves have illegitimately attributed to him. In either case, such accusations are so far wide of the mark that they do not even approach Nietzsche's position.

The foregoing discussion has, I believe, sufficiently answered Jaspers' charge of metaphysical dogmatizing and of absolutizing only a particular world-interpretation. However, Jaspers further observes a circularity in Nietzsche's argumentation, and to this we shall briefly address ourselves[39]. Nietzsche often states that the will to power is a process of interpretation. But while interpreting, the will to power is itself an interpretation. More specifically, Nietzsche presents us with a model of reality in which everything is construed in terms of power-relationships, and a criterion of truth such that "true" means an enchancement of that will to power which

---

[39] Ibid., p. 294.

we are. The "truth" of the ontological model itself, however, lies in the enhancing, strengthening effect which it has upon that will to power *which* we are. Thus the circularity which Jaspers observes (i. e. the interpretation of interpretation) becomes apparent. It would be a mistake, however, to regard this circularity as an objection to Nietzsche's view, or a self-contradiction on his part. As Wolfgang Müller-Lauter points out, "Solche Zirkelhaftigkeit gehört zu allem Verstehen[40]." If Nietzsche seeks to "verify" his model of reality on the basis of a truth-criterion already implicit to that model, this is the only consistent position possible for him. Nietzsche rejects entirely that correspondence paradigm in which an objective reality must be assumed which is independent of the act of interpretation or cognition. In rejecting this paradigm, Nietzsche also rejects those fundamental dichotomies which this view presupposes (subject-object, appearance-reality, etc.). This enables Nietzsche to radically unify all aspects of the cognitive act within one interpretative continuum which need not — indeed, cannot — seek beyond itself for a verifying ground. There are only interpretations, and this statement is itself an interpretation. That is Nietzsche's position, and it is a rigorously consistent one (which the correspondence theory is not). Nietzsche's view makes available to us an infinity of more useful, stronger, more beautiful interpretations, and provides a stimulus for growth in this general direction, something of which the traditional, correspondence-oriented philosophical systems are simply incapable. "Gesetzt, dass auch dies nur Interpretation ist — und ihr werdet eifrig genug sein, dies einzuwenden? — nun, um so besser[41]." —

---

[40] Wolfgang Müller-Lauter, "Nietzsches Lehre vom Willen zur Macht," *Nietzsche-Studien* III/1974, p. 49: "Wenn Nietzsche's Philosophie des Willens zur Macht die Wahrheit über die Wirklichkeit auszusagen beansprucht, so gerät sie also nicht in Widerspruch mit dem aus dieser Philosophie selber erwachsenden Wahrheitskriterium. Von diesem her gesehen ist sie sogar die einzige konsequente Weltdeutung. Wir bewegen uns im Zirkel. Solche Zirkelhaftigkeit gehört zu allem Verstehen. Nietzsche weiss das durchaus, sein Denken wird von diesem Wissen geleitet."
[41] JGB 22; KGW VI 2, 31.

CHAPTER FOUR

NIETZSCHE'S PERSPECTIVISM

I. The World as Illusion

Hans Vaihinger, in his *Die Philosophie des Als-Ob*, presents us with an elaborately documented account of one of the central features of Nietzsche's thought — his perspectivism or, as Vaihinger labels it, Nietzsche's philosophy of "conscious illusion" ("bewusstes Gewolltsein")[1]. In his early writings, notably *Die Geburt der Tragödie*, Nietzsche expressed a marked preference for "illusion" over "truth." His motives for this somewhat unorthodox preference were primarily aesthetic ones, the Greeks of the classical age being his model[2]. The Greeks of the classical period, according to Nietzsche, were able to tolerate the harsh, ugly realities of life only by seeking refuge in an imaginary realm of their own fashioning. This imaginary realm constituted the spiritual plane upon which the cultural appurtenances we associate with classical Greece (sculpture, tragedy, architecture, poetry, even philosophy) were conceived and enjoyed[3]. This illusory realm's lack of "objective reality" was not at all a short-coming, but rather, a high recommendation. Nietzsche did not consider the Greeks deluded or misguided in this regard. They were, he felt, very much aware of the illusory nature of the ideals which they conceived. Their illusions were conscious and deliberate.

This train of thought is to be found, as Vaihinger amply illustrates, throughout Nietzsche's writings. In the later writings, however, it

---

[1] Hans Vaihinger, "Nietzsches Lehre vom Bewussten Gewollt-Sein" in *Die Philosophie des Als-Ob* (Leipzig, 1911), p. 771 ff., hereinafter cited as Vaihinger, loc. cit. Cf. Walter del Negro, *Die Rolle der Fiktionen in der Erkenntnistheorie Friedrich Nietzsches* (München, 1923) especially pp. 132—137. It is somewhat disconcerting to note that del Negro analyzes Nietzsche in order to discover whether or not his "perspectival illusions" constitute "echte als-ob Annahmen" in Vaihinger's sense. I think it would be more to the point to ask whether or not Vaihinger's "als-ob Annahmen" constitute creative falsifications in Nietzsche's sense, and I feel that a strong case can be made that Vaihinger received his initial impetus in this epistemological direction from Nietzsche.

[2] Cf. Nietzsche's shorter and unpublished works on the classical Greeks in KGW III 2, especially "Die dionysische Weltanschauung," KGW III 2, 43—69.

[3] Cf. GA X, 124: "Der Inhalt der Kunst und der alten Philosophie fällt zusammen . . . ."

undergoes an important transformation: the "real" world is discarded, and comes to be regarded as nothing less than a fiction itself[4]. After having demonstrated that the "real" world of the metaphysicians and theologians is nothing but the creation of weak and decadent wills, Nietzsche goes on to claim that the world in which we live is itself an illusion, a fiction. It must be remembered that in demonstrating the "unreality" of any metaphysical world, Nietzsche is not necessarily arguing for the "reality" of a physical, material world. Both, as it turns out, are equally fictitious: "Die physische Welt wie die seelische beide falsch, aber dauerhafte Irrthümer[5]." Nietzsche's demonstrations for the "reality" of this world, overagainst the unreality of the "other world" are not intended to be metaphysical disproofs of a metaphysical world. What Nietzsche means, it would seem, is that there is only one world about which we even need concern ourselves. That is, there is only one world which is the case, and that is the world in which we, as individuals, factically experience ourselves as living. Any characterization we give this world, however, whether physical, biological, material, etc. is necessarily false. But, we ask, if this is the *only* world, how can it be false?

> Der Charakter der werdenden Welt als unformulirbar, als „falsch", als „sich widersprechend"
> Erkenntniss und Werden schliesst sich aus.
> Folglich muss „Erkenntniss" etwas anderes sein: es muss ein Wille zum Erkennbar-machen vorangehen, eine Art Werden selbst muss die Täuschung des Seienden schaffen[6].

Reality for Nietzsche is a turbulent, enigmatic chaos of power-quanta and power-constellations locked in combat with one another for more power. Since there is nothing stable in this scheme of things, nothing constant, Nietzsche feels justified in characterizing (somewhat dramatically, perhaps) everything we say about the world as false. As we saw earlier, the term "false" is normally regarded as applying only within a context wherein there exists something "true" to serve as a standard of comparison (viz. the context of the correspondence theory). What Nietzsche means, however, is this: since "reality" is constantly changing, anything we say or think about it is false, because any utterance is ultimately

---

[4] Cf. Nachlass Frühjahr—Sommer 1888, 16 [40]; KGW VIII 3, 296: " . . . wir haben die Kunst, damit wir nicht an der Wahrheit zu Grunde gehn." Even though this fragment dates from 1888, it expresses very well this view of the superiority of the "illusions" of art over the unpleasant "realities" of life. In the later works, however, the tendency is to strictly equate "illusion" and "reality."
[5] Nachlass August—September 1885, 39 [13]; KGW VII 3, 353.
[6] Nachlass Herbst 1887, 9 [89]; KGW VIII 2, 46.

incapable of adequately coming to grips with the ambiguity, contradiction, and incessant change of the will to power[7]. Any conceptual system (and language in particular) assumes the existence of stable entities to which its concepts apply. According to Nietzsche, no such stable things can meaningfully be said to exist, and therefore anything we think or say about the world entails a necessary "falsification" of way the world "really" is[8]. The fact that the only knowledge we have of the world is interpretation and falsification is not meant to be pejorative. False as our interpretations might be, they are all we have, all we can possibly have. Our erroneous judgements about the world are not to be thought of as "mistakes" for the simple reason that there is no "true" (i. e. unchanging) world about which we could be mistaken.

Vaihinger, in the best Neo-Kantian tradition, points out what he considers to be some fundamental similarities in the manner in which both Kant and Nietzsche regard the synthetic, creative function of the mind[9]. We might generalize and say that for both, the experiential world was conceived as a chaos of disparate phenomena which the mind organized into a consistent and meaningful world. For Kant, of course, the mind did this according to the pure, *a priori* categories of the understanding which he elaborated in the *Kritik der reinen Vernunft* and which he held to be universal. Kant further distinguished between the object as it appears to an observer and as it exists in itself (i. e., the "Ding an sich"). Nietzsche, of course, denies that there are any *a priori* categories common to all of us, or that there is any unseen noumenon lurking behind the phenomena of experience. Nevertheless he does regard the world as being in some fashion a chaos:

> Ursprünglich Chaos der Vorstellungen. Die Vorstellungen, die sich miteinander vertrugen, blieben übrig, die grösste Zahl ging zugrunde — und geht zugrunde[10].

Each individual power-center — and not only human individuals — edits, arranges, schematizes, and simplifies the chaos which surrounds it.

---

[7] This is, of course, highly reminiscent of Heraclitus' well-known adage about our being unable to step twice into the same stream (Diels-Kranz fr. 91, 12). It is impossible to give a detailed account here of Nietzsche's fascination with classical Greek thinkers or the influence of Heraclitus upon him, although the Heraclitean flavor of the present discussion is indisputable. See KGW III 2, which contains a number of unpublished works on the Greeks from the years 1870—1873. Of special interest is "Die Philosophie im tragischen Zeitalter der Griechen," pp. 294—366.

[8] This naturally applies to Nietzsche's own characterizations of reality, and the resolution of this paradox will be one of the major tasks of the following chapters.

[9] Vaihinger, loc. cit.

[10] GA XVI, 24.

Each individual interprets a world for himself by picking out those elements of his chaos of impressions which are of concern to him, and by simplifying, generalizing, and structuring them in the manner most conducive to his welfare[11]. This is not simply another way of expressing the banality that everyone has his own way of looking at the world. For Nietzsche, there is no world apart from interpretations of it: the world itself is an interpretative process.

> Der interpretative Charakter alles Geschehens. Es giebt kein Ereigniss an sich. Was geschieht, ist eine Gruppe von Erscheinungen ausgelesen und zusammengefasst von einem interpretirenden Wesen.[12]

This is what Nietzsche means by perspectivism.

> Der Perspektivismus ist nur eine complexe Form der Spezifität
> Meine Vorstellung ist, dass jeder spezifische Körper darnach strebt, über den ganzen Raum Herr zu werden und seine Kraft auszudehnen (— sein Wille zur Macht:) und Alles das zurückzustossen, was seiner Ausdehnung widerstrebt. Aber er stösst fortwährned auf gleiche Bestrebungen anderer Körper und endet, sich mit denen zu arrangiren („vereinigen"), welche ihm verwandt genug sind: — so conspiriren sie dann zusammen zur Macht. Und der Prozess geht weiter . . .[13]

The world has no univocal meaning. What meaning, what characteristics or qualities it does have are projected or interpreted into it by ourselves. Naturally, the world might be entirely different from the perspective of each interpreter. There is no world in itself, no things in themselves, no absolute and unchanging verities, and the desire to gain this sort of knowledge, Nietzsche regards as one of the perennial lunacies of philosophers and other crackpots. There is no "veil of illusion" which we must pierce before we can discover what the world is "really" like. Indeed,

> . . . die „Scheinbarkeit" gehört selbst zur Realität: sie ist eine Form ihres Seins d. h.
> in einer Welt, wo es kein Sein gibt, muss durch den Schein erst eine gewisse berechenbare Welt identischer Fälle geschaffen werden . . .
> „Scheinbarkeit" ist eine zurechtgemachte und vereinfachte Welt, an der unsere praktischen Instinkte gearbeitet haben: sie ist für uns vollkommen recht: nämlich wir leben, wir können in ihr leben: Beweis ihrer Wahrheit für uns . . .[14]

---

[11] Cf. Robert E. Ornstein, *The Psychology of Consciousness* (New York, 1972), especially pp. 15—48.
[12] Nachlass Herbst 1885—Frühjahr 1886, 1 [115]; KGW VIII 1, 34.
[13] Nachlass Frühjahr 1888, 14 [186]; KGW VIII 3, 165f.
[14] Nachlass Frühjahr 1888, 14 [93]; KGW VIII 3, 63.

II. Life as an Interpretative Process

If, as Nietzsche says, the world is an illusion, a falsification, a projection or interpretation from a particular perspective, why should we prefer one particular interpretation over any other? After all, they are all false, as Nietzsche constantly reminds us. Of course, the criterion to be met by any of these perspectival "errors" is not one of veracity, but rather one of utility. In point of usefulness there is a great deal of difference between interpretations, some of these "errors" having shown themselves to be practically indispenable. ". . . es könnte aber nöthige Irrthümer geben[15]."

It will be remembered from Chapter I that life itself is will to power, and that the fundamental motivation of any living thing is the drive to increase its power. To facilitate this drive, every living thing "interprets," arranges, organizes, etc. its world in the manner most conducive to the growth and enhancement of its power. This process of interpretation is not to be exclusively thought of as deliberate, conscious, reflective, or any such thing. Even though the notion of interpretation has many anthropomorphic associations for us, Nietzsche is not anthropomorphizing when he indicates an interpretative process in an entity or organism which we would consider to be incapable of such an activity.

> „Denken" im primitiven Zustande (vor-organisch) ist Gestalten-Durchsetzen, wie beim Crystalle. — In unserem Denken ist das Wesentliche das Einordnen des neuen Materials in die alten Schemata (= Prokrustesbett), das Gleichmachen des neuen[16].

> Das Gleichmachen ist dasselbe, was die Einverleibung der angeeigneten Materie in die Amoebe ist[17].

This interpretative process is not an "armchair adventure," nor is it "merely" imaginative. It is to be taken as a literal structuring and ordering of the world on the part of the individual; it is an "aktives Bestimmen" and "Zurechtmachung." Such an interpretative, perspectival process is necessary for the maintenance of life, and the organic process itself continually interprets[18]. For example, when an amoeba throws out a pseudopod or

[15] GA XI, 320.
[16] Nachlass August—September 1885, 41 [11]; KGW VII 3, 421f.
[17] Nachlass Sommer 1886—Herbst 1887, 5 [65]; KGW VIII 1, 213.
[18] "Der Wille zur Macht interpretirt: bei der Bildung eines Organs handelt es sich um eine Interpretation; er grenzt ab, bestimmt Grade, Machtverschiedenheiten. Blosse Machtverschiedenheiten könnten sich nicht als solche empfinden: es muss ein wachsen-wollendes Etwas da sein, das jedes andere wachsen-wollende Etwas auf seinen Werth hin interpretirt ... In Wahrheit ist Interpretation ein Mittel selbst, um Herr über etwas zu werden. (Der organische Prozess setzt fortwährendes *Interpretiren* voraus.)" Nachlass Herbst 1885—Herbst 1886, 2 [148]; KGW VIII 1, 137f.

a vine sends out a new tendril, both are actively interpreting and structuring their worlds, assimilating what they can from their environments for their own growth and ignoring everything else. Both organisms determine what their world shall be like, always with a view toward the increase and enhancement of their vital power. The manner in which a simple organism such as an amoeba does this is quite rudimentary, comparatively speaking. From the perspective of an amoeba, the world would consist probably of only two types of beings: those which are beneficial to it, and those which are not, i. e. things which are edible and things which are not. This would obviously be a vital distinction for an amoeba to make, but in all likelihood the only distinction which it is even capable of making. All the various differences which the microbiologist sees between the various types of microscopic organisms would simply not exist for the amoeba. When an amoeba encounters another microorganism, it is not concerned with its morphology, genus and species, reproductive processes, etc. It is concerned with whether or not it can eat the other organism. Thus, from our point of view our hypothetical amoeba must live in a rather simple world. From its own perspective, the amoeba interprets away any and all differences between the entities which it encounters. Color, noise, odor, etc. do not exist for the amoeba, because the only quality in which it is interested is edibility.

If we form a mental picture of what the world of an amoeba must be like, we see immediately that it is vastly oversimplified. It is, we would say, a false view of the world, because the amoeba is simply incapable of realizing the infinitely varied and complex nature of the world around it. Thus, this gross oversimplification of the world is a falsification, but a very necessary one for the amoeba, which might very well starve if it were suddenly forced to make the distinctions which we make between the various forms of microscopic life. The interpretative "error" which the amoeba makes is vital to its continued existence: it is a very useful error indeed[19].

Die Welt so und so gesehen, empfunden, ausgelegt, dass organisches Leben bei dieser Perspektive von Auslegung sich erhält. Der Mensch ist nicht nur ein Individuum, sondern das Fortlebende Gesammt-Organische in Einer be-

[19] Robert Ornstein offers another illustration of this point, that the cognitive processes are primarily for the reduction and simplification of data for the purpose of biological survival. Ornstein refers to an experiment conducted at the Massachusetts Institute of Technology by Lettvin, Maturana, McCulloch, and Pitts on data reduction in the visual processes of the frog. In this experiment visual stimuli were offered to an immobilized frog. These visual stimuli were monitored by means of electrodes implanted in the frog's eyes in order to determine "what the frog's eye tells the frog's brain." The results are most interesting within the present context. "There are thousands, millions of different visual patterns that one could present to a frog ...

stimmten Linie. Dass er besteht, damit ist bewiesen, dass eine Gattung von Interpretation (wenn auch immer fortgebaut) auch bestanden hat, dass das System der Interpretation nicht gewechselt hat. „Anpassung"[20]

Such perspectival falsification is indispensable for any living creature: we are no less guilty of such simplification and falsification than the amoeba. All of our vaunted "truths," "laws of nature," and the like are just as erroneous as the radical simplification which we have (perhaps unfairly) attributed to the amoeba. Nietzsche's point, however, is that we must perpetrate such fictions, such useful and necessary errors in order to survive at all. This is why he says,

> Wahrheit ist die Art von Irrthum, ohne welche eine bestimmte Art von lebendigen Wesen nicht leben könnte. Der Werth für das Leben entscheidet zuletzt[21].

Some examples of the useful fictions which mankind has utilized in maintaining itself and progressing are our beliefs in causality, matter, the subject-object distinction, not to mention various moral codes and religious creeds which have proven themselves to be of great utility[22]. All of these beliefs are perspectival errors in terms of which we interpret (i. e. construct) our world and conduct our lives. They are false, however, in any absolute sense, and do not correspond to any actually existing state of affairs independent of ourselves. Nevertheless, the fictions mentioned above have proven themselves indispensable to the continued survival of mankind, and to disbelieve in them would be suicidal. Nonetheless, to maintain that such useful fictions are universally valid, unchanging truths is a meaningless and undemonstrable assertion.

> NB. Die bestgeglaubten a priorischen „Wahrheiten" sind für mich — Annahmen bis auf Weiteres z. B. das Gesetz der Causalität sehr gut eingeübte Gewöhnungen des Glaubens, so einverleibt, dass nicht daran glauben das

choosing them from the almost infinite richness of the visual world of which humans are normally aware. However, in presenting many objects, colors, movements to the frog, the investigators observed a remarkable phenomenon: from all the different kinds of stimulation presented, only four different kinds of 'messages' were sent from the retina to the brain. In other words, no matter what complexity and subtle differences are present in the environment, the frog's eye is 'wired up' to send only a very few different messages. The frog's eye presumably evolved to *discard* the remainder of the information available." Ornstein, p. 22. The frog was chosen for this experiment because of the similarity of its eye to the human eye! Cf. JGB 188; KGW VI 2, 110 ff.

[20] Nachlass Ende 1886—Frühjahr 1887, 7 [2]; KGW VIII 1, 259.
[21] Nachlass April—Juni 1885, 34 [253]; KGW VII 3, 226.
[22] Cf. Nachlass Ende 1886—Frühjahr 1887, 7 [3—6]; KGW VIII 1, 262—291.

Geschlecht zu Grunde richten würde. Aber sind es deswegen Wahrheiten?
Welcher Schluss! Als ob die Wahrheit damit bewiesen würde, dass der Mensch
bestehen bleibt![23]

The usefulness of a particular belief (and all beliefs are ultimately false in
any absolute sense) for life is the sole criterion upon which we can judge it.
As we saw earlier, the "truth" of an idea lies in its utility for the growth and
enhancement of life and power, not in how adequately it corresponds to
some fixed, eternal standard. All of our beliefs about the world, the laws
of nature and so on are ultimately fictions — but many of these fictions
have proven themselves useful to the point of indispensability.

It might be objected that Nietzsche is arguing against a straw man in
this instance, and that no one but a fool would maintain for a moment
that his particular way of regarding the world was the only possible one.
History is full of jibes against just this sort of intellectual provincialism, for
example, Schopenhauer's admonition against making the limits of our
vision the limits of the world, or Montaigne's barb, that nothing
is so firmly believed as what we know least. It is doubtful, I think,
that any normal individual today would maintain the absolute impossibility of there being more than nine planets in our solar system, or
deny the possibility that there might be a number of elements which we have
not yet discovered, or that cancer might some day be eradicated. We must,
after all, keep an open mind about such things, for science is constantly
making advances and new discoveries which force a re-evaluation of our
former opinions. But this is nothing more than the polite sort of skepti-
cism which has come to be regarded as intellectual good manners.
Nietzsche's critique proceeds on a much more fundamental level than this
vapid sort of "Freigeisterei." Perhaps suspending judgement on the
final number of elements or planets in the solar system is a prudent thing
to do. But for Nietzsche, the principles of identity and sufficient reason,
the law of causality, etc. are equally provisional, equally illusory. And
while we are free to question, adjust, accept or reject the findings of
science or medicine, there remain a number of beliefs which are so firmly
rooted, so deeply embedded within our cognitive paradigm, that
disbelief in them is exceedingly difficult (if not outright impossible).
The belief in space and time, causality, identity, rationality, etc. is a fictitious
belief, but one which has proven to be of the very greatest utility. Even a
theoretical physicist, who realizes that our ordinary conception of the cause-
effect relationship is at best a crude and inadequate simplification, still

---

[23] Nachlass Sommer—Herbst 1884, 26 [12]; KGW VII 2, 150f.

accepts this cruder notion in his day to day life, and might find that belief in something he knows to be "false" is more vital to his continued welfare than his scientific "truth."

We have stated that all life interprets, that any living entity necessarily simplifies, falsifies, arranges and constructs his world for the purpose of controlling his environment and being able to live in it. The first example of such a simplification which we employed was that of an amoeba: man, however, simplifies and falsifies his own world in fundamentally the same way[24]. To illustrate this point let us use the example of the atomic theory of matter. I do not think anyone today would seriously argue with the statement that the constituent particles which form the objects of our experience are what modern physics calls atoms. Naturally, a lively argument could be generated among physicists as to the exact nature of these atoms, but we shall not concern ourselves with that for the time being. Let us regard an atom as one of those infinitesimally small particles of which all matter is composed, the atom itself being an aggregation of even smaller subatomic particles which exist in energy levels surrounding the central nucleus. The number of electrons which surround the nucleus, of course, determines the nature of the atom. In recent years it has become unfashionable to speak in terms of the Bohr model (i. e. the planetary model) of the atom, viz. a number of miniature billiard balls careening around a central clump of billiard balls. More recently the atom has come to be regarded as more like a cloud of energy, with points of charge surrounding it in only statistically predictable locations. Whichever model we choose, we still encounter a dilemma: the atom itself cannot meaningfully be said to possess any of those qualities which we attribute to the objects of our experience. It is quite unacceptable to say that an atom is red, soft, sweet, smooth — indeed, that it possesses *any* sensory qualities at all. Yet most of us would maintain that the sweet, red, smooth, etc. objects which we experience are comprised of elementary particles which lack any such characteristics. The conclusion we are thus forced to reach is this, that

---

[24] Cf. Ornstein, p. 17: "Personal consciousness is outward-oriented, involving action for the most part. It seems to have been evolved for the primary purpose of ensuring individual biological survival, for which active manipulation of discrete objects, sensitivity to forces which may pose a threat, separation of oneself from others, are very useful. We first *select* the sensory modalities of personal consciousness from the mass of information reaching us. This is done by a multilevel process of filtration, for the most part sorting out survival-related stimuli. We are then able to *construct* a stable consciousness from the filtered input. If we can realize ... that our ordinary consciousness is something we must of necessity construct or *create* in order to survive in the world, then we can understand that this consciousness is only *one* possible consciousness."

our senses must drastically simplify, organize, and interpret the experiences which impinge upon them[25]. If the physical objects which we perceive were, in fact, composed of atoms as described above, and if our senses could perceive these atoms, we would find ourselves not in a world of reassuringly solid objects, but in an incredible maze of particles vibrating at astronomical frequencies, and having no qualities at all which we could recognize. Obviously we would find such a world uncongenial. More than that, we would find it impossible to live in such a world. *If* we were to maintain that the atomic theory of matter corresponds accurately to the ultimate structure of matter, then we must maintain equally that our senses falsify and interpret the world for us to an amazing (but necessary) degree. Obviously we experience tables and chairs, and not vague clouds of swirling atoms.

In a similar vein, we might also remark that the light we see and are accustomed to calling red, green, blue, etc. actually has no "color" at all. As conceived by physics, light is a photon of radiant energy with a very high vibratory frequency and traveling at a prodigious rate of speed. Nevertheless, we do not "see" light in this fashion. Instead, we perceive colors, even though we might "know" that what we perceive as differences between colors are "really' only quantitative differences in vibratory frequency. If we accept this physical explanation of light, we are once again forced to the conclusion that our senses falsely interpret or distort this phenomenon. The fact that we see only a narrow spectrum of colors within the much larger spectrum of electromagnetic energy is further evidence of a selective process built into our perceptual apparatus, which allows us to perceive only what we must in order to survive. As Nietzsche frequently remarks, ". . . Unser Erkenntniss-Apparat nicht auf 'Erkenntniss' eingerichtet[26]."

Of course, no competent physiscist today would maintain for an instant that his descriptions of atoms, protons, mesons, quarks, etc. are intended to be literal descriptions of the way the world "really" is. Since before the

---

[25] The dilemma to which I am referring is this: if one accepts the atomic theory of matter, one must conclude that (a) the senses radically falsify and distort the world, because the way we "know" it to be is not at all the way we perceive it, or (b) that our reason is totally incapable of adequately knowing the nature of reality, and can put forth only speculative, interpretative, "best guess" models of how reality might be constituted.

[26] "Von der Vielartigkeit der Erkenntniss. Seine Relationen zu vielem Anderen spüren (oder die Relationen der Art) — wie sollte das 'Erkenntniss' des Anderen sein! Die Art zu kennen und zu erkennen ist selber schon unter den Existenz-Bedingungen: dabei ist der Schluss, dass es keine anderen Intellekt-Arten geben könnte (für uns selber) als die, welche uns erhält, eine Übereilung: diese thatsächliche Existenz-Bedingung ist vielleicht nur zufällig und vielleicht keineswegs nothwendig. Unser

turn of the last century, scientists (physicists in particular) have come to the realization that the further we extend the boundaries of our sense knowledge, the less we can be certain about, and have been perplexed by the discrepancy existing between the way science tells us the world "really" is, and the manner in which we actually experience it[27]. Scientists today are exceedingly reluctant to talk about "laws of nature," or to present their findings as literal, "correct" descriptions of the manner in which the world, independent of ourselves, functions. Even something as basic as an atom is no longer looked upon as a concrete entity; rather, it has come to be regarded as an hypothetical entity which has proven itself of great value in predicting and interpreting experimental data. It has become a commonplace today within the scientific community to hold that any sort of scientific knowledge we may obtain is, by its very nature, interpretative and perspectival: a datum cannot be encountered apart from an observer, who in the very act of observation influences the data, and can only observe the data from his own particular perspective. In the words of Werner Heisenberg, ". . . we have to remember that what we observe is not nature in itself but nature exposed to our method of questioning[29]."

It is not my wish here to maintain that Nietzsche's notion of perspectivism exercised any influence upon the subsequent development of the physical sciences, although that is not inconceivable. It is interesting to note, however, that many of Nietzsche's ideas (which surely must have

Erkenntniss-Apparat nicht auf 'Erkenntniss' eingerichtet." Nachlass Sommer—Herbst 1884, 26 [127]; KGW VII 2, 181f. Cf. Ornstein, p. 220f.: "The structure of our nervous system allows us only a limited selection from the available stimulation. Our eyes, ears, brain, each select, and we must then construct a stable personal consciousness from this limited input ... The lineal sequence of events is our own personal, cultural, and scientific construction. It is certainly convenient, and is perhaps necessary for biological survival and the development of a complex, technological society — but it is only one of the many possible constructions of consciousness available to man."

[27] See Henry Margenau, *The Nature of Physical Reality* (New York, 1950). Cf. Ornstein, p. 20f.: "Consider the most important avenue of personal consciousness, the eye. It responds to radiant electromagnetic energy in the visible spectrum. If we consult a chart of the electromagnetic spectrum, we note that the 'visible' spectrum is but one tiny slit in the entire energy band. The entire spectrum ranges in wavelength from less than one billionth of a meter to more than a thousand meters; yet we can 'see' only the tiny portion between 400 and 700 billionths of a meter ... We cannot possibly experience the world as it fully exists — we would be overwhelmed. We are restricted by our physical evolution to only a few sensory dimensions. If we do not possess a 'sense' for a given energy-form, we do not experience its existence. It is almost impossible for us to imagine an energy-form or an object outside our normal receptive range. What would infrared radiation or an X-ray 'look' like? What is the 'sound' of a one-cycle note?"

[28] See Margenau, pp. 58—63.

[29] Werner Heisenberg, *Physics and Philosophy* (New York, 1958), p. 28.

seemed extravagant when he first expressed them) are accepted today
without cavil by scientists and those who pride themselves on their
"scientific" knowledge. The purpose of this scientific digression has been
to give more or less concrete examples for Nietzsche's assertions that
a) we (as well as all other life forms) necessarily simplify, arrange, edit,
and otherwise interpret our experiential world, b) that we do not derive
knowledge "from" the world of our experience, but rather project our
interpretations upon this world, c) that such interpretation, such useful
falsification, is necessary for the maintenance of life, and d) that the world
which is the case is our construction[30].

> Auslegung, nicht Erklärung. Es giebt keinen Thatbestand, alles ist flüssig,
> unfassbar, zurückweichend; das Dauerhafteste sind noch unsere Meinungen.
> Sinn-hineinlegen — in den meisten Fällen eine neue Auslegung über eine
> alte unverständlich gewordene Auslegung, die jetzt selbst nur Zeichen ist[31].

> — der Mensch findet zuletzt in den Dingen nichts wieder als was er selbst in
> sie hineingesteckt hat: das Wiederfinden heisst sich Wissenschaft, das Hinein-
> stecken — Kunst, Religion, Liebe, Stolz . . .[32]

III. Logic as a Perspectival Falsification

We shall now examine in greater detail some of the necessary errors
which, because of their utility, have come to be regarded as unchanging
"truths" or laws of nature and laws of reason. One such system of
perspectival falsifications is logic, which since the time of Aristotle has
been the core and the foundation of the Western cognitive paradigm.
I should like to add that we are not concerned here with the intricacies of
symbolic, multivalued or modal logic, but with those fundamental
principles such as the principles of identity, non-contradiction, and
sufficient reason, which permeate our entire mode of thought and speech.
  Logic and logical (i. e. rational, analytic, disjunctive) thought have
traditionally been regarded as the standards by which to measure the

---

[30] Cf. Ornstein, p. 182: "We know, for instance, that our 'normal' consciousness is not
    complete, but is an exquisitely evolved, selective, personal construction whose pri-
    mary purpose is to ensure biological survival. But this mode, although necessary
    for survival, is not necessarily the only one in which consciousness can operate. As
    the material success of our culture eases the task of survival, it provides a secure
    basis for the development of another mode of consciousness. The essence of the
    active mode of survival is selection and limitation. If we were indiscriminately aware
    of each quantum of energy reaching us, we would likely be dead within a day."
[31] Nachlass Herbst 1885—Herbst 1886, 2 [82]; KGW VIII 1, 98.
[32] Nachlass Herbst 1885—Herbst 1886, 2 [174]; KGW VIII 1, 151f.

truth or falsity of our statements. Logic is a system of formal propositions and operations which are regarded as true *a priori*. The propositions of logic are not derived from experience, but are in all cases applicable to experience. Since the propositions and rules of logic are formal and general, they apply to all cases i. e., they are regarded as universally valid. In order for this to be the case, however, there must exist identical objects, identical cases and events to which the procedures of logic can apply. According to Nietzsche, however, there is no constancy whatever in the world. Reality is in a ceaseless state of flux and nothing remains the same from one instant to the next. Thus logic rests upon a fundamentally false proposition viz., that there exist identical cases to which its procedures are applicable.

> Die Logik ist geknüpft an die Bedingung: gesetzt, es giebt identische Fälle. Thatsächlich, damit logisch gedacht und geschlossen werde, muss diese Bedingung erst als erfüllt fingirt werden. Das heisst: der Wille zur logischen Wahrheit kann erst sich vollziehen, nachdem eine grundsätzliche Fälschung alles Geschehens vorgenommen ist. Woraus sich ergiebt, dass hier ein Trieb waltet, der beider Mittel fähig ist, zuerst der Fälschung und dann der Durchführung Eines Gesichtspunktes: die Logik stammt nicht aus dem Willen zur Wahrheit[33].

Nevertheless, the tendency to act as though there were constancy and identity in the world was very likely instrumental in ensuring the continued survival of the human species. Our paleolithic ancestors who could generalize about weather conditions, which animals were harmful and which could be hunted, etc. might quite conceivably have been more successful in keeping themselves alive than their more acute brethren who noticed, e. g., that no two sabertooth tigers were exactly identical or behaved in precisely the same manner, and in view of this refused to make sweeping generalizations about their inherent unfriendliness. In this way a more superficial, inexact mode of thinking might have been more useful than a more precise and difficult mode of thought.

> Das oberflächlichste, vereinfachteste Denken ist in Hinsicht auf Auslösung des Willens das am meisten nützliche . . .
> die Präcision des Handelns steht in Antagonismus mit der weitblickenden und oft ungewiss urtheilenden Vorsorglichkeit: letztere durch den tieferen Instinkt geführt[34].

Nietzsche regards logic and logical thinking as having arisen out of the fundamental urge to control and dominate our environment by making

---

[33] Nachlass August—September 1885, 40 [13]; KGW VII 3, 365f.
[34] Nachlass Sommer 1886—Herbst 1887, 5 [68]; KGW VIII 1, 214.

it as simple, predictable, and amenable to our control as possible. There is no sameness in the world, but we must posit sameness nevertheless, because we could not survive in a world in which everything was constantly changing and nothing predictable.

> Das Leben ist auf die Voraussetzung eines Glaubens an Dauerndes und Regulär-Wiederkehrendes gegründet; je mächtiger das Leben, um so breiter muss die errathbare, gleichsam seiend gemachte Welt sein. Logisirung, Rationalisirung, Systematisirung als Hülfsmittel des Lebens[35].

The positing of sameness and regularity in the world by logical thinking is, of course, a falsification and gross oversimplification, but this is not meant as a deprecation of logic and rationality. On the contrary, such simplification and falsification is necessary for life to exist at all. We have constructed for ourselves, by means of a perspectival falsification, a world of identical objects and regular occurrences, and this is the only kind of world in which we could survive. The utility of this way of viewing the world is its justification, not its "correctness."

Nietzsche does, however, take issue with the belief that our particular manner of regarding the world is in any ultimate or absolute sense true (i. e., that it correctly corresponds to an actual and independent state of affairs). Behaving as though there were regularity and sameness in the world has proven to be most beneficial for man, but we must not think that we merely discovered regularity and sameness already existing in the world. Rather, we are responsible for these features of the world.

> Unsre subjektive Nöthigung, an die Logik zu glauben, drückt nur aus, dass wir, längst bevor uns die Logik selber zum Bewusstsein kam, nichts gethan haben als ihre Postulate in das Geschehen *hineinlegen*: jezt finden wir sie in dem Geschehen vor — wir können nicht mehr anders — und vermeinen nun, diese Nöthigung verbürge etwas über die „Wahrheit". Wir sind es, die „das Ding", das „gleiche Ding", das Subjekt, das Prädikat, das Thun, das Objekt, die Substanz, die Form geschaffen haben, nachdem wir das Gleichmachen, das Grob- und Einfachmachen am längsten getrieben haben.
> Die Welt erscheint uns logisch, weil wir erst logisirt haben . . .[36]

I should like to emphasize once more that what Nietzsche takes issue with are not the individual results of a particular scientific or rational discipline, but with the unquestioned methodological assumptions which lead to a particular conclusion in the first place. Most scientists today are rather reluctant to claim any absolute validity for their findings. Still, if a scientist such as a biologist or a chemist experimentally demonstrates a

[35] Nachlass Herbst 1887, 9 [91]; KGW VIII 2, 49. Cf. Ornstein, p. 40 ff.
[36] Nachlass Herbst 1887, 9 [144]; KGW VIII 2, 82.

relationship or causal connection between two pieces of data, he does not doubt that such a relationship actually does exist between the entities or processes in question, and not merely within his own methodological assumptions and precedures[37]. A scientist today would probably not apodictically declare that there existed a necessary ontological connection between a logical demonstration and an empirical state of affairs, but his methodological assumptions force him to act as though this were in fact the case. Nietzsche himself was a great admirer of the exact sciences because of their stringency, precision, and *relative* freedom from human prejudices. Nevertheless, these sciences have their own unexamined presuppositions which determine to a large degree the nature of their findings, and their subsequent reflections upon these findings[38].

> ... nicht „erkennen", sondern schematisiren, dem Chaos so viel Regulari-
> tät und Formen auferlegen, als es unserem praktischen Bedürfniss genug thut
>   In der Bildung der Vernunft, der Logik, der Kategorien ist das Be-
> dürfniss maassgebend gewesen: das Bedürfniss, nicht zu „erkennen", son-
> dern zu subsumiren, zu schematisiren, zum Zweck der Verständigung,
> der Berechnung ...
> Die Kategorien sind „Wahrheiten" nur in dem Sinne, als sie lebenbedingend
> für uns sind: wie der Euklidische Raum eine solche bedingte „Wahrheit"
> ist[39].

The fact that some of the "fictions" which we have been discussing have proven to be of great utility is no guarantee that they are a) un-changingly, absolutely true, or b) that they will continue to be of utility. Traditionally, these useful fictions have, however, come to be regarded as truths and — *qua* truths — unchanging. Here Nietzsche sees a real disadvantage. As long as we regard our useful fictions, our perspectival falsifications, as leading to unchanging truths, there is neither the need nor the desire to fashion for ourselves even more useful fictions, and thereby reach an even higher stage of development or greater degree of power over our world. When we become convinced of the absolute truth of our methods and modes of thinking, we become less adventurous and less creative, and allow our useful fictions to petrify into absolute truths or laws of nature[40]. Since change, contradiction, contrast, danger, etc. are essential as stimulants to the increased power and enhancement of life, Nietzsche views the tendency to postulate one particular mode of thought

---

[37] Cf. Ernest Nagel, *The Structure of Science* (New York, 1961), pp. 1—14.
[38] Cf. Alwin Mittasch, *Friedrich Nietzsche als Naturphilosoph* (Stuttgart, 1952).
[39] Nachlass Frühjahr 1888, 14 [152]; KGW VIII 3, 125f. Cf. Heidegger, *Nietzsche* I, pp. 551—562.
[40] GD III "Die Vernunft in der Philosophie"; KGW VI 3, 68—73.

— the rational, logical mode — as the only possible one as profoundly negative[41].

> Das vernünftige Denken ist ein Interpretiren nach einem Schema, welches wir nicht abwerfen können[42].

The ancient Greeks, Nietzsche felt, were implicitly aware of the provisional, illusory nature of their ideals, and were thus able to actively employ their own creative energies to shape and structure a world reflective of their own buoyant vitality and sublime aesthetic sensibilities. We, on the other hand, have bound ourselves to a particular interpretation of the world, which we have further come to regard as the only possible one. This petrification of our perspective ensures, if nothing else, that man will remain human, all-too human, and this Nietzsche regards as a horror to be eschewed.

> Das der Werth der Welt in unserer Interpretation liegt (— dass vielleicht irgendwo noch andere Interpretationen möglich sind als bloss menschliche —) dass die bisherigen Interpretationen perspektivische Schätzungen sind, vermöge deren wir uns im Leben, dass heisst, im Willen zur Macht, zum Wachsthum der Macht erhalten, dass jede Erhöhung des Menschen die Überwindung engerer Interpretationen mit sich bringt, dass jede erreichte Verstärkung und Machterweiterung neue Perspektiven aufthut und an neue Horizonte glauben heisst — dies geht durch meine Schriften. Die Welt, die uns etwas angeht, ist falsch d. h. ist kein Thatbestand, sondern eine Ausdichtung und Rundung über eine mageren Summe von Beobachtungen; sie ist „im Flusse", als etwas Werdendes, als eine sich immer neue verschiebende Falschheit, die sich niemals der Wahrheit nähert: denn — es giebt keine „Wahrheit"[43].

The world is precisely as we have made it: it need not remain that way.

IV. The Subject-Object Distinction

One of the most important, perhaps the most fundamental, of these perspectival falsifications or necessary errors is the distinction we take for granted between subjects and objects. This distinction lies at the basis of a vast number of other convenient fictions, and by clarifying it at this point, we may *a fortiori* dispense with individual treatment of these derivative fictions. The subject-object distinction, for Nietzsche, is considerably more than a logical convenience: it is the fundamental distinction which we make

[41] Nachlass Herbst 1887, 9 [60]; KGW VIII 2, 30 ff.
[42] Nachlass Sommer 1886—Herbst 1887, 5 [522]; KGW VIII 1, 198.
[43] Nachlass Herbst 1885—Herbst 1886, 2 [108]; KGW VIII 1, 112.

between action and actor, from which are derived such notions as causality, substantiality, the unity of consciousness, the principle of sufficient reason, etc.

> Die Auslegung eines Geschehens als entweder Thun oder Leiden — also jedes Thun ein Leiden — sagt: jede Veränderung, jedes Anderswerden setzt einen Urheber voraus und einen, an dem „verändert" wird.

The etymology of our words "subject" and "object" is illuminating in this regard. An object, in the strict sense of the word (viz. "that which is cast against") is the recipient of an act or an effect, the subject being that which acts upon or produces an effect upon the object. Carried one step further, an object is anything of which we are aware i. e., anything which impinges upon our senses. From here it is but a short step to notions of tangibility, visibility, and the more rarified philosophical notions of substance and materiality. All this rests upon a fundamental falsification, according to Nietzsche, viz. the separation of act from actor which leads to the separation of action from that which is acted upon.

> Subjekt, Objekt, ein Thäter zum Thun, das Thun und das, was es thut, gesondert: vergessen wir nicht, dass das eine blosse Semiotik und nichts Reales bezeichnet[46].

It will be remembered from Chapter I that all entities, all phenomena are reducible to particular quanta and configurations of the will to power, and the relationships existing between them. The power-quanta and power-constellations discussed earlier are not things which *have* will to power or *exercise* will to power in the sense in which an agent is thought to discharge its activity. Rather, these power-quanta and -constellations *are* precisely what they *do*: to isolate a particular power-quantum from its activities and relationships with other power-quanta is to annihilate it. For Nietzsche, there is no agent left after its activity has been abstracted from it. Agent (or subject) and act are identical, and Nietzsche would rather drop the static notion of "agent" altogether, implying as it does that an agent or subject might be capable of *not* acting. Of course, this erroneous distinction has been built into our language and become so commonplace (and useful) that we can no longer get by without it. Statements such as "lightning flashes" or "thunder crashes" or "fire burns" make sense grammatically (i. e. we understand them), but are completely

---

[44] Cf. Heidegger, *Nietzsche* I, pp. 602—606.
[45] Nachlass Herbst 1885—Herbst 1886, 2 [145]; KGW VIII 1, 136.
[46] Nachlass Frühjahr 1888, 14 [79]; KGW VIII 3, 50.

redundant, and therefore illustrative of Nietzsche's point. There *is* no
lightning without the flash, nor *is* there thunder without the crashing,
while fire *is itself* the burning.

> Unsere Unart, ein Erinnerungs-Zeichen, eine abkürzende Formel als Wesen
> zu nehmen, schliesslich als Ursache z. B. vom Blitz zu sagen: „er leuchtet".
> Oder gar das Wörtchen „ich". Eine Art von Perspektive im Sehen wieder
> als Ursache des Sehens selbst zu setzen: das war das Kunststück in der Erfin-
> dung des „Subjekts", des „Ichs"![47]

Ultimately it is just as redundant to say "I do" or "I am" as it is to say
"the sun shines" or "the wind blows[48]." Just as there is no wind (except
in an abstract, and therefore irrelevant sense) without the blowing, there is
no subject or actor left when the activity has been thought away.
Furthermore, if we regard an object as something which might in itself be
regarded as a subject, objectivity becomes a species of subjectivity, and the
whole distinction becomes meaningless.

> Dass zwischen Subjekt und Objekt eine Art adäquater Relation stattfinde;
> dass das Objekt etwas ist, das von Innen gesehn Subjekt wäre, ist eine gut-
> müthige Erfindung, die, wie ich denke, ihre Zeit gehabt hat. Das Maass dessen,
> was uns überhaupt bewusst ⟨wird⟩, ist ja ganz und gar abhängig von grober
> Nützlichkeit des Bewusstwerdens: wie erlaubte uns diese Winkelperspektive
> des Bewusstseins irgendwie über „Subjekt" und „Objekt" Aussagen, mit
> denen die Realität berührt würde! —[49]

That Nietzsche completely rejects any artificial separation between
action and actor was, I think, sufficiently elaborated in the first and third
chapters, and we need not go into a redundant elaboration here. This
still does not disprove, it might be objected, that there are objects upon
which we, in some subjective fashion, do act. In other words, if we accept
Nietzsche's assertion that action and actor (i. e. subject) are identical, there
still remains the objective half of the distinction which remains, apparently,
unaffected. To this, Nietzsche would reply that without subjects there can
be no objects, and that objectivity is but a subspecies of the concept

[47] Nachlass Herbst 1885—Herbst 1886, 2 [193]; KGW VIII 1, 160.
[48] The influence of Schopenhauer is unmistakable here. One is reminded of Schopenhauer's jibe at Spinoza: "Spinoza sagt (epist. 62), dass der durch einen Stoss in die
Luft fliegende Stein, wenn er Bewusstsein hätte, meinen würde, aus seinem eignen
Willen zu fliegen. Ich setze nur noch hinzu, dass der Stein recht hätte." (*Die Welt
als Wille und Vorstellung* I 24). Even though Nietzsche often criticizes Schopenhauer's concept of will as entirely too psychological, there would seem to be more
than a superficial resemblance between Schopenhauer's notion of the objectification
of the will, and Nietzsche's identification of action and actor.
[49] Nachlass November 1887—März 1888, 11 [120]; KGW VIII 2, 299.

"subjectivity[50]." If we analyze the conventional subject-object distinction with all that it implies in sufficient detail, we notice that three moments may be distinguished within it: a) subject; b) act; and c) object, or a) actor; b) act; and c) that which is acted upon. We have seen that Nietzsche strictly identifies the first two moments of this distinction. However, if we bear in mind that there are no things at all left after activity has been abstracted from them, there is no object remaining after the abstraction of the first two moments.

> Die Eigenschaften eines Dings sind Wirkungen auf andere „Dinge": denkt man andere „Dinge" weg, so hat ein Ding keine Eigenschaften d. h. es giebt kein Ding ohne andere Dinge d. h. es giebt kein „Ding an sich"[51].

If we were to retain the terminology of our example, we might say that there are neither actors, nor is there any thing which is acted upon, but only action itself. In ordinary language, of course, the very word action implies the other two moments, and is therefore useless except for purposes of illustration. In the Nietzschean scheme of things there are neither actors nor acts nor things which are acted upon, but only turbulent and dynamic quanta of will to power, and our notions of subject, object, etc. are the result of a perspectival simplification and falsification of this chaos of power-quanta.

V. Causality

Another of the perspectival falsifications or useful errors which we have erroneously regarded as a "truth" i. e., as an actual relationship existing among actual entities, is the notion of causality. According to Nietzsche, every judgement involving a subject and predicate (which would seem to include all judgements) rests upon the fundamental belief in the validity of the subject-object distinction, from which is derived the notion of cause and effect[52]. For Nietzsche, this means that the assertion is made, implicitly or explicitly, that every activity is the effect of an acting agent i. e., that any activity (*qua* effect) presupposes an agent (*qua* cause). This has been a very useful belief, to be sure, but there are no grounds for maintaining, simply because we can think in no other way, that our notion of causality represents an actual feature of reality, independent of ourselves.

---

[50] Nachlass Herbst 1887, 9 [40]; KGW VIII 2, 17.
[51] Nachlass Herbst 1885—Herbst 1886, 2 [85]; KGW VIII 1, 102.
[52] Nachlass Herbst 1885—Herbst 1886, 2 [85]; KGW VIII 1, 99 ff.

„Ursache" kommt gar nicht vor: von einigen Fällen, wo sie uns gegeben
schien und von wo aus wir sie projicirt haben zum Verständniss des Geschehens, ist die Selbsttäuschung nachgewiesen.
Unser „Verständniss eines Geschehens" bestand darin, dass wir ein Subjekt
erfanden welches verantwortlich wurde dafür, dass etwas geschah und wie
es geschah.
Wir haben unser Willens-Gefühl, unser „Freiheits-Gefühl", unser Verant-
wortlichkeits-Gefühl und unsere Absicht vom einem Thun in den Begriff
„Ursache" zusammengefasst:
: causa efficiens und finalis ist in der Grundconception Eins[53].

Any and all interpretations are ultimately carried out for the purpose
of increasing or enhancing power. In the case of causality, this takes the
form of interpreting any new or unfamiliar experience in terms of what
one already "knows," i. e. in terms of something familiar and reassuring.
A "law of nature" such as causality is an aid to understanding — and
thereby controlling — our environment. We are confident that no matter
how strange, how unexpected or frightening a particular event might seem,
we are at least capable of discovering its cause. When we have isolated a
"cause," we know the reason why the event occurred in the manner it
did, and can predict its future occurrence. Carried to its conclusion, the
belief in causality maintains that nothing occurs which has not been
previously caused or occasioned by something else, and that everything
which occurs is fundamentally predictable and explainable, granting only
that one has the requisite knowledge of the necessary and sufficient conditions governing the occurrence of any particular event (which, in turn,
might be construed as a specific application of the principle of sufficient
reason). This naturally means that the world must be a stable and predictable world, in which nothing takes place arbitrarily or fortuitously. If it
appears that an event does occur arbitrarily or "for no reason," this is
attributed simply to ignorance on our part of the true causes of that event.
The notion that there might exist anomalies, that events might take place
"for no reason" is unsettling and obnoxious to us, and is dismissed.

... es giebt nicht was Kant meint, keinen Causalitäts-Sinn
man wundert sich, man ist beunruhigt, man will etwas Bekanntes, woran
man sich halten kann ...
sobald im Neuen uns etwas Altes aufgezeigt wird, sind wir beruhigt.
Der angebliche Causalitäts-Instinkt ist nur die Furcht vor dem Ungewohnten
und der Versuch, in ihm etwas Bekanntes zu entdecken ...[54]

[53] Nachlass Frühjahr 1888, 19 [98]; KGW VIII 3, 66f.
[54] Ibid. Cf. Thomas S. Kuhn, *The Structure of Scientific Revolutions* (Chicago, 1962). Kuhn
brings into very sharp focus the great reluctance we have toward altering our
accepted, conventional manner of viewing the world (i. e. our paradigm).

Thus far it might appear that Nietzsche is giving us a "psychologistic" account of causality, which bears considerable resemblance to David Hume's (and, to a certain extent, even to Kant's)[55]. Yet, even granting the psychological origin of our belief in causality, one might object that this in no way disproves the existence of the corresponding relationship between things and events independent of our observation. However, such an objection still assumes the validity of the subject-object distinction and, if we accept Nietzsche's destruction of this distinction, such an objection ceases to be interesting.

> Die Causalitäts-Interpretation eine Täuschung . . .
> ein „Ding" ist eine Summe seiner Wirkungen, synthetisch gebunden durch einen Begriff, Bild . . .
> Es giebt weder Ursachen noch Wirkungen.
> Sprachlich wissen wir davon nicht loszukommen. Aber daran liegt nichts. Wenn ich den Muskel von seinen „Wirkungen" getrennt denke, so habe ich ihn negirt . . .
> In summa: ein Geschehen ist weder bewirkt, noch bewirkend . . .
> Thatsächlich hat die Wissenschaft den Begriff der Causalität seines Inhalts entleert und ihn übrig behalten zu einer Gleichnissformel, bei der es im Grunde gleichgültig geworden ist, auf welcher Seite Ursache oder Wirkung. Es wird behauptet, dass in zwei Complexen Zuständen (Kraftconstellationen) die Quanten Kraft gleich bleiben[56].

The reader will recall from our earlier discussion that what a thing is, for Nietzsche, is the sum total of its activities and relationships with other "things." There is no thing, no agent, no subject apart from these activities and relationships. On this basis Nietzsche can maintain that, even though the concept of causality might be a useful interpretative scheme, it involves a falsification of the dynamic continuum of power-quanta into agents (or subjects) which discharge an activity, the activity being something distinct or separable from the agent.

> Endlich begreifen wir, dass Dinge, folglich auch Atome nichts wirken: weil sie gar nicht da sind . . . dass der Begriff Causalität vollkommen unbrauchbar ist — Aus einer nothwendigen Reihenfolge von Zuständen folgt nicht deren Causal-Verhältniss (— das hiesse deren wirkende Vermögen von 1 auf 2, auf 3, auf 4, auf 5 springen zu machen) . . .[57]

> Das Gesetz der Causalität a priori — dass es geglaubt wird, kann eine Existenzbedingung unserer Art sein; damit ist es nicht bewiesen[58].

---

[55] Cf. Edmund Husserl, *Logische Untersuchungen* I: *Prolegomena zur reinen Logik* (Tübingen, 1968), pp. 58—198. See Nachlass Herbst 1885—Herbst 1886, 2 [83]; KG WVIII 1, 99 ff.
[56] Nachlass Frühjahr 1888, 14 [98]; KGW VIII 3, 67.
[57] Ibid.
[58] Nachlass Sommer—Herbst 1884, 26 [74]; KGW VII 2, 166.

VI. The Thinking Subject as Agent

Nietzsche's rejection of the subject-object distinction may not, at first glance, appear as radical and sweeping as it actually is. Yet when we realize how much in our Western cognitive paradigm depends upon this seemingly obvious and simple distinction, we must also realize that Nietzsche's rejection of it has far-reaching consequences indeed. To illustrate this point, let us take the case of Descartes. Nietzsche is rather critical of Descartes (as might be expected), and for a number of reasons which do not concern us here. Of more immediate concern to us is the development and the implications of Descartes' principle *cogito, ergo sum* in *Meditations* II.

> „Es wird gedacht: folglich giebt es Denkendes": darauf läuft die argumenta-
> tio des Cartesius hinaus. Aber das heisst, unsern Glauben an den Substanz-
> begriff schon als „wahr a priori" ansetzen: — dass, wenn gedacht wird, es
> etwas geben muss, „das denkt", ist aber einfach eine Formulirung unserer
> grammatischen Gewöhnung, welche zu einem Thun einen Thäter setzt. Kurz,
> es wird hier bereits ein logisch-metaphysisches Postulat gemacht — und nicht
> nur constatirt... Auf dem Wege des Cartesius kommt man nicht zu etwas
> absolut Gewissem, sondern nur zu einem Faktum eines starken Glaubens.
> Reduzirt man den Satz auf „es wird gedacht, folglich giebt es Gedanken" so
> hat man eine blosse Tautologie: und gerade das, was in Frage steht die „Re-
> alität des Gedankens" ist nicht berührt...[59]

Descartes, of course, inherited a long tradition of substance-based scholastic metaphysics with all its attendant difficulties, and should not be regarded as an intellectual villain (as some recent commentators seem to do)[60] who introduced that pernicious mind-body dualism into Western philosophy. In fact, the two major features of the *Meditations on First Philosophy*, the *cogito* and the ontological argument for the existence of God, were not original with Descartes[61]. But even if Descartes was not entirely original in these instances, he throws into sharp relief a very

---

[59] Nachlass Herbst 1887, 10 [158]; KGW VIII 2, 215.

[60] Cf. *Descartes: A Collection of Critical Essays*, ed. by Willis Doney (Garden City, N.Y., 1967).

[61] An argument practically identical with the *cogito* is to be found in St. Augustine's *Contra Academicos* where it is utilized as a refutation of the Pyrrhonian variety of scepticism. The ontological argument for the existence of God was formulated by St. Anselm of Canterbury in the 11th century, in his *Proslogium*. See Windelband, pp. 237 ff. and p. 250. It appears, however, that Descartes was ignorant of both of the above mentioned writings and, if not entirely original, he was at least honest. See the "Objections and Replies" to the *Meditations* in *The Philosophical Works of Descartes*, trans. by Elizabeth Haldane and G. R. T. Ross (Cambridge, 1970), Vol. II.

deep-seated tendency in Western thought as a whole, and it is this tendency, this presupposition, against which Nietzsche argues.

The *cogito* does in fact, as Nietzsche points out, imply a separability of thought from thinking (or thinker), this separability being crucial to Descartes' inductive proof of his own existence. Descartes argues from the existence of a thought (or the activity of thinking) to the necessary existence of a thinker (i. e. a substance of which the essential attribute is thinking). Nietzsche, however, maintains that this argument is simply tautologous. If we were to say "There are thoughts, therefore there is thinking," clearly this argument would be redundant, since there obviously would be no thoughts without thinking. But to argue in this manner that because of the existence of thoughts, there must exist an agent or subject who performs the act of thinking must be equally tautologous. The distinction between thought, thinker, and thinking is, for Nietzsche, a purely grammatical distinction.

In all fairness to Descartes, it must be allowed that he never said that thoughts, thinking, and thinkers existed separately. And yet, his proof for the existence of a thinking ego implicitly rests upon such a distinction, and does indeed imply that the thinker and his thoughts are separable, as subject and object at least. An argument which proceeds from the existence of entity *a* to the necessary existence of entity *b* must presuppose that *a* and *b* are separate and discrete entities. If this separateness is not upheld, then the argument loses all force and becomes a purely analytical or tautologous assertion. Descartes must uphold a distinction of this sort, for the notion that the thinker *is* the activity of thinking or that the mind *is* a self-thinking thought would most likely have struck him as absurd. The force of Descartes' demonstration of the *cogito* rests upon the supposed necessary connection existing between ideas (as objects or acts), and the existence of mind as an agent or substance which is the necessary precondition for the existence of thoughts or ideas. If, on this basis, we accept the existence of thoughts or ideas as given, then *a fortiori* mind or some sort of thinking substance must also exist. Thus reasoned Descartes. But according to Nietzsche, all of this rests upon a false assumption.

> Der „Geist" etwas, das denkt: womöglich gar „der Geist absolut, rein, pur" — diese Conception ist eine abgeleitete zweite Folge der falschen Selbstbeobachtung, welche an „Denken" glaubt: hier ist erst ein Akt imaginirt, der gar nicht vorkommt, „das Denken" und zweitens ein Subjekt-Substrat imaginirt in dem jeder Akt dieses Denkens und sonst nichts Anderes seinen Ursprung hat: d. h. sowohl das Thun, als der Thäter sind fingirt[62].

[62] Nachlass November 1887—März 1888, 11 [113]; KGW VIII 2, 296.

Whether one conceives man's intellectual faculties in terms of a thinking substance, mind, or soul, the basic implication is the same, viz. that there exists some perduring substance, some "thing" which remains fundamentally unchanged, regardless of the passions, affects, growth, decline, etc. to which an individual may be subject. Man has learned to explicate his experiences with reference to an unchanging "I," which is thought to be the spiritual and intellectual center of gravity, in terms of which the phenomenal world is perceived, understood, and rendered meaningful. According to Nietzsche, however, this perspectival falsification is carried over into our understanding of the world, so that we posit some sort of perduring, substantial substrate underlying the myriad changes and transformations of the material world. This is the "reality" underlying the "appearances" of the phenomenal world, and ensures for us the stability, predictability, and continuity of that world. This substrate has been variously conceived: for Aristotle it was *hyle* (as distinct from *morphe*); for Spinoza, the spiritual substance of God; for Hegel, "Geist," and in terms of contemporary physics, energy. This whole notion of an unchanging reality underlying and supporting the phenomenal world, however, rests upon a false subject-object distinction, which is perspectivally superimposed upon the "real" world[63].

> Die logisch-metaphysischen Postulate, der Glaube an Substanz, Accidens, Attribut usw. hat seine Überzeugungskraft in der Gewohnheit, all unser Thun als Folge unseres Willens zu betrachten: — so dass das Ich, als Substanz, nicht eingeht in die Vielheit der Veränderung. — Aber es giebt keinen Willen. —[64]

Thus we see how an apparently innocuous distinction such as that between subject and object, doer and deed, agent and patient, etc. has far-reaching implications indeed[65]. Man's primitive experience of himself as a corporeal entity in various relationships with other things, gives rise to the perspectival distinction between doer and deed etc., and, as Nietzsche says,

---

[63] It might be objected at this point that Nietzsche's principle of the will to power is nothing other than another expression of the supposed "reality" underlying the phenomena we observe. There is a degree of validity to this objection, but one must remember that Nietzsche does not regard the will to power as something "underlying" phenomena, but as the phenomena themselves.

[64] Nachlass Herbst 1887, 9 [98]; KGW VIII 2, 55. That will, of which Nietzsche here denies the existence, is the egocentric, psychological sort of will, conceived as an attribute of a "thinking thing."

[65] "Subjekt: das ist die Terminologie unsres Glaubens an eine Einheit unter all den verschiedenen Momenten höchsten Realitätsgefühls: wir verstehn diesen Glauben als Wirkung Einer Ursache, — wir glauben an unseren Glauben so weit, dass wir um seinetwillen die 'Wahrheit', 'Wirklichkeit', 'Substanzialität' überhaupt imaginiren.

> Der Leib, das Ding, das vom Auge construirte „Ganze" erweckt die Unterscheidung von einem Thun und einem Thuenden; der Thuende, die Ursache des Thuns immer feiner gefasst, hat zuletzt das „Subjekt" übrig gelassen[66].

This primitive notion of subjectivity is, in turn, rarified and abstracted into a general notion of substantiality, and this has led to an all-embracing world-view common to philosophy, science, even the language we speak. Naturally, Nietzsche regards all this as simply a perspectival falsification of the world which has nevertheless proven itself to be of considerable utility for mankind's growth and development.

However efficacious a particular „illusion" or "falsehood" might be, it is nevertheless an illegitimate step to claim absolute, correspondential validity for it. When our useful errors petrify into "truths," they preclude any further advancement or growth in power. If there is a didactic element in Nietzsche's scathing attacks upon our most cherished „truths," it is this: by bringing home to us the finite, erroneous, and perspectival nature of our hallowed logical truths and laws of nature, we might conceivably be forced into a much more plastic and creative view of reality, thereby becoming capable of transcending what have heretofore been human limitations, and growing toward Nietzsche's vague but intoxicating ideal of the "Übermensch."

Let us speculate with Nietzsche on what the consequences might be if we were to cast off that elementary distinction between subject and object, with all that it has come to imply for us:

> B) Hat man begriffen, dass das „Subjekt" nichts ist, was wirkt, sondern nur eine Fiktion, so folgt Vielerlei.
> Wir haben nur nach dem Vorbilde des Subjekts die Dinglichkeit erfunden und in den Sensationen-Wirwarr hineininterpretirt. Glauben wir nicht mehr an das wirkende Subjekt, so fällt auch der Glaube an wirkende Dinge, an Wechselwirkung, Ursache und Wirkung zwischen jenen Phänomenen, die wir Dinge nennen . . .
> Es fällt endlich auch das „*Ding an sich*": weil dies im Grunde die Conception eines „Subjekts an sich" ist. Der Gegensatz „Ding an sich" und „Erscheinung" ist unhaltbar; damit aber fällt auch der Begriff „Erscheinung" dahin.
> C) Geben wir das wirkende Subjekt auf, so auch das Objekt, auf das gewirkt wird. Die Dauer, die Gleichheit mit sich selbst, das Sein inhärirt weder dem, was Subjekt, noch dem, was Objekt genannt wird: es sind Complexe des Ge-

---

'Subjekt' ist die Fiktion, als ob viele gleiche Zustände an uns die Wirkung Eines Substrats wären: aber wir haben erst die 'Gleichheit' dieser Zustände geschaffen; das Gleichsetzen und Zurechtmachen derselben ist der Thatbestand, nicht die Gleichheit (— diese ist vielmehr zu leugnen —)" Nachlass Herbst 1887, 10 [19]; KGW VIII 2, 131.

[66] Nachlass Herbst 1885—Herbst 1886, 2 [158]; KGW VIII 1, 141.

schehens, in Hinsicht auf andere Complexe scheinbar dauerhaft — also z. B.
durch eine Verschiedenheit im tempo des Geschehens, (Ruhe-Bewegung,
fest-locker: alles Gegensätze, die nicht an sich existiren und mit denen that-
sächlich nur Gradverschiedenheiten ausgedrückt werden, die für ein ge-
wisses Maass von Optik sich als Gegensätze ausnehmen.
Es giebt keine Gegensätze: nur von denen der Logik her haben wir den Begriff des Gegensatzes — und von denen aus fälschlich in die Dinge übertragen.
D) Geben wir den Begriff „Subjekt" und objekt" auf, dann auch den Begriff „Substanz" — und folglich auch dessen verschiedene Modificationen
z. B. „Materie" „Geist" und andere hypothetische Wesen „Ewigkeit und
Unveränderlichkeit des Stoffes" usw. Wir sind die Stofflichkeit los ...[67]

VII. Conclusion

We saw at the beginning of this chapter on Nietzsche's perspectivism
that we (as well as all other entities), as complexes and centers of power,
necessarily interpret a world for ourselves out of the flux and chaos of
power-quanta. However, this interpretation or perspectival falsification
is not an interpretation *of* some underlying reality which continues to
exist regardless of how we happen to interpret. The world *is* our interpretation, and nothing else[68]. We create certain perspectives (i. e.
falsifications) of the world in order to simplify, regulate, and control it,
thereby enabling ourselves to exist and grow in this "illusory" world. Any
such perspectives or interpretations are ultimately false, of course, as they
imply some degree of regularity, permanence, and predictability as inherent
in the nature of things. Nietzsche, however, characterizes the world
(insofar as he characterizes it at all) as a chaotic maze of power-quanta,
which is constantly changing and about which any statement is already
an interpretation, a falsification. Obviously any interpretation of the world
which claims to be universally valid, to correctly correspond to the
ultimate nature of reality, or to be unchangingly true in any sense whatever
is simply inadequate to express that perplexing and enigmatic fundamental
reality, the will to power.

---

[67] Nachlass Herbst 1887, 9 [91]; KGW VIII 2, 47f. The "Ewigkeit und Unveränderlichkeit des Stoffes" is not, of course, a scientific hypothesis which can be seriously
maintained any more in view of the current state of nuclear physics. It is interesting
to note that this particular notion, which Nietzsche wished to discard as a no longer
useful fiction, has in fact been discarded by modern science, and for much the same
reason.

[68] "Soweit überhaupt das Wort 'Erkenntniss' Sinn hat, ist die Welt erkennbar: aber
sie ist anders deutbar, sie hat keinen Sinn hinter sich, sondern unzählige Sinne
'Perspektivismus'." Nachlass Ende 1886—Frühjahr 1887, 7 [60]; KGW VIII 1, 323.

This must not be regarded as nihilistic, however, or as yet another expression of the futility of man's efforts to come to grips with that world which is the case. Nietzsche is urging us to cast off our outmoded perspectives, regardless of how useful they once were or how entrenched they have become, and create for ourselves new, more vigorous, more sublime, and more useful interpretations of the world. In this way, we not only overcome our human, all-too-human limitations, but literally create a new world for ourselves, a new world which itself is a product of our increased vitality and heightened sensibilities. Nietzsche's perspectivism, far from being a pessimistic denial of the possibility of knowledge, is a vigorous and bracing challenge to us to literally become more than we were. And in this, its proper sense, Nietzsche's perspectivism is wholly positive.

> Die Erkenntniss wird, bei höherer Art von Wesen, auch neue Formen haben, welche jetzt noch nicht nöthig sind[69].

[69] Nachlass Sommer—Herbst 1884, 26 [236]; KGW VII 2, 208.

CHAPTER FIVE

NIETZSCHE AND THE PROBLEM OF LANGUAGE

I have already made repeated references to the great linguistic difficulties encountered in attempting to work out Nietzsche's theory of knowledge. Nietzsche certainly employs ordinary language in order to express himself, yet uses it in a most extraordinary fashion, so that one is often uncertain about what it is that he is attempting to communicate. Certainly the paradoxes, contradictions, metaphors, hyperboles, etc. which we encounter in Nietzsche's writings do little to promote a clear, logical, unequivocal understanding of his ideas. And while from the vantage of contemporary Anglo-American linguistic analysis this may elicit charges of uttering nonsense or of sheer unintelligibility, to dismiss Nietzsche on such grounds would be dogmatism with a vengeance (as well as a complete misunderstanding). The purpose of this chapter shall be to demonstrate that such paradoxes, contradictions, etc. are not simply lapses on Nietzsche's part, i. e. evidence of muddled thinking. Rather, I propose to show that such contrariety is an essential feature of Nietzsche's way of thinking, and that he employed language with a great degree of skill and care in formulating his ideas. These linguistic difficulties are put into their proper perspective only when we realize that that which Nietzsche seeks to express through language is something which that language is ultimately incapable of expressing. Thus, Nietzsche has only inappropriate linguistic resources available to him, and this means that he is forced to formulate his ideas within an inauthentic framework. Far from being evidence of sloppy or inconsistent thinking, the contraries and paradoxes we encounter in Nietzsche's writings are indications of his constant struggle to create a new linguistic paradigm, to open up levels of meaning and intelligibility which lie outside our normal sphere of discourse and thought. In short, Nietzsche wishes to say what has never been said before, and could not have been said within ordinary language.

By education and profession Nietzsche was a classical philologist. He had therefore been initiated into a demanding and exacting science, and was well aware of the nature and the capabilities of language. I mention this only to make clear from the outset that a possible objection to Nietzsche's position on language e. g., that Nietzsche's unique use of language stems from an inadequate acquaintance with the structure and workings of language, is not to be taken seriously. Of even greater importance is that in addition to his scholarly and professional interest in language, Nietzsche was a brilliant writer. Even his severest critics must allow that Nietzsche was a master of German prose. Indeed, the wit and grace — and often savage irony — which characterize Nietzsche's works may sometimes be an obstacle to a deeper understanding of his ideas, since they invite casual and superficial reading. Thus, in view of these two facts, I would assert that Nietzsche was more than adequately equipped to transform ordinary language into an extraordinary medium.

I. The Early Works

We find an early sketch of Nietzsche's views on language in the unpublished essay, *Ueber Wahrheit und Lüge im aussermoralischen Sinne*. In this brief essay, Nietzsche embraces a rigorous nominalism (reminiscent of David Hume), and makes the point that language, by its very nature, is incapable of telling us anything about things as they really are. In this essay Nietzsche characterizes language as resting upon the metaphorical translation of sense impressions into a series of wholly dissimilar media.

> Ein Nervenreiz zuerst übertragen in ein Bild! erste Metapher. Das Bild wieder nachgeformt in einem Laut! Zweite Metapher. Und jedesmal vollständiges Ueberspringen der Sphäre, mitten hinein in eine ganz andere und neue[1].

An image is nothing more than a metaphor for a sense impression. A word is likewise simply a metaphor for the image i. e., a metaphor for a metaphor, and therefore twice removed from the original datum. Finally, concepts or general ideas are once more regarded as metaphors, but metaphors which have nothing more in common with our experiences, metaphors which have been scrupulously purged of the uniqueness and immediacy of an actual experience, and which therefore designate — nothing.

> Denken wir besonders noch an die Bildung der Begriffe: jedes Wort wird so-fort dadurch Begriff, dass es eben nicht für das einmalige ganz und gar individualisirte Urerlebnis, dem es sein Entstehen verdankt, etwa als Erinnerung dienen soll, sondern zugleich für zahllose, mehr oder weniger ähnliche, d. h. streng genommen niemals gleiche, also auf lauter ungleiche Fälle passen muss. Jeder Begriff entsteht durch Gleichsetzen des Nicht-Gleichen[2].

---

[1] *Ueber Wahrheit und Lüge im aussermoralischen Sinne*, KGW III 2, 373. Hereinafter cited as *Wahrheit und Lüge*.
[2] Ibid., p. 373f.

Truthfulness or veracity within this context is nothing more than "lying" according to a customary and accepted scheme. To characterize conventional truthfulness as a species of lying has obvious rhetorical appeal, but what Nietzsche means is this: if language rests upon the metaphorical translation of actual experiences into radically dissimilar media (i. e. images, words), then language can tell us nothing about the way things really are in themselves. If we then assume a correspondence theory of truth (as Nietzsche seems to do here to make his point), we are justified in maintaining that our statements do not mirror reality at all. And if our words and statements do not mirror reality, then nothing we say is really true in the correspondence sense of truth. And, if nothing that we say can legitimately be regarded as true, then everything we say must be false, i. e. any statement about reality which claims to be a truth is actually a lie. Naturally we all lie in basically the same way, and therefore lying consistently within an arbitrary linguistic scheme becomes the standard for "truthfulness." Those rascals whom we designate as "liars" are reprehensible because they use the metaphorical signs of language incorrectly, i. e. in an inconsistent manner which is regarded as producing undesirable consequences within the social context and therefore unacceptable. The "liar's" real transgression is inconsistent linguistic usage, and the moral opprobrium associated with lying is entirely arbitrary. This is the "extra-moral" sense of truth and lie indicated in the title of the work which we are considering.

Our entire intellectual, verbal, rational scheme rests upon metaphors, i. e. metaphorical translations of actual experiences into images, then words, and finally, concepts. Nietzsche says, however, that we have forgotten the metaphorical nature of our words and concepts, and that only by forgetting the origin of our language are we able to lay claim to some sort of truth about the "real" world. The "truths" of language, logic, science, and philosophy are therefore simply analytical or tautologous: they tell us nothing more than what we originally built into them[4]. It is a common,

---

[3] It is interesting to note that in an attack upon ethical utilitarianism, Nietzsche argues against an analogous form of forgetfulness of the origins of our words. According to Nietzsche, the English utilitarians claimed that the word "good" originally meant simply "useful," and that we have subsequently forgotten the utility of so-called "moral" behavior and have illegitimately associated such behavior with transcendental values. Nietzsche ridicules the notion that we could have somehow forgotten the obvious fact that useful actions are useful. See GM I 1—2; KGW VI 2, 272 ff.

[4] Cf. Nachlass Herbst 1885—Herbst 1886, 2 [174]; KGW VIII 1, 152 f.: " ... — der Mensch findet zuletzt in den Dingen nichts wieder als was er selbst in sie hinein-gesteckt hat: das Wiederfinden heisst sich Wissenschaft, das Hineinstecken — Kunst, Religion, Liebe, Stolz ... ."

although mistaken, assumption that we gain truths about the real world, i. e. about things as they really are in themselves, through language. The truths of language are indicative only of the relationships between various metaphors or the manner in which we customarily use those metaphors.

> Man kann sich einen Menschen denken, der ganz taub ist, und nie eine Emp-findung des Tones und der Musik gehabt hat: wie dieser etwa die Chlad-nischen Klangfiguren im Sande anstaunt, ihre Ursachen im Erzittern der Saite findet und nun darauf schwören wird, jetzt müsse er wissen, was die Menschen den Ton nennen, so geht es uns allen mit der Sprache. Wir glauben etwas von den Dingen selbst zu wissen, wenn wir von Bäumen, Farben, Schnee und Blumen reden und besitzen doch nichts als Metaphern der Dinge, die den ursprünglichen Wesenheiten ganz und gar nicht entsprechen. Wie der Ton als Sandfigur, so nimmt sich das räthselhafte X des Dings an sich einmal als Nervenreiz, dann als Bild, endlich als Laut aus. Logisch geht es also jeden-falls nicht bei der Entstehung der Sprache zu; und das ganze Material worin und womit später der Mensch der Wahrheit, der Forscher, der Philosoph arbeitet und baut, stammt, wenn nicht aus Wolkenkukuksheim, so doch jeden-falls nicht aus dem Wesen der Dinge[5].

Nietzsche's critique of language in *Ueber Wahrheit und Lüge im ausser-moralischen Sinne* quite obviously incorporates that critique of the correspon-dence theory which was outlined in Chapter III. But Nietzsche is perceptive enough to realize that the assertion that language does not, in fact, corres-pond to objects in the real world is just as dogmatic and just as inadmissable as the contrary assertion. To claim that words do *not* correspond to things in themselves obviously presupposes a firsthand acquaintance with these things, and this is impossible.

> Das Uebersehen des Individuellen und Wirklichen giebt uns den Begriff, wie es uns auch die Form giebt, wohingegen die Natur keine Formen und Be-griffe, also auch keine Gattungen kennt, sondern nur ein für uns unzugäng-liches und undefinirbares X. Denn auch unser Gegensatz von Individuum und Gattung ist anthropomorphisch und entstammt nicht dem Wesen der Dinge, wenn wir auch nicht zu sagen wagen, dass er ihm nicht entspricht: das wäre nämlich eine dogmatische Behauptung und als solche unerweislich wie ihr Gegentheil[6].

Nietzsche seems to have in mind here the same problematic to which David Hume addressed himself in *A Treatise of Human Nature*, viz. what causes our sense impressions, or what is it, of which we see only the "appearances?" Hume's answer was basically this, that all we can say with certainty is that we *have* impressions, all speculation regarding what might

---

[5] *Wahrheit und Lüge*, KGW III 2, 373.
[6] Ibid., p. 374.

"cause" them or "where" they might come from being futile. Nietzsche takes a similar position[7]. Ultimately, we should have to say that even the original sense impression can only be a metaphor for its corresponding object, and this position still begs a much larger epistemological question: to claim that even sense impressions are metaphors for objects presupposes a non-metaphorical acquaintance with those objects. Nietzsche's reluctance to talk about "appearances" indicates an awareness on his part of this situation. Of course, in subsequent works, Nietzsche very neatly avoids the inconsistencies of the correspondence theory by positing an identity between all the components of the cognitive act.

Even though *Ueber Wahrheit und Lüge im aussermoralischen Sinne* seems to be, at least in part, a polemic against the positivism of the late nineteenth century, it would be ultimately incorrect to maintain that Nietzsche's intent in this essay is to impugn the value of language as a "merely" metaphorical medium which is incapable of yielding any truths about reality. Although this certainly appears to be the tone of this work, the brunt of Nietzsche's attack — if it is an attack — is directed toward our forgetfulness of the creative, artistic nature of language. By allowing our freely created metaphors to petrify into linguistic conventions, we have perhaps created for ourselves the illusion of possessing objective, universal truths, but we have thereby also robbed ourselves of the ability to create better, more useful, more sublime metaphors.

> Nur durch das Vergessen jener primitiven Metapherwelt, nur durch das Hart- und Starr-Werden einer ursprünglich in hitziger Flüssigkeit aus dem Urvermögen menschlicher Phantasie hervorströmenden Bildermasse, nur durch den unbesiegbaren Glauben, diese Sonne, dieses Fenster, dieser Tisch sei eine Wahrheit an sich, kurz nur dadurch, dass der Mensch sich als Sub-

---

[7] "Schon dies kostet ihm Mühe, sich einzugestehen, wie das Insekt oder der Vogel eine ganz andere Welt percipiren als der Mensch, und dass die Frage, welche von beiden Weltperceptionen richtiger ist, eine ganz sinnlose ist, da hierzu bereits mit dem Maassstabe der richtigen Perception d. h. mit einem nicht vorhandenen Maassstabe gemessen werden müsste. Ueberhaupt aber scheint mir die richtige Perception — das würde heissen der adäquate Ausdruck eines Objekts im Subjekt — ein widerspruchsvolles Unding: denn zwischen zwei absolut verschiedenen Sphären wie zwischen Subjekt und Objekt giebt es keine Causalität, keine Richtigkeit, keinen Ausdruck, sondern höchstens ein ästhetisches Verhalten, ich meine eine andeutende Uebertragung, eine nachstammelnde Uebersetzung in eine ganz fremde Sprache. Wozu es aber jedenfalls einer frei dichtenden und frei erfindenden Mittel-Sphäre und Mittelkraft bedarf. Das Wort Erscheinung enthält viele Verführungen, weshalb ich es möglichst vermeide: denn es ist nicht wahr, dass das Wesen der Dinge in der empirischen Welt erscheint ... Selbst das Verhältniss eines Nervenreizes zu dem hervorgebrachten Bilde ist an sich kein nothwendiges ... Aber das Hart- und Starr-Werden einer Metapher verbürgt durchaus nichts für die Nothwendigkeit und ausschliessliche Berichtigung dieser Metapher." *Wahrheit und Lüge*, p. 378. Cf. Ornstein, op. cit., pp. 16—46.

jekt, und zwar als künstlerisch schaffendes Subjekt vergisst, lebt er mit einiger Ruhe, Sicherheit und Konsequenz . . .[8]

One can view Nietzsche's characterization of language as exclusively metaphorical as a criticism only if one accepts the existence of an extra-cognitive world of things in themselves (itself a questionable assumption), and then adds that language tells us nothing about this world. Superficially, this would seem to be Nietzsche's position in the work under consideration. However, in subsequent works, Nietzsche strenuously rejects any and all forms of epistemological dualism. This enables him to cut off at its very roots all speculation regarding how accurately our words and ideas correspond to objects. Once Nietzsche has broken out of the epistemological labyrinth created by the dualism of the correspondence theory, he is free to positively embrace the creative, metaphorical nature of language, not as a peephole through which we hope to catch a glimpse of things in themselves, but as an intensely dynamic and creative medium through we can literally reshape and restructure that world which we are.

II. Language and Science in the "Positivistic Phase"

In the Nietzsche-literature one often encounters the attempt to divide his works into three phases or periods. Whether or not such a division is justified lies beyond the scope of the present chapter, and I shall explore the historical development of Nietzsche's theory of knowledge in a subsequent chapter. For present purposes, however, I shall provisionally adopt this division. With this in mind, we could say that we have already dealt with Nietzsche's views on language in his "first period," and must now turn a consideration of how these views are developed during Nietzsche's "second period." This is the period which is usually (and misleadingly) referred to as Nietzsche's "positivistic phase." Some clarification is in order on this point.

The most obvious departure from his earlier views which strikes us in the works of this "positivistic phase" (*Menschliches, Allzumenschliches, Morgenröte, Also sprach Zarathustra, Die fröhliche Wissenschaft*) is the increasingly unfavorable position which Nietzsche adopts toward art, religion, metaphysics, morality, etc., and the rather positive attitude he takes toward "science[9]." Nietzsche's chief objections to metaphysics, religion, etc.

---

[8] *Wahrheit und Lüge*, p. 377.
[9] The word which Nietzsche uses is naturally "Wissenschaft," which has a much broader scope than does the ordinary usage of the English word "science." Nietzsche

here are their lack of honesty, their pronounced tendency to perpetuate useless and pernicious views of man and the world, and their hostility to the unprejudiced and courageous spirit of scientific inquiry. What Nietzsche finds so admirable in science is its (relative) freedom from human prejudices and foibles, its objectivity, and the clarity and rigor of its procedures. Within this context, the "scientific spirit" denotes a willingness to tenaciously pursue an investigation as far as possible, even if the "truths" thereby discovered prove to be inexpedient, unpleasant, or otherwise offensive to conventional pieties. Naturally all this is lacking in religion, morality, metaphysics, and other associated superstitions. Obviously Nietzsche has an idealized sort of science in mind here, and he is quite aware of this. What he finds praiseworthy is the motivating spirit of scientific inquiry, rather than any particular scientific position[10]. Nietzsche's views on language during this period do not greatly differ from those already discussed, although there is generally a difference of emphasis in the context wherein they occur.

generally appears to have in mind the natural sciences, although he often speaks of philology as a science within this context. This is also the period during which Nietzsche made some of his most remarkable psychological discoveries i. e., transformed traditional philosophical anthropology into a "science."

[10] See FW. I think that we are justified in regarding classical philology as paradigmatic for Nietzsche's view of "science" as a whole, and his various utterances concerning classical philology are most illuminating in light of the present discussion. In his earliest works, in which he was still primarily concerned with classical Greece, Nietzsche often alludes to the paradox implicit to classical philology viz., that a strict adherence to the letter of a given text usually precludes an understanding or appreciation of the spirit, the context, which gave rise to that text. (See KGW III 2, which contains a number of these early, unpublished philological essays.) This is quite in keeping with his view of language during this period i. e., language as a metaphorical structure, and certainly implies that the philologist must "read between the lines" i. e., read a given text as metaphorical in order to gain an adequate understanding of that context in which it was written. This "unscientific" sort of philology, of which *Die Geburt der Tragödie* is certainly the best known example, brought Nietzsche into disrepute among the classical philologists of his day, most notably Ulrich von Willamowitz-Moellendorf (see K. Gründer, *Der Streit um Nietzsches „Geburt der Tragödie"*). In the works of Nietzsche's second creative period, however, we notice an important change of emphasis. Classical philology now comes to be viewed as the paradigm of the exact sciences. Nietzsche makes repeated references to the necessity of precise, accurate, unprejudiced reading (cf. MAM I 270—272) and praises the sceptical, manly spirit of the great German historians and philologists who, in spite of the muddle-headedness of romanticism, boldly and with open minds, plumbed the depths of their respective disciplines, without distorting their findings to suit popular prejudice (JGB 209). Nietzsche sharply criticizes the philology of Christianity (MR I 84) for reading whatever it pleases into a text such as the New Testament. "Der Mangel an Philologie: man verwechselt beständig die Erklärung mit dem Text — und was für eine 'Erklärung'!" (Nachlass Frühjahr 1888, 15 [82]; KGW VIII 3, 250). There is yet another important shift of emphasis which takes place in the works of Nietzsche's last creative period, which can be stated quite succinctly: "Derselbe Text

Nietzsche's basic position during this second phase is still that language is a construct of metaphors, illusions, interpretations, etc. In the earlier works, however, this feature of language was viewed in a positive fashion, i. e. language was viewed as an aesthetic, creative, plastic medium through which man could and did create for himself sublime and comforting illusions, thus enabling himself to tolerate a basically unpleasant reality. In the second period, Nietzsche came to regard our predilection to forget or deny the metaphorical, illusory nature of language as reprehensible, for the reason that this constituted a great obstacle to the fearless and impartial investigation of reality.

> Die Bedeutung der Sprache für die Entwicklung der Cultur liegt darin, dass in ihr der Mensch eine eigene Welt neben die andere stellte, einen Ort, welchen er für so fest hielt, um von ihm aus die übrige Welt aus den Angeln zu heben und sich zum Herrn derselben zu machen. Insofern der Mensch an die Begriffe und Namen der Dinge als an aeternae veritates durch lange Zeitstrecken hindurch geglaubt hat, hat er sich jenen Stolz angeeignet, mit dem er sich über das Thier erhob: er meinte wirklich in der Sprache die Erkenntniss der Welt zu haben. Der Sprachbildner war nicht so bescheiden, zu glauben, dass er den Dingen nur Bezeichnungen gebe, er drückte vielmehr, wie er wähnte, das höchste Wissen über die Dinge mit den Worten aus; in der That ist die Sprache die erste Stufe der Bemühung um die Wissenschaft. Der Glaube an die gefundene Wahrheit ist es auch hier, aus dem die mächtigsten Kraftquellen geflossen sind. Sehr nachträglich . . . dämmert es den Menschen auf, dass sie einen ungeheuren Irrthum in ihrem Glauben an die Sprache propagirt haben[11].

Nietzsche's criticism during the period under discussion is directed toward the forgetfulness of ordinary language (more properly, on the part of those who use it) of its origin and status. If, as Nietzsche indicates, language is exclusively a construct of metaphors, anthropomorphisms, interpretations, etc., there is nothing to be done about that, except perhaps

---

erlaubt unzählige Auslegungen: es giebt keine 'richtige' Auslegung." (Nachlass Herbst 1885—Frühjahr 1886, 1 [120]; KGW VIII 1, 35.) The careful reader will have noticed that the views expressed in these quotations do not fit particularly well into the usual division of Nietzsche's work into three periods, i. e. he appears to be saying something other than what he should have been saying at a particular time. But this only underscores the folly of insisting too strictly on the validity of such a division. Thus, we may venture the following outline of Nietzsche's views on philology and, by association, science: 1) since language is metaphorical, the philologist must read a text "metaphorically" or "between the lines" in order to understand that context in which the text was conceived; 2) the task of the philologist is to read a text as closely, dispassionately, and accurately as possible without reading his own opinions or prejudices into it; 3) there can be no "correct" reading of a text: a text is subject to innumerable interpretations. If we substitute "world" for "text", the epistemological relevance of this outline becomes quite obvious.

[11] MAM I 11; KGW IV 2, 26f.

to remember what it is which we actually have in language. And what we have in language is not a description of the ultimate nature of things, nor even a means of getting such information. What we have in language is a system of metaphors, interpretations, or linguistic signs ("Bezeichnungen") which simply designate or otherwise point to things within that world which, for us, is the case, but which certainly cannot be regarded as objective descriptions. To name a thing, to give it a label, is not at all the same as explaining or describing that thing. Yet due to our congenital forgetfulness, we constantly ignore this vital distinction and mistakenly think that possessing names for the objects of our experience is the equivalent of objective, explanatory knowledge of the the things as such.

Those interpretations and metaphors which constitute our language, Nietzsche argues, must originally have been made for purely utilitarian ends such as survival and simply getting on in the world. In this capacity, ordinary language seems to have succeeded admirably in allowing our forbears to distinguish the useful, beneficial aspects of their environment from the harmful, and thereby survive and grow. However, once such a useful linguistic metaphor or interpretation is created, we promptly forget that it is nothing more than an interpretation, carried out from a particular perspective for a particular purpose. It is this process of petrification and conceptualization which transforms our once fluid and malleable metaphors — which could always be replaced by even more useful metaphors — into a rigid conceptual scheme which, because of its apparent stability and reliability, is mistakenly thought to reflect an equally stable and reliable reality. In this fashion, what were at one point useful metaphors remain within language long after their usefulness has passed, and become crude assumptions and presuppositions. These crude presuppositions are far more than the mores, folkways, religious and political institutions embedded in the language and mode of thought of a particular group. Language contains a very definite view of reality. Because we are accustomed to expressing ourselves in terms of subject and object, substance and accidence, I and thou, spirit and nature, etc., we have allowed these once useful interpretations to harden into an inflexible structure which now represents a considerable obstacle to the creation of better, more useful interpretations[12]. We are no longer able to think except in terms of that

---

[12] Cf. Thomas S. Kuhn, *The Structure of Scientific Revolutions* (Chicago, 1962). I have made repeated references to the resemblance between Kuhn's notion of paradigm shifts, and Nietzsche's perspectivism. Of particular interest here is Kuhn's account of the enormous resistance to any change in the dominant paradigm, and the lengths to which investigators will sometimes go to make the "facts" fit the "theory." See Kuhn, pp. 43—135.

particular interpretation of reality which is inherent in the language we speak.

> Die Sprache und die Vorurtheile, auf denen die Sprache aufgebaut ist, sind uns vielfach in der Ergründung innerer Vorgänge und Triebe hinderlich: zum Beispiel dadurch, dass eigentlich Worte allein für superlativische Grade dieser Vorgänge und Triebe da sind —; nun aber sind wir gewohnt, dort, wo uns Worte fehlen, nicht mehr genau zu beobachten, weil es peinlich ist, dort noch genau zu denken; ja ehedem schloss man unwillkürlich, wo das Reich der Worte aufhöre, höre auch das Reich des Daseins auf . . .[13]

Rules of grammar have become laws of nature. Names and labels have become explanations of the inner nature of things. We have forced reality into our linguistic, conceptual scheme to such an extent that if we encounter an anomalous phenomenon (i. e. a phenomenon which does not fit into our predetermined linguistic mould), we almost invariably attribute this to faulty observation and not to an inadequacy on the part of our cognitive-linguistic paradigm. We habitually speak of lightning flashing or of fire burning, when a moment of reflection would show these to be completely tautologous formulations. Likewise we habitually speak of an object as having qualities, when all we experience are those very qualities, and not the object (cf. Locke's distinction between primary and secondary qualities). These linguistic habits have become so firmly entrenched within our mode of thinking and speaking that, as Nietzsche has it, we would rather break a leg than a word.

> Die Worte liegen uns im Wege! — Überall, wo die Uralten ein Wort hin-stellten, da glaubten sie eine Entdeckung zu haben. Wie anders stand es in Wahrheit! — sie hatten an ein Problem geführt, und indem sie wähnten, es gelöst zu haben, hatten sie ein Hemmnis der Lösung geschaffen, — Jetzt muss man bei jeder Erkenntniss über steinharte verewigte Worte stolpern, und wird dabei eher ein Bein brechen als ein Wort[14].

Considerations such as these led Nietzsche to, perhaps overenthusiastically, embrace "science" during his middle phase. His position was that science — even if it was not entirely free from presuppositions and dogma — was nevertheless motivated by the desire to investigate that world which is the case as objectively and as free from prejudice as possible, even if the results of such investigations exploded our worn-out metaphors or proved damaging to the sacred cows of convention. Perhaps Nietzsche had in mind figures such as Galileo, who tempted both fate and the inquisition by

---

[13] MR II 115; KGW V 1, 105.
[14] MR I 47; KGW V 1, 49.

scientifically demonstrating the untenability of the then current (and ecclesiastically endorsed) geocentric cosmology. *Eppur si muove!* Nevertheless it moves. It is this motivating spirit which interests Nietzsche, this dispassionate willingness to follow the path of inquiry wherever it might lead, even if the "truths" thereby laid bare proved to be unpleasant, unpopular, or destructive.

Nietzsche's favorable attitude toward the sciences during this period is not to be construed as that sort of optimism which was characteristic of the Enlightenment, viz. that science was ultimately capable of answering all questions and solving all problems. (This, I think, would be more applicable to the nineteenth century positivists, against whom Nietzsche raged.) As Alois Riehl has it, Nietzsche was never an "Enlightenment thinker," but rather an "enlightened thinker[15]." The manner in which science used its cognitive-linguistic resources was far more free, far more creative than the conventional mode of thought and discourse. This latter mode of thought and discourse — ordinary language, common sense, as well as religion, metaphysics, morality — was incapable of freeing itself from the worn-out metaphors, the assumptions and presuppositions of our linguistic tradition. Yet science, according to Nietzsche, at least makes the attempt to break out of the predetermined pattern of thought inherent in our language, and is thus capable of offering us fresh, new perspectives on the world. Even if science cannot provide us with access to the things in themselves or give us fixed, ultimate truths, it can at least demonstrate the complete groundlessness of conventional religion, morality, etc., and thus make way for newer and more useful "regulative fictions."

> In der Wissenschaft haben die Überzeugungen kein Bürgerrecht, so sagt man mit gutem Grunde: erst wenn sie sich entschliessen, zur Bescheidenheit einer Hypothese, eines vorläufigen Versuchs-Standpunktes, einer regulativen Fiktion herabzusteigen, darf ihnen der Zutritt und sogar ein gewisser Werth innerhalb des Reiches der Erkenntniss zugestanden werden ,— wenn immerhin mit der Beschränkung, unter polizeiliche Aufsicht gestellt zu bleiben, unter die Polizei des Misstrauens. — Heisst das aber nicht, genauer besehen: erst wenn die Überzeugung aufhört, Überzeugung zu sein, darf sie Eintritt in die Wissenschaft erlangen? Finge damit nicht die Zucht des wissenschaftlichen Geistes an, sich keine Überzeugungen mehr zu gestatten? . . .[16]

We see that Nietzsche's preference for science here is really of a formal, methodological nature. Science, in Nietzsche's view, makes a more authentic use of the epistemological, linguistic tools at its disposal. The

---

[15] Alois Riehl, *Friedrich Nietzsche: Der Künstler und der Denker* (Stuttgart, 1923), p. 62.
[16] FW V 344; KGW V 2, 256f.

continuity here between these considerations and Nietzsche's earlier views on language is readily seen: Nietzsche still regards language as a construct of metaphors and interpretations which is incapable of telling us anything about ultimate reality or things in themselves. But science, it would seem, is implicitly aware of this, and utilizes this awareness within its methodology. The scientist is aware of the theoretical, provisional (i. e. metaphorical) nature of his statements, and this awareness enables him to cast off his no longer useful metaphors for newer, more satisfactory ones. The theologian, the metaphysician, the moralist, can trade only in the worn-out currency of linguistic tradition. The scientist, on the other hand, is free to strike new coins which, even if they are no closer to absolute truth than those of his predecessors, at least do not claim to be what they are not, and can be exchanged for an even better currency, should the need arise.

We might view that group of disciplines which Nietzsche loosely designated as "science" as a test case: what can be accomplished when authentic use is made of language? What can be accomplished when the users of language become aware that what they posses are signs, metaphors, or interpretations, and not veridical statements about ultimate reality? Clearly a great deal can be accomplished. From this perspective a vastly more flexible, creative use can be made of language. New and more useful metaphors can be created to more successfully master our environment, and this creative process can be carried out indefinitely, so long as we do not mistakenly regard a highly useful metaphor (or scientific hypothesis) as a fixed and ultimate truth. In this way, man can repossess himself of language and use it creatively as a tool, rather than being possessed by language and forced into a static and unyielding *Weltanschauung*. At one point in his creative career Nietzsche seemed to feel that science was the embodiment of this point of view. That he came to revise this opinion goes almost without saying.

> Sind nicht den Dingen Namen und Töne geschenkt, dass der Mensch sich an den Dingen erquicke? Es ist eine schöne Narretei, das Sprechen: damit tanzt der Mensch über alle Dinge[17].

III. Language in the "Umwertungszeit"

Nietzsche did not embrace "science" because he felt that the discoveries of science were somehow closer to the absolute truth then the traditional views of religion or philosophy. Science was preferable because it made

[17] Z III 13: 2; KGW VI 1, 268. Lest the reader suspect that Nietzsche is illegitimately smuggling in a correspondence theory here, I hasten to add that this excerpt from

more authentic use of its linguistic-cognitive resources. However, that science which Nietzsche had in mind was not so much physical or natural science, but rather a "fröhliche Wissenschaft." He soon came to the realization that the scientists of his day were far from being the "free spirits" of *Die fröhliche Wissenschaft*. If they had succeeded in discrediting many of the anachronistic prejudices and assumptions of tradition, they tended simply to replace old dogmas with new dogmas. Science was perhaps closer to Nietzsche's ideal of freely creating hypotheses and regulative fictions than, say, religion or philosophy, but Nietzsche was entirely disenchanted with the positivistic attitude which so many nineteenth-century scientists adopted, which led them to become even more zealous and dogmatic than their predecessors[18]. The often critical attitude which Nietzsche displayed toward the sciences in his later works appears to be a reversal of his former point of view only if one fails to realize that Nietzsche's preference for science was all along a preference for a more flexible, more creative, and more authentic cognitive-linguistic paradigm, i. e. a method, an attitude, rather than for the concrete results of any particular discipline[19]. Science had indeed developed a healthy sense of scepticism, had indeed created a number of new and useful metaphors, but tended to defeat itself by once again becoming dogmatic and inflexible[20]. Even if science had made some headway toward the creation of a new cognitive-linguistic paradigm, it had not entirely succeeded, and still fell victim to many of the "crude assumptions" inherent in our language, thus abandoning the flexibility and creativity which Nietzsche valued. Even though Nietzsche tended to disassociate himself from science in his later works, he continued to explore and develop that linguistic model which remained quite consistent throughout his early and middle works.

The major theme of Nietzsche's later works, the works of the so-called "Umwertungszeit," is the will to power. During the 1880's Nietzsche had begun to develop his own model of reality, his own cognitive paradigm, and his views on the nature and function of language are an integral part of these formulations. Throughout this book we have concentrated on Nietzsche's mature ontological and epistemological views, and it will be recalled from earlier chapters that Nietzsche's mature model of reality

Also sprach Zarathustra is preceded by the following: "Für mich — wie gäbe es ein Ausser-mir? Es giebt kein Aussen! Aber das vergessen wir bei allen Tönen; wie lieblich ist es, dass wir vergessen!" I think that this makes it evident that Nietzsche's mention of "Dinge" does not presuppose correspondence criteria here.

[18] See JGB VI 204; KGW VI 2, 133ff.
[19] Nachlass Frühjahr 1888, 15 [51]; KGW VIII 3, 236.
[20] GM I 13; KGW VI 2, 292ff.

was that of a turbulent, constantly changing flux of power-quanta. The leading motive of Nietzsche's critique of language during this period may be expressed quite succinctly:

> Die Ausdrucksmittel der Sprache sind unbrauchbar, um das „Werden" aus-
> zudrücken; es gehört zu unserm unablöslichen Bedürfniss der Erhaltung, be-
> ständig eine gröbere Welt von Bleibenden, von „Dingen" usw. zu setzen[21].

If, for the moment, we accept Nietzsche's flux ontology, and if we agree that a fundamental presupposition of ordinary language is that its signs designate consistent, self-identical objects or events in the world, then obviously language is incapable of authentically grasping the change, paradox and ambiguity which characterize that world which is the case. Nietzsche makes this point somewhat more succinctly in *Götzen-dämmerung*, in a section entitled "Die Vernunft in der Philosophie":

> Die Sprache gehört ihrer Entstehung nach in die Zeit der rudimentärsten
> Form von Psychologie: wir kommen in ein grobes Fetischwesen hinein,
> wenn wir uns die Grundvoraussetzungen der Sprach-Metaphysik, auf deutsch:
> der Vernunft, zum Bewusstsein bringen. Das sieht überall Thäter und Thun:
> das glaubt an Willen als Ursache überhaupt; das glaubt an's „Ich", an's Ich als
> Sein, an's Ich als Substanz und projicirt den Glauben an die Ich-Substanz auf
> alle Dinge — es schafft erst damit den Begriff „Ding" ... Die „Vernunft" in
> der Sprache: oh was für eine alte betrügerische Weibsperson! Ich fürchte,
> wir werden Gott nicht los, weil wir noch an die Grammatik glauben...[22].

This passage from *Götzendämmerung* is preceded by a section — surely one of Nietzsche's most delightful — in which he analyzes the development of concepts within language. His view there is basically the same sort of nominalism which was dealt with earlier, but now grounded within the flux ontology of the will to power. A concept, Nietzsche feels, is a general term which because of its generality, is held to be applicable to any number of identical cases. But for Nietzsche there can be no identical cases, and the creation and use of concepts involves a radical falsification of our experi-ence. To become a concept, a sign, a metaphor, is wrenched out of that context of immediate experience in which it arose. The concept is thus divorced from that changing stream of lived experience in which it function-ed as perhaps a useful metaphor, squeezed dry of its original vitality and — as Nietzsche expresses it — "mummified." When a linguistic metaphor is taken out of that specific context in which it arose and is generalized to fit more than one case, it applies *ipso facto* to no cases. A concept, a general terminus, thus has nothing more to do with experiential reality. This, however, is not yet the substance of Nietzsche's critique.

---

[21] Nachlass November 1887—März 1888, 11 [73]; KGW VIII 2, 278.
[22] GD III 5; KGW VI 3, 71f.

Language, as a construct of metaphors, signs, interpretations, etc., may not yield veridical judgements in the correspondence sense, but it is useful. If the use of concepts involves a somewhat cavalier ignoring of the uniqueness of a particular experience, we might make a similar observation about the rest of our words, signs, and metaphors. If the world is a constantly changing stream of power-quanta, then any statement at all will be false in the referential sense the moment it is uttered, because the situation in which the statement was applied will have changed in the meantime. But this does not constitute an objection. Nietzsche is not interested in how well our linguistic metaphors correspond to an unchanging reality, because he denies that it is meaningful to talk about such a reality and claims further that that cognitive paradigm which embodies such an epistemological dualism and referential truth-criterion is self-referentially inconsistent. Nietzsche is concerned with how well our linguistic constructs increase or or otherwise enhance our will to power, and nothing else. He is not concerned with a word's reference or a concept's logical content. He is exclusively concerned with how well these linguistic metaphors work for us as flexible, creative tools. Even if a concept says nothing about reality, it is useful insofar as it is a linguistic rule or connecting link between the other signs or metaphors of language.

The legitimate use of a concept, therefore, would be as a regulative fiction which enables us to effectively employ the other fictions of language. This use of concepts is certainly justifiable because it is more useful and efficient to employ general fictions than to create on-the-spot specific fictions for the multifarious aspects of our experience. Nevertheless, Nietzsche sees our entire intellectual tradition as having made an illegitimate use of concepts and this has caused great mischief. For the most part we have illegitimately regarded concepts, the conceptual "truths" of reason and language, as necessarily reflecting some feature of reality. Because our concepts seem to be stable and consistent within language, we have come to believe that they must correspond to equally stable and equally consistent aspects of reality. Furthermore, we have come to regard the rules of linguistic usage as yielding reality-criteria, such that a statement which is in violation of linguistic usage cannot be a "true" statement, and therefore cannot correspond to any actual state of affairs[23]. Once this πρῶτον

---

[23] This is a very brief synopsis of that destruction of the correspondence theory (*as adequatio intellectu et rei*) which was elaborated in Chapter III. As it stands here, it might appear a bit facile, but Nietzsche's point is this: a fundamental presupposition of language within our tradition is that language has a metaphysical function. We ordinarily never doubt that the statements which we formulate within language refer to some reality separate from language and from those who use it. The assumption here is that language is grounded in entities which exist independently of our

ψεῦδος has been made, once the internal rules of language are equated with "laws of nature," the internal rules of language and reason become yard-sticks for evaluating reality. If a concept is held to have some sort of priority within language i. e., if a concept is regarded as being somehow "superior" to, or "more true" than a particular terminus because of its generality, then there must exist correspondingly general structures within reality as such. How else could we have arrived at the concepts? Since the realities which must correspond to our concepts are not directly encountered in experience, the fault must lie with our sensory apparatus. The senses must be incapable of giving us a true picture of reality, and for this reason we must rely exclusively upon conceptual rationality to inform us as to the true nature of reality. Needless to say, such views are odious to Nietzsche, whose term of collective opprobrium for them is "Sprach-Metaphysik."

For Nietzsche, this mode of thought has led to some highly unpalatable positions. It has led us to completely invert our reality criteria to the point where we now confuse what is "most real" (i. e. immediate, pre-conceptual experience) with what is "least real" (i. e. conceptualism, reason, logic). For this reason, we now possess a large number of linguistic metaphors (e. g. subject and object, cause and effect, substance and accidence, appearance and reality, ego, will, thing, to name but a few) which masquerade as unalterable features of reality, and which have become so

cognitive-linguistic faculties. Nietzsche regards this assumption as paradigmatic for our entire Western mode of thinking and speaking. It is this which leads us to formulate propositions such as "fire burns," "wind blows," *cogito ergo sum*, or even scientific propositions about atoms and forces. In such cases we have interpreted the linguistic subject-verb distinction into our experiential world and unnecessarily multi-plied reality by construing the same phenomenon once as an activity, and then as an agent which performs that activity. Nietzsche demonstrates that the correspon-dence theory which is assumed here is self-referentially inconsistent, and that it is nonsensical to argue from linguistic propositions to an extra-linguistic reality. Our alternatives are these: a) if we wish to maintain that language is about extra-linguistic reality, we are committed to a self-referentially inconsistent truth-criterion; b) if we drop the implication-laden term "truth" entirely and talk instead about "meaning," we are committed to the position that language says nothing about extra-linguistic "things," that all propositions are analytical in nature, and that "truth" (sic) is nothing more than a measure of how consistently one follows the internal rules of a particular language game. A number of recent linguistic analysts have opted for this second alternative (e. g. Gilbert Ryle), and this would seem to corroborate Nietzsche's point: meaning, significance, "thinghood," etc. are internally constituted in interpretative (i. e. cognitive-linguistic) activity, not by reference to some separate and independent realm of entities. It would probably not be incorrect to maintain that Nietzsche is denying the truth-functionality of language, but it would be ana-chronistic. Arthur Danto draws some interesting parallels between Nietzsche's approach in this regard and contemporary linguistic analysis. See Danto, pp. 83—87, 96—98, 106—107. Cf. also John T. Wilcox, *Truth and Value in Nietzsche* (Ann Arbor, 1974).

firmly entrenched within our mode of thinking and speaking that we can no longer exchange them for more useful metaphors. Indeed, we can scarcely regard such notions as metaphors at all, because that very language in which such a proceeding must be carried out already presupposes that which is to be called into question. That we now seem to find identical cases or regular occurrences in the world is not especially noteworthy: all we are doing in such instances is pretending to discover something which was implicit to our world-interpretation in the first place. We might say that for Nietzsche, an alleged statement of fact about reality is actually nothing more than a statement about how our linguistic metaphors relate to one another. I should like to re-emphasize here that Nietzsche's criticism is not directed toward the metaphorical nature of language, but rather toward our forgetfulness of this characteristic. It is this forgetfulness, this linguistic inauthenticity, which leads us to debase our once fluid and creative metaphors and allow them to harden into concepts and facts.

Nietzsche distinguishes between signs ("Zeichen," "Bezeichnungen," metaphors, interpretations) and explanations, a distinction which our ordinary use of language has blurred. One of the idiosyncrasies of our rational-linguistic paradigm is that we commonly think that we have "explained" something when all we have done is to supply a label or name. It one were to ask, "What is a dog?" and receive by way of an explanation that a dog is a carniverous, domesticated mammal of the family *Canidae*, such an answer might ordinarily assuage our curiosity, but obviously tells us nothing about the nature of dogs. Our "explanation" of what a dog is is simply analytical in nature i. e., it is simply the substitution of one linguistic metaphor for another[24]. Nietzsche felt that all of our rational, linguistic "explanations" follow a similar pattern. We make the same *gaffe* when we regard a scientific or mathematical "Bezeichnung" as an explanation of events in the world. To maintain that what water "really" is is H_2O, or that a dropped object always falls "because of" gravity are both simply descriptions of how our language functions, not factual statements about reality. It is not inconsistent to claim that a sleeping draught works because of its dormitive virtue, but a statement such as this is not terribly illuminating either.

Auslegung, nicht Erklärung. Es giebt keinen Thatbestand, alles ist flüssig, unfassbar, zurückweichend; das Dauerhafteste sind noch unsere Meinungen.

---

[24] What we have done in such a case is to clarify the meaning of the word "dog," and this is entirely an intra-linguistic affair. Cf. Willard van Orman Quine, *Ontological Relativity and Other Essays* (New York, 1969) and *Word and Object* (Cambridge, Mass., 1960).

Sinn-hineinlegen — in den meisten Fällen eine neue Auslegung über eine alte unverständlich gewordene Auslegung, die jetzt nur Zeichen ist[25].

Illusion, dass etwas erkannt sei, wo wir eine mathematische Formel für das Geschehen haben: es ist nur bezeichnet, beschrieben: nichts mehr![26]

If we accept Nietzsche's view that language is metaphorical in nature, we see that one metaphor is not preferable to another because one represents reality more accurately than another, and Nietzsche views such epistemological considerations as completely idle. The criterion upon which we must evaluate our linguistic metaphors is their utility within a given context. It is not likely that the chemical formula for water would be of much use to someone dying of thirst or drowning at sea, but this same metaphor might be quite useful to the chemist in his laboratory. In the epistemological sense, it is an idle question to ask "yes, but what is water *really*?" because such a question presupposes that we can meaningfully talk about water in absolute terms, outside of any specific context in which water is of interest to us. As a request for unobtainable metaphysical information, Nietzsche would disallow the question as meaningless, and would, in all liklihood, construe it as a request for a more useful metaphor.

Since Nietzsche rejects the correspondence theory of truth, he can dismiss any questions about which metaphor, which interpretation is the "correct" one. There can be no "correct" interpretation, if by correct we mean "corresponding exactly to reality," because Nietzsche denies that it is either meaningful or consistent to talk about any such realm of stable, self-identical entities to which statements could correspond. Even if there were such a realm, to intelligibly make statements about it would presuppose a transcendent mode of cognition which is unavailable to us.

IV. Toward a New Linguistic Paradigm

A brief synopsis of the preceding discussion of Nietzsche's views upon language will be helpful at this point before entertaining considerations of what this implies with regard to Nietzsche's own position. We have seen that in his earliest critical reflections upon language, Nietzsche took a fundamentally nominalistic position. This was to remain his basic position with regard to language throughout his creative career, although there were some changes of the context in which this view was put forth. In

[25] Nachlass Herbst 1885—Frühjahr 1886, 2 [82]; KGW VIII 1, 98.
[26] Nachlass Herbst 1885—Frühjahr 1886, 2 [89]; KGW VIII 1, 103.

Ueber Wahrheit und Lüge im aussermoralischen Sinne Nietzsche maintains that language is a purely metaphorical structure which can say nothing about the ultimate nature of things. His account there of the genesis of language is basically this: our primordial, preconceptual sense impressions (themselves metaphors) are translated into images or representations, i. e. metaphors. These metaphorical images are, in turn, translated into sounds i. e. words which are again metaphorical. Concepts are general metaphors which govern the use of specific metaphors, but which are also quite remote from the given data of lived experience. Nietzsche appears to be thinking in terms of the Kantian noumenon-phenomenon distinction here, the implication being that language (which includes "pure reason" as its most rarified and abstract metaphors) can have only phenomenal validity. Words are only metaphors which tell us nothing about things in themselves, but this is not regarded as a shortcoming. For Nietzsche, the metaphorical nature of language represents a vast, creative resource for man, and he laments only our forgetting of this fundamental characteristic of language which leads us to chain ourselves to one particular set of metaphors, thereby abandoning our potential to create new and better (i. e., more useful) metaphors.

During his second creative period, the so-called "positivistic phase," Nietzsche maintained this basic view of language. His favorable attitude toward "science" in the works of this period stems largely from his belief that science embodied a more authentic and creative (i. e. consciously metaphorical) use of language. Science had apparently freed itself from the naive belief that our customary manner of regarding the world is the only possible one. Science pursued its inquiries in a fearless and open-minded manner, unfettered by and sceptical toward the conventional pieties of tradition. Since science dealt with theories and hypotheses, it could view its own metaphors as provisional, and could cast them aside in order to create even more useful interpretations. In this way, science appeared to have overcome that naive presumptiousness which insists that one particular point of view is the only possible, indeed, the "true" point of view[27]. Nonetheless, Nietzsche became somewhat disenchanted with science with the realization that the positivistic scientists of his day tended to become just as unyielding and dogmatic about the "correctness" of their views as their predecessors had been. Thus, even science seemed to have abandoned what had been its greatest asset, a more authentic and flexible use of linguistic metaphors.

---

[27] Cf. Walter del Negro, *Die Rolle der Fiktionen in der Erkenntnistheorie Friedrich Nietzsches* (München, 1923).

These linguistic considerations are consistently maintained in Nietzsche's last creative period. In the works of this period, the "Umwertungszeit," Nietzsche's linguistic views become an integral part of the context of the will to power, and are supported and amplified by Nietzsche's mature views on cognition and reality. Because of his destruction of the correspondence theory, Nietzsche rejects any considerations of the ultimate "correctness" of any particular metaphor or interpretation as futile. Indeed, Nietzsche's characterization of reality as a continually changing flux of power-quanta undermines the possibility of any stable state of affairs to which our linguistic metaphors could meaningfully correspond. He is thus free to wholeheartedly embrace the fluid, metaphorical nature of language as a valuable creative tool through which we can radically restructure and reinterpret our world. The criterion for evaluating a particular linguistic formulation becomes its utility in a given context, and considerations of epistemological correctness, reference, denotation etc. are dismissed as irrelevant. Nietzsche's major criticism of our conventional use of language is once more directed toward our forgetfulness of its creative, metaphorical nature. This forgetfulness has led us to insist upon the truth, the correctness of what is only one possible set of metaphors, and to confuse the structure of language with the structure of reality. On this basis, Nietzsche can claim that that particular mode of rational, conceptual thinking which is an essential feature of our linguistic paradigm — far from being an adequate representation of external reality — is nothing more than a particular metaphorical scheme, a scheme whose metaphorical nature we have forgotten and which we can therefore no longer exchange for a more useful one.

> Wir hören auf zu denken, wenn wir es nicht in dem sprachlichen Zwange tun wollen, wir langen gerade noch bei dem Zweifel an, hier eine Grenze als Grenze zu sehen.
> Das vernünftige Denken ist Interpretiren nach einem Schema, welches wir nicht abwerfen können[28].

Whether or not Nietzsche himself entirely succeeded in casting off this restrictive scheme and creating a more authentic and more flexible linguistic paradigm must now be considered.

V. Nietzsche's Linguistic Model as a Formal Structure

I think that the paradox implicit to Nietzsche's view of language will by now have become obvious. If language is metaphorical, if every state-

[28] Nachlass Sommer 1886—Herbst 1887, 5 [22]; KGW VIII 1, 197f.

ment is already an interpretation, then are not Nietzsche's own statements equally interpretation, equally metaphorical? We might even extend this paradox and say that since all statements are interpretative and therefore not literally "true" or "correct," they are all literally "false," and that therefore Nietzsche's own statements are false as well.

I doubt that Nietzsche would deny the "falsity" of his own views because, as we saw earlier, he uses the terms "true" and "false" in a very special way. To claim that all statements are metaphorical, are interpretative and therefore "false" is only Nietzsche's way of emphasizing the fluid, creative, and perspectival nature of all knowledge. The word "false" is used rhetorically in this regard, to underscore the untenability of the correspondence theory. Our views are not true in the way we have traditionally believed. Indeed, they are all false according to correspondence criteria, but this serves only to reveal the fundamental uselessness of the correspondence theory, and does not affect the utility of our "useful fictions" at all. Nietzsche's views are indeed interpretations and metaphors, but not "mere" interpretations or "only" metaphors. The words "mere" or "only" are entirely unjustified if, as Nietzsche claims, interpretations are all that we can possibly have.

To disparage an interpretation as a biased, incomplete, or otherwise inadequate view of reality is not admissable. To reject an interpretation on these grounds presupposes the appearance-reality distinction and assumes that we can know "reality," overagainst which an interpretation could then be seen as inadequate or incorrect. This in turn presupposes the correspondence theory which, as we have argued, is inconsistent with itself. To argue the point that interpretations are inadequate because they do not accurately and objectively represent reality is to tacitly lay claim to some sort of transcendental, extra-cognitive knowledge, and this is impossible. Therefore, to dismiss an interpretation as an inadequate representation of reality is an inconsistent and self-defeating argument. There can be more useful or less useful interpretations, but not correct and incorrect interpretations.

Nietzsche is saved the bother or refuting the referential or correspondence theory of truth simply by demonstrating that this position must deny its own assumptions in order to function at all. Nietzsche's own position, on the other hand, is quite consistent with itself, which the correspondence theory is not. By claiming that all statements are metaphorical and interpretative, and by allowing that this statement is itself an interpretation, Nietzsche is taking the only possible consistent position. His position also avoids the self-contradiction of the correspondence theory by not claiming to have knowledge of what it denies can be known. All statements are interpretations, this statement is itself an interpretation, and that is the end of the matter.

Granting the consistency of Nietzsche's linguistic model, it still might be objected that his basic philosophical position is nevertheless not consistent with itself. After having denied that there is a stable, external reality in which our statements are grounded through a relationship of correspondence, it might be argued that Nietzsche inconsistently supplies a model of reality (the will to power) such that interpretative statements somehow correspond to it. By claiming on the one hand that reality is ultimately unknowable, but then supplying an explanatory model to clarify this unknowability, is Nietzsche not contradicting himself in exactly the same way that the correspondence theory contradicts itself? Is he not claiming "knowledge" of what he denies can be known?

Not at all, and this unfortunately common "refutation" of Nietzsche's position is a symptom of nothing more than a failure to understand what that position actually is. The will to power as an ontological model is not a snapshot of ultimate reality, on the basis of which we might make "correct" statements. The will to power is itself a metaphor, an interpretation, a regulative fiction, which functions as an explanatory model or heuristic rule within Nietzsche's theory of knowledge. What Nietzsche appears to be saying is that if we need a model of what reality must be like, in order that all statements about it must be interpretations, the will to power is such a model. But this is certainly a far cry from the world-models of traditional metaphysics. The will to power is itself a metaphor, which governs the use of our other metaphors. Its advantage over traditional models is not its correctness, but its utility and flexibility. The will to power does not purport to correspond to reality because it claims that there is no reality to correspond to. Stripped to its bare essentials, the position which Nietzsche advances states simply that all statements are interpretative and perspectival, including itself, and the will to power functions as a metaphorical illustration of this, without claiming ultimacy or correctness for itself.

Another possible objection at this point might be that Nietzsche's position is circular i. e., tautologous. In the formal, logical sense it certainly is circular, in basically the same way that all necessary truths are (e. g., p v ~p). Nietzsche's position is undoubtedly circular, but it is not for that reason vacuous. Nietzsche did not attempt to tailor his explanatory model to fit "facts." Indeed, what we ordinarily call "facts" are themselves interpretative structures — what we might call stale metaphors. The major theme of Nietzsche's cognitive paradigm is that we freely create "facts" rather than discover them ready-made. We are not passive spectators who simply report facts about eternal verities which lie somewhere beyond ourselves. The cognitive process for Nietzsche is creative and dynamic, and he seems to feel that we have been most unjust toward ourselves in disowning that world which we have made for ourselves. We have, it appears, forgotten our original role as active creators of knowledge, thereby alienating ourselves from our own creative potentialities.

In keeping with the enormous creative potential which he feels is available to man, Nietzsche's linguistic paradigm of metaphors is formal and empty, but not vacuous. By this I mean only that the position that all statements are interpretations can be viewed as a formal structure which can be applied to any given experience, and give that experience whatever interpretative character we choose. Nor is this to be misconstrued as a form of epistemological nihilism, which bemoans the relative and non-ultimate nature of human knowledge (although weaklings and decadents might very well make this negative interpretation). The proper and positive use of Nietzsche's cognitive-linguistic paradigm (as a formal structure) is as a means of freeing ourselves from the impossible task of tailoring our statements to fit the entities of some noumenal realm somewhere beyond ourselves, and to exploit this cognitive freedom in a creative manner. In this way, our interpretations are not restricted to any particular world-view, but are themselves constitutive of new world-views, i. e. new and more useful interpretations.

Within this context, truth becomes a function of how well a particular interpretation works, and not of how adequately it corresponds to an unknowable reality. Since truth is viewed as a pragmatic function rather than a logical property, we are presented with a neat solution for logical problems such as contradiction or paradox. It is quite conceivable that the same person could usefully employ both of two mutually exclusive propositions in different situations, thereby illustrating the greater flexibility and comprehensiveness of Nietzsche's criteria over conventional semantic-logical truth criteria. Since I have already dealt with Nietzsche's views on truth in considerable detail, I do not feel that additional comment is required here.

Nietzsche's position has an additional advantage over traditional epistemological positions, which I choose to call its *philosophical economy*. By this I mean that Nietzsche's cognitive-linguistic paradigm can include opposing views without having to negate or refute them, and without doing violence to itself. With his flexible criterion for truth and metaphorical linguistic scheme, Nietzsche does not need to refute opposing philosophical positions or reject them as failing to correspond adequately to reality. He can accommodate them within the formal structure of his own position by viewing opposing positions as interpretative schemes which are ultimately no more correct or incorrect than his own. Of course Nietzsche would claim a greater utility for his position since this is the only criterion he accepts, but in this case we are dealing with more and less useful interpretations, and not correct and incorrect representations of reality. Nietzsche's position does not require him to expose opposing views as false, but merely to indicate their relative lack of utility over-against his own. For this reason, an epistemological position which contradicted Nietzsche's on the logical or semantic level, could still be compatible with his model if it contributed to the enhancement of our creative powers. In order to remain consistent, Nietzsche would have to allow that a more useful position than his own would, for that very reason, be preferable, but this in no way undermines his model. For example, if were to accept a philosophical position which logically excluded Nietzsche's (e. g., language is not interpretative, the world is not will to power), and if this position proved to be of greater utility than our interpretation of Nietzsche's position, then it would be preferable as an interpretative model while remaining entirely consistent with the formal structure of Nietzsche's scheme. In other words, since the only criterion Nietzsche accepts is that of the enhancement of power, *his model can include its own refutation insofar as that refutation constitutes a more useful interpretation: a logical-semantic refutation of Nietzsche's position could very well be a pragmatic verification of that position.* Logical contradiction is not a problem for Nietzsche. In fact, he often uses contradiction and paradox as techniques in formulating his position. Even if it sometimes appears that Nietzsche does claim to be "right," and that therefore everyone else must be "wrong," this must be viewed in context because it is a matter of Nietzsche's mode of expression, and not a formal inconsistency. If one succeeds in grasping the formal structure of Nietzsche's cognitive linguistic model, as I have outlined it, one becomes aware that Nietzsche's position is not nearly so truculently dogmatic as many of his detractors maintain. Indeed, Nietzsche's position is far more flexible and ultimately far less dogmatic than what philosophers are generally accustomed to.

VI. The Question of Technique

We have now examined Nietzsche's position on language and the implications of this position at some length. It remains to be seen how Nietzsche utilizes this position in the formulation of his own statements. I do not intend to give a stylistic analysis of Nietzsche's various writings, but only to indicate some of the linguistic techniques he himself uses, which arise out of his view of language as such and serve to illustrate it. The three techniques which I have chosen for the present discussion are a) presupposing that position which is being argued against; b) the deliberate use of contradiction and paradox; and c) the non-conceptual use of termini.

We have already seen Nietzsche's use of the first technique mentioned here in his destruction of the correspondence theory of truth. Briefly, his method of attack in this regard is this: by presupposing that truth = *adequatio intellectus et rei*, Nietzsche demonstrates that this position is untenable on grounds of its own presuppositions, or in other words, it represents a position on truth which cannot be verified according to that criterion which it contains. This demonstration of inner inconsistency is, of course, a much more effective destruction than a mere rejection or denial of that position would be. If Nietzsche were to reject the correspondence theory simply because of its formal incompatibility with his own position, this would obviously beg the larger question of the validity of Nietzsche's own position. But by operating within the correspondence theory and demonstrating its internal inconsistency, it is not necessary for Nietzsche to attempt a refutation of this position from a vantage point which would itself be open to question.

A more neutral example, at least for present purposes, of this technique is encountered in Nietzsche's critique of conventional morality.

> Der Sieg eines moralischen Ideals wird durch dieselben „unmoralischen" Mittel errungen wie jeder Sieg: Gewalt, Lüge, Verleumdung, Ungerechtigkeit[29].

> Die Moral ist gerade so „unmoralisch" wie jedwedes andre Ding auf Erden; die Moralität selbst als eine Form der Unmoralität[30].

By provisionally accepting conventional moral standards such as honesty, truthfulness, altruism, etc., Nietzsche intends to demonstrate that these moral standards originated in judgements and motives which — according to the very standards in question — are immoral. By presupposing conventional standards such as honesty, truthfulness and altruism, and then demonstrating that such standards arise, for the most part, out of deceit,

---

[29] Nachlass Ende 1886—Frühjahr 1887, 7 [6]; KGW VIII 1, 281.
[30] Nachlass Herbst 1887, 9 [140]; KGW VIII 2, 79. See also MR II; KGW V 1, 87—138.
[31] In contemporary philosophical jargon one might say that what Nietzsche does here is demonstrate the self-referential inconsistency of such positions. See Joseph M. Boyle, Jr., "Self-Referential Inconsistency, Inevitable Falsity and Metaphysical Argumentation," *Metaphilosophy* III/1 (January, 1972), pp. 25—42. Alois Riehl has a rather different view of this procedure: "Wer endlich, wie Nietzsche, die Irrtümlichkeit der Welt, in der wir zu leben glauben, für das 'Sicherste und Festeste' hält, 'dessen unser

dissimulation, and self-interest, Nietzsche uses this moral position to under-
cut itself. Thus he can declare, in his familiar paradoxical manner, that
morality is itself a special case of immorality. What he means, of course,
is that conventional morality would be forced to find its own origins
immoral if it were interested in consistency, which it is not. Again, we see
how Nietzsche employs this technique of presupposing a position and
analyzing that position *on its own terms* until its internal inconsistencies
become apparent. I hasten to add that since we are exclusively concerned
with method here, this must remain an utterly inadequate account of
Nietzsche's moral philosophy. From Nietzsche's perspective, such logical
inconsistency does not in itself constitute a shortcoming, but for the two
positions in question (the correspondence theory and conventional morality) this internal inconsistency proves to be disastrous.

The second technique mentioned above, that of deliberately creating
paradoxes and contradictions, has often been introduced as evidence that
Nietzsche is simply not to be regarded as a serious philosopher. My contention is that to make this charge is simply to be ignorant of Nietzsche's
theory of language. Certainly Nietzsche's writings abound in paradoxes,
but to construe this as evidence of muddled thinking is a bit too facile[32].
By entertaining both of two logically exclusive propositions, Nietzsche's
intent is to reveal the basic inadequacies (or uselessness) of those criteria
according to which the propositions in question necessarily exclude one
another. Perhaps a better way of expressing this would be to say that
Nietzsche's use of contradiction and paradox intends to illustrate the
narrow and arbitrary limits which ordinary, logical rationality imposes
upon us. Why should the logical exclusiveness of two propositions compel
us to choose only one of them, when we might usefully employ both them
as circumstances warrant? The statesman who privately believes lying to
be reprehensible may nevertheless find the telling of untruths to his constituents to be in their best interest. The theoretical physicist who realizes
that the notion of efficient causality is at best a crude and inaccurate
metaphor will nevertheless step out of the way of a speeding automobile,
knowing that failure to do so would "cause" him to have a most unpleas-

---

Auge noch habhaft werden kann', muss wissen, was Wahrheit ist und folglich
anerkennen, dass es Wahrheit gibt. Wie könnte er sonst irgend etwas als Irrtum
erkennen, wie überhaupt den Begriff des Irrtums bilden? . . . Man braucht die Logik,
selbst um die Logik zu verneinen, so unmöglich ist es, sie zu verneinen." Riehl,
op. cit., p. 130. *Oculos habent, et non videbunt.*

[32] Cf. Riehl, p. 17: "Der aphoristische Stil eignet sich nicht für grosse geistige Bau-
werke. Wie er den Gedanken isoliert, ihn aus dem Zusammenhang mit dem Ganzen
herausstellt, so verlangt er auch vom Leser nicht zusammenhängendes, in ein Ganzes
sich versenkendes Denken. Ein isolierter Gedanke ist aber in den meisten Fällen

ant afternoon. A nation founded in the belief that the liberties of its citizens are inviolate generally does not hesitate to abrogate some of those liberties for the sake of maintaining the others. In all of these examples (my own), the logical incompatibility of two propositions is no barrier to their practical utilization, and this is intended to demonstrate nothing more than the functional inadequacy of purely logical criteria. This may appear to be suspiciously cynical (due mainly to my choice of examples), but Nietzsche's employment of this technique goes considerably beyond mere cynicism.

Nietzsche's real purpose in playing off contradictory positions against one another is to indicate relationships, connections, levels of meaning which remain inaccessible as long as one insists upon regarding logically incompatible propositions disjunctively. This is not meant to imply that the contradictions which Nietzsche employs are not real: they most certainly are contradictions on the logical-semantic level of discourse, and Nietzsche's purpose is in part to demonstrate the severe, but by no means insuperable, limitations of that level of discourse[33]. We find an example of such a contradiction in Nietzsche's discussions of "will." His statements about the will fall into two broad categories, those in which the will is characterized as a fundamental creative principle, and those in which the will is characterized as a fiction, a fable, and its very existence denied. I have chosen this particular example because these two conflicting themes are found in many of Nietzsche's writings, and therefore it does not constitute an isolated instance. The following quotations are illustrative of the first theme. In *Also sprach Zarathustra* we read:

> Weg führte ich euch von diesen Fabelliedern, als ich euch lehrte: „der Wille ist ein Schaffender".
> Alles „Es war" ist ein Bruchstück, ein Räthsel, ein grausamer Zufall — bis der schaffende Wille dazu sagt: „aber so wollte ich es!"
> — Bis der schaffende Wille dazu sagt: „Aber so will ich es! So werde ich's wollen!"[34]

In *Zur Genealogie der Moral* the will is regarded as so fundamental that " . . . lieber will noch der Mensch das Nichts wollen, als nicht wollen . . . ."[35] If we allow that will is part of our cognitive apparatus, these quotations

---

zugleich ein einseitiger, durch die Loslösung aus dem Ganzen, wozu er gehört, halb-wahr gewordener Gedanke." Such a position, as I intend to demonstrate in this chapter, is a serious misunderstanding of both Nietzsche's intent and his method.

[33] See JGB I, "Von den Vorurtheilen der Philosophen"; KGW VI 2, 9—33.

[34] Z II 20; KGW VI 1, 177.

[35] GM III 28; KGW VI 2, 430.

would certainly bear out what my thesis has been throughout this book, that cognition for Nietzsche is a process of creation (or creative willing). Yet there exists a second view of the will which would appear to refute this thesis:

> Schwäche des Willens: das ist ein Gleichniss, das irreführen kann. Denn es giebt keinen Willen, und folglich weder einen starken noch schwachen Willen[36].

> Unfreiheit oder Freiheit des Willens? — Es giebt keinen „Willen"; das ist nur eine vereinfachende Conzeption des Verstandes . . .[37]

> Ich lache eures freien Willens und auch eures unfreien: Wahn ist mir das, was ihr Willen heisst, es giebt keinen Willen . . .[38]

On the one hand, it appears that Nietzsche views the will as a fundamental creative principle, while on the other hand he denies its very existence. He thus appears to be both affirming and denying the same thing, which is a patent self-contradiction. What are to make of this?

It would be a mistake to say to ourselves, "Either Nietzsche means this, or he means that, but he cannot mean both." Nietzsche does indeed mean both, and the wary reader will view a contradiction of this sort as a signal that more careful reading and deeper reflection is called for. If we view the two positions illustrated above in the proper context, we find that what Nietzsche is denying is the psychological, egocentric, conscious sort of will which still figured prominently in the philosophical anthropology of his day. Nietzsche regards all of our psychological faculties (ego, will, thinking, reason, consciousness) as being products or consequences of a more fundamental and unconscious driving force. Nietzsche argues against the Enlightenment concept of man, according to which the conscious ego-functions (will, reason, intellect, etc.) were held to be man's noblest part, capable of overcoming and suppressing his baser urgings, and thereby enabling him to rationally and dispassionately explore the secrets of the Newtonian cosmos. Nietzsche's own psychological explorations showed this traditional view to be wholly inadequate, a view which was useless insofar as it prevented man from gaining a deeper self-understanding and — by ignoring them — placing man at the mercy of unconscious drives and affects of which he remained oblivious. In this regard, Nietzsche may legitimately be regarded as a pioneer of dynamic psychology and psychoanalysis[39].

---

[36] Nachlass Frühjahr 1888, 14 [219]; KGW VIII 3, 186.
[37] GA XVI, 135.
[38] GA XII, 267.
[39] See Henri Ellenberger, *The Discovery of the Unconscious* (New York, 1970), especially pp. 271—278.

The sort of will which Nietzsche affirms and characterizes as creative is a non-rational, non-egoistical, unconscious will, and Nietzsche views the psychological sort of will, consciousness, reason, intellect, ego, etc. as superficial functionaries, "Werkzeuge" of this more basic creative force, of which the word "will" is naturally only a metaphor. These structures do not themselves carry out the creative acts of cognitive interpretation which constitute an individual's reality: they are themselves "interpretations" on the part of a more fundamental and creative "will." That will which was traditionally regarded as enabling man to freely and rationally gain knowledge and plan his actions, that sort of will does not exist according to Nietzsche. But a turbulently creative, unconscious, irrational will does exist.

One might be tempted to explain away the contradiction in question here by pointing out that it rests upon an equivocation, and is therefore only an apparent contradiction. There is certainly an equivocation present in Nietzsche's two views of the will, but the manner in which he brings us to realize this is precisely by means of a contradiction. Nietzsche could have, we might suppose, laboriously distinguished between a psychological will and a creative will, between a will[1] and a will[2], but this was not his style. Instead of a more conventional, scholarly, discursive method, Nietzsche audaciously flings contradictions at his reader. This forces the careful reader to grasp both horns of the logical dilemma, to read carefully and reflect deeply. Only after the conventions of ordinary discourse have been fractured does Nietzsche's insight become accessible, and that on a new level of meaning[40]. Nietzsche's arguments derive a considerable part of their forcefulness from the effort required to see through his deliberate contradictions and paradoxes to that which he intended by them. This, in turn, means that we are forced to develop a different mode of reading and understanding before we become capable of authentically appropriating Nietzsche's insights. In spite of their almost casual, aphoristic style, Nietzsche's works are not intended to be read casually. In fact, Nietzsche's works demand an enormous effort in order to be assimilated and understood, and this is particularly evident with regard to his method of contradiction and paradox. If one had encountered the contradiction in question

---

[40] Instead of rationally discoursing about an irrational will, Nietzsche forces us to abandon conventional, rational discourse before we can grasp his insight. Whatever else we might think about such a novel approach, we might at least claim that — in the present context — it is more appropriate and more productive of an authentic insight to approach the irrational in an extra-rational manner. The nearest analogy I can offer to such a procedure is the Zen koan. Cf. Martin Heidegger, *Unterwegs zur Sprache* (Pfullingen, 1971), especially pp. 83—156.

and viewed it disjunctively (viz., either he means this, or he means that, but he cannot mean both), one would have grasped only a fragment of Nietzsche's argument and have overlooked one of his most valuable psychological insights. Doubtless Nietzsche could have employed more conventional means to express this particular insight, but then he would not have been the uniquely fascinating thinker that he is[41].

The final linguistic technique which we must still consider is Nietzsche's own metaphorical, non-conceptual use of termini. If, as Nietzsche claims, language is an inherently metaphorical, interpretative structure, it is only consistency on his part to use his own terms metaphorically, and not claim conceptual status for them[42]. We saw earlier that Nietzsche regarded concepts as stale metaphors which, because of their generality, can say nothing about a reality consisting of particulars. Nietzsche does not deny the utility of concepts within language as such, insofar as they perform the function of regulative fictions which govern the use of the other fictions (i. e. metaphors) of language. But since Nietzsche rejects the correspondence theory of truth, he also rejects the view that, as general structures, concepts represent correspondingly general features of reality. Reality for Nietzsche is a tumultuous, ever-changing flux of power-quanta. Since a concept is by its very nature static, it is useless for expressing such a model of reality. Moreover, a concept supposedly has one and only one definitive, univocal meaning: it admits of no interpretation (or of only one interpretation, which amounts to the same thing). The view of reality which Nietzsche seeks to express, however, is changing, paradoxical, fluid, mobile, and — whatever else it might be — it is not static. Since concepts are static, since they are bound by one particular definition, they are of no use in expressing a position such as Nietzsche's. "Aus dem Begriff führt kein Weg in das Wesen der Dinge[43]."

Ordinarily we would not think of a concept as being all that static and inflexible. After all, one need only open a dictionary to find that many of the concepts within it have a variety of meanings (i. e. equivocal con-

---

[41] I am basically in agreement with W. Müller-Lauter, who argues persuasively that Nietzsche's use of paradox and contradiction is a direct and consistent outgrowth of that "Gegensätzlichkeit" which is a fundamental feature of the will to power. See Müller-Lauter, op. cit., pp. 10—33.

[42] Eugen Fink repeats this not uncommon criticism that, while Nietzsche's insights are indeed profound, his failure to conceptually elaborate them is a serious shortcoming. I hope to have demonstrated in this chapter that, so far from being a shortcoming, this is the only consistent position which Nietzsche could take. It is inappropriate to demand that Nietzsche conceptually elaborate an anti-conceptual position. See E. Fink, *Nietzsches Philosophie* (Stuttgart, 1960), pp. 149, 160 ff.

[43] GA IX, 264.

cepts). A concept such as "tree" we might say is very flexible indeed, and can meaningfully accommodate a vast number of individual things. But this is not the sort of linguistic flexibility which Nietzsche strives for, because no matter how many particulars a concept may accommodate, particular things must still be deprived of their unique and essential differences before they can be made to fit the concept. The real reason that Nietzsche cannot adequately express himself in ordinary, conceptual language is this: a concept seeks to communicate a fixed, determinate, and univocal content: Nietzsche does not. Nietzsche does not wish to formulate his statements in such a way that they could purport to fix and univocally communicate one determinate feature of reality. To do this would be equivalent to insisting upon the correspondential correctness of only one possible interpretation, and thus preclude the possibility of actively creating new and more useful interpretations, in effect standing still while reality continues to change. For this reason, Nietzsche's termini (will, power, individual, knowledge, world, etc.) must not be regarded as intending to express a single fixed, logical content. They are intended to be signs, metaphors, or indicators, to be used in actively constructing an individually useful interpretation, and nothing else. Nietzsche is not interested in giving a fixed and unyielding description of a static reality. Rather, he attempts to provide us with a means, a tool, with which we may take an active and creative part in structuring that reality which is of concern to us. To do this he must maximize the plasticity, fluidity, and, of course, the ambiguity of his own language and use his termini not as concepts (which can have only one meaning) but as signs and metaphors, which can have a multitude of meanings.

There is a vast paradox in all this, a paradox of which Nietzsche is very well aware. In the strictest sense, this means that we may not regard Nietzsche's statements about reality as factual, veridical, correct, or even true in any sense other than his own. It further means that we are to regard a notion such as the will to power, for example, as intended to provide nothing less than a metaphorical structure which we may use to create a more satisfactory, more useful world-interpretation for ourselves. Once we have begun this process, it is entirely conceivable that we will also no longer require Nietzsche. As he himself says, with incredible modesty, in the preface to that most immodest of books, *Ecce Homo*, "Hier redet kein Fanatiker, hier wird nicht ‚gepredigt‘, hier wird nicht Glauben verlangt ... "[44] and, quoting from *Also sprach Zarathustra*, reminds us that "Man vergilt einem Lehrer schlecht, wenn man immer

[44] EH Vorwort 4; KGW VI 3, 258.

nur der Schüler bleibt"[45]. We find a striking parallel to this at the conclusion of Wittgenstein's *Tractatus Logico-Philosophicus* which will serve here both as a clarification and a conclusion:

> My propositions serve as elucidations in the following way: anyone who understands me eventually recognizes them as nonsensical, when he has used them — as steps — to climb up beyond them. (He must, so to speak, throw away the ladder after he has climbed it.)
>
> He must transcend these propositions, and then he will see the world aright[46].

To this I would only add Nietzsche's insight, that to see the world "aright" is to realize that there is ultimately no "right" way to see it.

---

[45] Since this passage is particularly striking in this context, I quote it in its entirety:
"Allein gehe ich nun, meine Jünger! Auch ihr geht nun davon und allein! So will ich es.

Geht fort von mir und wehrt euch gegen Zarathustra! Und besser noch: schämt euch seiner! Vielleicht betrog er euch.

Der Mensch der Erkenntniss muss nicht nur seine Feinde lieben, er muss auch seine Freunde hassen können.

Man vergilt einem Lehrer schlecht, wenn man immer nur der Schüler bleibt. Und warum wollt ihr nicht an meinem Kranze rupfen?

Ihr verehrt mich: aber wie, wenn eure Verehrung eines Tages umfällt? Hütet euch, dass euch nicht eine Bildsäule erschlage!

Ihr sagt, ihr glaubt an Zarathustra? Aber was liegt an Zarathustra! Ihr seid meine Gläubigen, aber was liegt an allen Gläubigen!

Ihr hattet euch noch nicht gesucht: da fandet ihr mich. So thun alle Gläubigen; darum ist es so wenig mit allem Glauben.

Nun heisse ich euch, mich verlieren und euch finden; und erst, wenn ihr mich Alle verleugnet habt, will ich euch wiederkehren." EH Vorwort 4; KGW VI 3, 258. Quoted from Z I 22:3; KGW VI 1, 97.

[46] Ludwig Wittgenstein, *Tractatus Logico-Philosophicus*, trans. by D. F. Pears and B. F. McGuiness (London, 1961), 6.54. Cf. Erich Heller, "Wittgenstein and Nietzsche" in *The Artist's Journey into the Interior and other essays* (New York, 1968), pp. 201—226

CHAPTER SIX

NIETZSCHE'S WAY OF THINKING

I. The Traditional Cognitive Paradigm

We turn now to an analysis of what precisely *thinking* means for
Nietzsche. More specifically, we shall inquire into what status the traditional epistemological categories of thought, knowledge, perception, etc.
have within the framework of Nietzsche's theory of knowledge. The
question to which we shall first address ourselves is not so much "How
did Nietzsche himself think?" but rather, what does he consider to be
involved in the cognitive process itself: what is the nature, scope, and
function of that human activity which we call thinking? As our analysis
proceeds, I think that it will become clear that Nietzsche's own intellectual
activity coincides to a very large degree with his characterization of what
authentic, i. e. creative, aesthetic thinking is (or ought to be). It is of utmost
importance that the reader realize that what Nietzsche is really attacking
and seeking to undermine in his various analyses is an entire cognitive
paradigm, an entire mode of thinking. One fails to grasp the urgency and
radicality of Nietzsche's thinking if one regards him as simply seeking to
restructure or rearrange the structures of the traditional cognitive paradigm from within, while nevertheless presupposing that paradigm in its
broader outlines. The difficulties of such an undertaking are enormous.
Nietzsche is forced to employ the language, categories, and procedures of
that very paradigm which he seeks to undermine, and this naturally
imparts a highly unusual, paradoxical character to many of his utterances.
One must bear in mind that in a paradigm shift of this nature, the criteria
of the old paradigm are inapplicable to the new, but I think that this will
become clearer as our investigation proceeds.

Since the time of Plato and Aristotle, Western man has come to regard
himself as *homo sapiens*, i. e. as that animal whose capacity for rational
thought and abstract intellection is his defining characteristic. Rational
thought, in turn, has been conceived as logical, analytical, disjunctive and
discursive thought, and has been grounded in a correspondence theory of
truth (not a theory of meaning). Within this general structure language
has been regarded as having a metaphysical function (i. e. language as

truth-functional), which is only to say that language was regarded as capable of yielding true propositions about an extra-linguistic reality. In the last several hundred years, this traditional mode of thought has been incorporated with the goals and methods of experimental science, and has thus constituted a mode of thought and a manner of regarding the world which is distinctly Western. Generalizations of this sort are, to be sure, fraught with the danger of inaccuracy, but for purposes of contrast, I feel that such a generalization is not unwarranted in the present instance. I do not mean to imply that there exists a single, all-embracing, universally accepted mode of thought in Western culture: that a general pattern, paradigm, or parameter exists, however, cannot be doubted. It is this paradigm itself which Nietzsche challenges[1].

The character of the traditional Western mode of thought (or cognitive paradigm), then, insofar as it can be characterized at all, has tended to be rational, analytical, discursive, disjunctive, has employed a correspondence theory of truth, and has regarded language as truth-functional. Valid knowledge has come to be regarded as the product of a process of investigation and/or experimentation, in which phenomena or objects are analyzed into their simpler components until a general level of clarity, conceptual distinctness and intelligibility has been achieved. Essential to this explanatory procedure is that the moments or components of the explicandum be made as distinct as possible, and that any blurring of conceptual outlines is to be scrupulously avoided. An object is identified and defined by means of a process of analysis and isolation from other, similar objects, i. e. an object is defined by showing precisely what it is which makes it distinct from everything else. Only then are an object's connections and relationships with other things thrown into the proper sharp relief necessary for intelligibility[2]. The assumption is made that when the particular parts are clearly understood, our understanding of the whole will be equally clear[3]. The further assumption is made that those statements in

---

[1] One cannot help but be reminded of Heidegger's characterization of Western thought in its entirety as metaphysical, and I would assert that Heidegger received substantial hints in this regard from Nietzsche. Many of Heidegger's individual analyses in his destruction of Western ontology dovetail quite neatly with Nietzsche's views. Cf. Martin Heidegger, *Nietzsche* I, II, *Sein und Zeit*. Cf. also Otto Pöggeler, "Sein als Ereignis," *Zeitschrift für philosophische Forschung* XIII/4 (1959), pp. 599—632.
[2] See Errol E. Harris, *Nature, Mind, and Modern Science* (New York and London, 1954). See also Hans Reichenbach, *The Rise of Scientific Philosophy* (Berkeley and Los Angeles, 1963).
[3] But cf. Erich Heller, *The Disinherited Mind* (Philadelphia, 1952), p. 57f.: "For the modern mind, in some of its most vocal representatives has yielded to the inferior magic of facts, numbers, statistics, and to that sort of empiricism which, in its passion for concreteness, paradoxically reduces experience to a purely abstract notion of

which such analyses are carried out have valid reference to independent, external "things." This is true whether we are speaking of an inductive or a deductive pattern of explanation. A deductive explanatory pattern verifies itself by demonstrating its applicability to particulars, while an inductive explanation begins with those very particulars and seeks to incorporate them into a more general structure. This mode of thinking and its accompanying explanatory procedures has demonstrated its practical efficacity in the growth of modern experimental science and our own technological civilization.

Certainly there exist numerous exceptions to the schematic characterization given above, and the danger of such a generalization is that one may find few individuals who fit into it in all particulars. If we regard rational, disjunctive, discursive thought and truth-functional (metaphysical) discourse as one moment in the Western intellectual tradition, there certainly exists a complementary moment of synthesis and generalization, which seeks to organize particular bits of information into a comprehensive and meaningful whole[4]. The findings of experimental science, for example, are useless unless they can be related to one another within a coherent body of knowledge and brought into harmony with man's aesthetic and spiritual inclinations. Nevertheless, I do not think this invalidates our original contention, that Western thought has become increasingly preoccupied with facts, with particulars, with categories and distinctions. Within such a context, thinkers (which in the popular mind has come to mean a scientific thinker) are extremely reluctant to make any broad, sweeping statements unless they can somehow be instantiated[5]. Even such historical figures as Thomas Aquinas, René Descartes, Hegel, Schopenhauer, or even scientists such as Werner Heisenberg or Friedrich von Weizsäcker, who in various ways have performed a broad, inclusive activity of synthesis, are properly regarded as arising out of or reacting against an intellectual tradition as characterized above. Figures such as these reinforce, rather than invalidate, our characterization of the Western cog-

---

measurable data, having cast aside the 'immeasurable wealth' of authentic experiences of the spirit and imagination. The specialization in trifles which results from such abstractions, seeks its justification not only in the arithmetical deception that a thousand futilities add up to a large piece of significance, but also in the strange belief that the great issues have all been fully explored and the outstanding sources exhausted."

[4] Cf. Pöggeler, op. cit., p. 603: "Die griechisch geborene Metaphysik ist zwar im Abendland zur herrschenden Tradition geworden, aber sie hat bestimmte Denkmotive, wie sie vor allem der jüdisch-christlichen Tradition entstammen, nicht in sich aufheben können. So blieb sie von einem antimetaphysischen Denken wie von ihrem Schatten begleitet."

[5] Cf. Harris, pp. 256—352; cf. also Reichenbach, pp. 27—50 and 74—125.

nitive paradigm as a whole. A paradigm such as this can accommodate a great deal of diversity within itself, and this might give rise to the illusion that there is no common paradigm. But the constitutive elements of such a paradigm are such fundamental presuppositions, that they are never really called into question themselves and we are usually unaware of those assumptions upon which our cognitive activity rests. And it is this very ground, these very assumptions, this entire cognitive paradigm which Nietzsche calls into question[6].

II. Nietzsche's Critique of the Traditional Cognitive Paradigm

From what has already been said in the foregoing chapters, a substantial portion of Nietzsche's critique of our traditional mode of thought will already have been anticipated. Nevertheless, since we ourselves, for better or worse, all function within this cognitive paradigm, it will be helpful to reiterate some of the essential points of Nietzsche's critique so that our own analysis and conceptual distinctions remain as clear as possible.

From our discussion of Nietzsche's model of reality in Chapter I, it will be recalled that the world was held to be a formless, turbulent chaos of power-quanta which are ceaselessly combining or separating from one another, overpowering or being overpowered, assimilating or being assimilated. If we accept this model of reality, then obviously any statements about the world, descriptions of it, or generalizations about how this power-chaos now functions or will function in the future, will be false the moment they are uttered: if we accept Nietzsche's model, we are also committed to a metaphorical (i. e. non-metaphysical, non-truth-functional) view of language[7].

Within the cognitive paradigm of our tradition, it is generally held that for any type of knowledge to qualify as valid knowledge, that piece of knowledge must be somehow verifiable in any number of instances and communicable. Since there can be no knowledge of particulars, our knowledge is necessarily of a general or universal nature[8]. If we maintain that the statement "Water seeks its own level" is a true statement and represents a valid bit of knowledge, implied by this is that the statement is true

---

[6] We might regard the presuppositions of the traditional cognitive paradigm as something like what is called a "horizon" in the phenomenological literature, i. e. that backdrop overagainst which an object is constituted and made thematically meaningful, while the horizon itself is neither thematized nor objectified. On this basis, a paradigm shift becomes a shift in horizon.

[7] I am reminded here of W. Heisenberg's well-known principle of indeterminacy, although this may be stretching a point. Cf. Werner Heisenberg, op. cit.

[8] Cf. Aristotle, *Metaphysics*.

of all water, everywhere, and not merely one quantity of water in a particular situation at a particular time. We assume that there exist identical, or at least fundamentally similar situations and entities to which our general, rational, scientific knowledge will correspond.

Within the Nietzschean scheme of things, of course, the existence of identical (or even closely similar) situations or entities is denied. The quanta of the will to power are constantly flowing, shifting, and realigning themselves, and no configuration or alignment remains static or even identical with itself. Thus, any statement, any rule or law, any type of epistemological statement which claims to be valid for more than one instance is simply mistaken. If knowledge is necessarily universal and timeless, there is nothing in the world of power-quanta to which it could even apply. As Nietzsche so frequently reminds us, there are no facts, there are no identical cases, and therefore there are no laws or rules which would be applicable to them. And since Western thinkers since Aristotle have generally shared that paradigm according to which there can be no knowledge of particulars, Nietzsche is quite plainly denying the possibility of knowledge in the traditional, paradigmatic sense.

> Erkenntniss an sich im Werden unmöglich; wie ist also Erkenntniss möglich? Als Irrthum über sich selbst, als Wille zur Macht, als Wille zur Täuschung. Werden als Erfinden Wollen Selbstverneinen, Sich-selbst-Überwinden: kein Subjekt, sondern ein Thun, Setzen, schöpferisch . . .[9]

We have sufficiently dealt with the notion that there can be no knowledge (in the traditional, paradigmatic sense) of a constantly changing world in the preceding chapters, so that a detailed recapitulation here would serve no purpose. It should be pointed out, however, that Nietzsche does not consider knowledge to be of particulars, either:

> . . . es giebt keine dauerhaften letzten Einheiten, keine Atome, keine Monaden: auch hier ist „das Seiende" erst von uns hineingelegt, (aus praktischen, nützlichen perspektivischen Gründen) . . .
> — die Ausdrucksmittel der Sprache sind unbrauchbar, um das Werden auszudrücken: es gehört zu unserem unablöslichen Bedürfnis der Erhaltung, beständig die eine gröbere Welt von Bleibend⟨em⟩, von „Dingen" usw. zu setzen . . .[10]

III. Nietzsche's Critique of the Natural Attitude

Another paradigmatic assumption (or perhaps, necessary error) within our traditional mode of thinking is the notion that what knowledge we

---

[9] Nachlass Ende 1886—Frühjahr 1887, 7 [54]; KGW VIII 1, 321.
[10] Nachlass November 1887—März 1888, 11 [73]; KGW VIII 2, 278.

possess is derived from the objects surrounding us through the senses. Perhaps it would be more accurate to say that our knowledge is assumed to be grounded in the information we derive from the senses, and that this knowledge or sense data is further assumed to correspond to the real, external, self-identical, and perduring objects in the world around us. The fundamental presupposition of this correspondence view is that material things do exist and do constitute the furnishings of our world. It is further presupposed that these objects are perceived more or less identically by everyone, and that these material objects have a separate and independent existence, i. e. they would still exist as they are if there were no one present to observe them. This is the "natural attitude" (to borrow a phrase from Edmund Husserl) in which most of us live our daily lives, including the philosophers and scientists who would take violent issue with this "natural attitude" on theoretical grounds. A corollary of this naive realism is that the world appears more or less identically to everyone[11].

Once again, Nietzsche views this as a perspectival falsification, but one which has become so common and so ingrained within our mode of thinking that it is uncritically regarded as a self-evident truth. But for Nietzsche, there are no "things" (in the sense of substantial, self-identical, perduring entities) at all, let alone "identical things." What we customarily refer to as an object or a thing is a simplified, falsified, perspectival interpretation of an infinitely more complicated system of power-aggregates and power-relationships. "Alles, was als 'Einheit' ins Bewusstsein tritt, ist bereits ungeheur complizirt: wir haben immer nur einen Anschein von Einheit[12]." The following passage from the *Nachlass* of 1887 is particularly noteworthy in this regard, and I quote it in its entirety:

> Unsre psychologische Optik ist dadurch bestimmt
> 1) dass Mittheilung nöthig ist, und dass zur Mittheilung etwas fest, verein-facht, präcisirbar sein muss (vor allem im identischen Fall . . .) Damit es aber mittheilbar sein kann, muss es zurechtgemacht empfunden werden, als „wieder erkennbar". Das Material der Sinne vom Verstande zurechtgemacht, reduzirt auf grobe Hauptstriche, ähnlich gemacht, subsumirt unter Verwandtes. Also: die Undeutlichkeit und das Chaos des Sinneseindrucks wird gleichsam logisirt.
> 2) die Welt der „Phänomene" ist die zurechtgemachte Welt, die wir als real empfinden. Die „Realität" liegt in dem beständigen Wiederkommen gleicher, bekannter, verwandter Dinge, in ihrem logisirten Charakter, im Glauben, dass wir hier rechnen, berechnen können.

---

[11] Language makes and perpetuates this assumption. When I say "dog" to you, I ordinarily assume that corresponding image in your mind is that of a furry canine quadruped, or if I say "green," that your experience of that color is the same as mine. See Chapter V. Cf. Alfred Schutz, *The Phenomonology of the Social World*, trans. by G. Walsh and F. Lehnert (Evanston, Ill., 1967), especially pp. 97—139.

[12] Nachlass Sommer 1886—Herbst 1887, 5 [56]; KGW VIII 1, 209.

3) der Gegensatz dieser Phänomenal-Welt ist nicht „die wahre Welt", sondern die formlos-unformulirbare Welt des Sensations-Chaos, — also eine andere Art Phänomenal-Welt, eine für uns „unerkennbare".

4) Fragen, wie die „Dinge an sich" sein mögen, ganz abgesehen von unserer Sinnen-Receptivität und Verstandes-Aktivität, muss man mit der Frage zurückweisen: woher könnten wir wissen, dass es Dinge giebt? Die „Dingheit" ist erst von uns geschaffen. Die Frage ist, ob es nicht noch viele Art⟨en⟩ geben könnte, eine solche scheinbare Welt zu schaffen — und ob nicht dieses Schaffen, Logisiren, Zurechtmachen, Fälschen die bestgarantirte Realität selbst ist: kurz, ob nicht das, was „Dinge setzt", allein real ist; und ob nicht die „Wirkung der äusseren Welt auf uns" auch nur die Folge solcher wollenden Subjekte ist . . .

„Ursache und Wirkung" falsche Auslegung eines Kriegs und eines relativen Siegs

die anderen „Wesen" agiren auf uns; unsere zurechtgemachte Scheinwelt ist eine Zurechtmachung und Überwältigung von deren Aktionen; eine Art Defensiv-Maassregel.

Das Subjekt allein ist beweisbar: *Hypothese*, dass es nur Subjekte giebt — dass „Objekt" nur eine Art Wirkung von Subjekt auf Subjekt ist . . . ein Modus des Subjekts[13].

The individual knower simplifies, organizes, regulates, i. e. interprets and falsifies his world, and it is this synthetic, creative function of the knower which furnishes the world with stable objects and bestows upon them their respective characters and qualities[14]. Our hypothetical individual in the "natural attitude" assumes that the world already is the way he perceives it, and that he is deriving what he knows from things as they already are. Nietzsche radically reverses this situation, since he maintains that whatever character, qualities, or regularity the world has, have been bestowed upon it by ourselves, the "knowers." Knowledge, insofar as that term still has meaning within this context, is a wholly synthetic, wholly creative function[15]. This will be dealt with in greater detail in the second portion of this chapter, and in the following chapters.

The major fault which Nietzsche finds with that mode of thinking which we have been describing is not that it is false, wrong, incorrect, or any other such thing: it is a perspectival falsification, like any other interpretation of the world, and one interpretation is no more true or false

---

[13] Nachlass Herbst 1887, 9 [106]; KGW VIII 2, 59 f.

[14] The neo-Kantian Hans Vaihinger points out the apparent similarity between Nietzsche's notion of the creative, form-giving power of the mind and the similar concept developed by Kant in the *Kritik der reinen Vernunft*. See Vaihinger, loc. cit.

[15] Cf. Nachlass Herbst 1885—Herbst 1886, 2 [152]; KGW VIII 1, 139: "Die Entstehung der 'Dinge' ist ganz und gar das Werk der Vorstellenden, Denkenden, Wollenden, Erfindenden. Der Begriff 'Ding' selbst ebenso als alle Eigenschaften." This passage is very typical.

(in the correspondence sense) than any other. The difference between interpretations lies in the degree of power, of utility, which they represent. No interpretation (and here we must include Nietzsche's own) is adequate to express the seething, turbulent chaos of power-quanta which for Nietzsche is the world[16]. Some interpretations, however, through an implicit awareness of the ambiguous nature of reality, capitalize upon its lack of univocal meaning and utilize this for the growth and enhancement of power. Thus, Nietzsche does not inveigh against the traditional, Western cognitive paradigm because it is intellectually mistaken, but rather, because it makes things too easy for itself. It limits our understanding of the world to only one possible interpretation, and minimizes the ambiguity and change which Nietzsche regards as stimulants to growth and development.

> 1. Satz. Die leichtere Denkweise siegt über die schwierige — als Dogma: simplex sigillum veri. — Dico: dass die Deutlichkeit etwas für Wahrheit aus-weisen soll, ist eine vollkommene Kinderei . . .
> 2. Satz. Die Lehre vom Sein, vom Ding, von lauter festen Einheiten ist hundert Mal leichter als die Lehre vom Werden, von der Entwicklung
> 3. Satz. Die Logik war als Erleichterung gemeint: als Ausdrucksmittel, — nicht als Wahrheit . . . Später wirkte sie als Wahrheit . . .[17]

Our conventional way of regarding the world is one interpretation out of an infinite number of possible interpretations, and by no means the only possible one. Nietzsche speculates that there were undoubtedly very practical reasons for our particular *Weltanschauung* developing in the manner it did, and yet, when it petrifies into "truth," into "reality," the possibility of growth, of further development, of creating even more useful interpretations is precluded[18]. Nietzsche regards our conventional world-view, our dominant cognitive paradigm, as robbing man of the unlimited possibilities to which he is entitled (or perhaps, condemned). Naturally, if the stable, reliable, predictable form which we have imposed upon the world were somehow to be removed, it would very likely destroy most individuals, who would be incapable of surviving in a world of ceaseless change and ambiguity. Our view of the world, we think, is the only possible one, the "true" world view. But, Nietzsche asks,

> Was ist Wahrheit? (inertia, die Hypothese, bei der Befriedigung entsteht, geringster Verbrauch von geistiger Kraft usw.)[19].

---

[16] The paradox here is, I think, quite obvious. Nietzsche's characterization of the world should perhaps be regarded as a dramatic statement of the ultimate futility of *any* interpretation which regards itself as anything more than an interpretation.

[17] Nachlass Juli—August 1888, 18 [13]; KGW VIII 3, 335f.

[18] Cf. GD III; KGW VI 3, 68—73.

[19] Nachlass Herbst 1885—Herbst 1886, 2 [126]; KGW VIII 1, 123.

Nietzsche regards even the desire for "truth," the desire for unchanging, objective knowledge, as a symptom of weakness. To preclude any possible confusion here, I remind the reader that the criterion for truth " . . . liegt in der Steigerung des Machtgefühls,[20]" and that the variety of "truth" under attack here is the traditional static, correspondential variety. However, as we saw earlier, once Nietzsche has redefined and re-evaluated "truth," he has little further use for it.

> „Wille zur Wahrheit" — als Ohnmacht des Willens zum Schaffen . . . Wer seinen Willen nicht in Dinge zu legen vermag, der Willens- und Kraftlose, der legt wenigstens noch seinen Sinn hinein: d. h. den Glauben, das schon ein Wille da sei, der in den Dingen will oder wollen soll.
>
> Es ist ein Gradmesser von Willenskraft, wie weit man des Sinnes in den Dingen entbehren kann, wie weit man in einer sinnlosen Welt zu leben aushält: weil man ein kleines Stück von ihr selbst organisirt.
>
> Das philosophische Objektiv-Blicken kann somit ein Zeichen von Willens- und Kraft-Armuth sein. Denn die Kraft organisirt das Nähere und Nächste; die „Erkennenden", welche nur fest-stellen wollen, was ist, sind solche, die nichts festsetzen können, wie es sein soll[21].

IV. Nietzsche's Attitude toward the Sciences

Nietzsche's attitude toward the sciences (both natural and humane) is extremely complex. This was already briefly touched upon in the last chapter, and we saw there some of Nietzsche's reasons for regarding science from two very different points of view: as an edifice built out of stale metaphors, or as a means of authentically utilizing the provisional, metaphorical nature of language in a creative manner. On the one hand, Nietzsche views the sciences as utilizing the naively realistic "natural attitude" as their point of departure, and perpetuating many of those convenient fictions which they might be better advised to overthrow[22]. On the other hand, he maintained a keen interest in the natural sciences as he neared the untimely end of his own creative career, and even formulated

---

[20] GA XVI, 45.

[21] Nachlass Herbst 1887, 9 [60]; KGW VIII 2, 29 ff.

[22] See Chapter IV. The convenient fictions which the sciences perpetuate are the subject-object distinction, the notion of causality, the primacy of reason, the correspondence theory of truth, to mention but a few. One should keep in mind that the sort of science with which we are dealing here is that of the late ninteenth century. A good many canons of rational or scientific thought which Nietzsche exposed as nothing more than prejudices or perspectives have also been accepted as such by an appreciable number of contemporary scientists. One need only consider the revolutionary impact of Einstein's general theory of relativity or the advent of quantum theory upon our established ways of thinking. Cf. Kuhn, op. cit. and Jaspers, op. cit., pp. 171—184.

some plans for perfecting himself in mathematics and physics, in order to give a "scientific" verification for his notion of the eternal recurrence[23]. As with so many other things, Nietzsche was capable of regarding the sciences from two very different points of view. We have already seen Nietzsche's negative critique of science and its accompanying mode of thought, as well as his favorable attitude toward science as incorporating a more authentic, flexible, and creative use of language. But since science is such a prominent part of our dominant cognitive paradigm, that paradigm which Nietzsche seeks to undermine, we must deal with Nietzsche's motives for taking a positive, favorable stance toward science in greater detail[24].

> Der Nihilism als normales Phänomen kann ein Symptom wachsender Stärke sein oder wachsender Schwäche
> theils dass die Kraft zu schaffen, zu wollen so gewachsen ist, dass sie diese Gesamt-Ausdeutungen und Sinn-Einlegungen nicht mehr braucht („nähere Aufgaben", Staat, usw.)
> theils, dass selbst die schöpferische Kraft, Sinn zu schaffen, nachlässt, und die Enttäuschung der herrschende Zustand ⟨wird⟩. Die Unfähigkeit zum Glauben an einen „Sinn", der „Unglaube"
> Was die Wissenschaft in Hinsicht auf beide Möglichkeiten bedeutet?
> 1) Als Zeichen von Stärke und Selbst-Herrschung, als Entbehrenkönnen von heilenden tröstlichen Illusions-Welten
> 2) als untergrabend, secirend, enttäuschend, schwächend . . .[25]

As Nietzsche indicates here, in its negative aspect science perpetuates the naively realistic world-view that knowledge is to be gleaned from things, breaks the world up into neatly compartmentalized bits of data and, by maintaining that there is a stable world order or an unchanging "Nature," prevents us from taking an active, potent role in constructing a more satisfactory world for ourselves. In his own time, however, Nietzsche observed that natural science was beginning to destroy outmoded perspectives[26], to dissolve the naively optimistic world-view which the nine-

---

[23] See Oskar Becker, "Nietzsches Beweise für seine Lehre von der ewigen Wiederkunft," *Blätter für deutsche Philosophie* IX (1936), pp. 368—387. See also W. Müller-Lauter, op. cit., pp. 164—181.

[24] There is a regrettable ambiguity present in the word "science" which, in ordinary usage, designates only the natural sciences. The German word "Wissenschaft" includes all the natural sciences, but also mathematics, philology, philosophy, history, etc. and it would be erroneous to regard these disciplines as exempt from Nietzsche's attacks. Nietzsche was himself a "Wissenschaftler," although we might hesitate to call him a "scientist."

[25] Nachlass Herbst 1887, 9 [60]; KGW VIII 2, 31f.

[26] One need only think of the impact which Darwin's theories of the descent of man and of natural selection had upon established religious beliefs.

teenth century had inherited from the eighteenth, and was beginning to hint that the world was far more ambiguous and far less knowable than had previously been believed. Nietzsche's own writings proved to be a great stimulus to psychoanalysts such as Carl G. Jung and — indirectly — Sigmund Freud, both of whom demonstrated through their researches into the human psyche that even man himself is very much a mystery and an enigma[27].

> Die Wissenschaft — das war bisher die Beseitigung der vollkommenen Verworrenheit der Dinge durch Hypothesen, welches alles „erklären", — also aus dem Widerwillen des Intellekts an dem Chaos. — Dieser selbe Widerwille ergreift mich bei der Betrachtung meiner selbst: die innere Welt möchte ich auch durch ein Schema mir bildlich vorstellen und über die intellektuelle Verworrenheit hinauskommen. Die Moral war eine solche Vereinfachung: sie lehrte den Menschen als erkannt, als bekannt. — Nun haben wir die Moral vernichtet — wir selber sind uns wieder völlig dunkel geworden! Ich weiss, dass ich von mir nichts weiss. Die Physik ergiebt sich als eine Wohltat für das Gemüt: die Wissenschaft (als der Weg zur Kenntnis) bekommt einen neuen Zauber nach der Beseitigung der Moral — und weil wir hier allein Konsequenz finden, so müssen wir unser Leben darauf einrichten, sie uns zu erhalten. Dies ergiebt eine Art praktischen Nachdenkens über unsere Existenzbedingungen als Erkennende[28].

In addition to giving us a very revealing glimpse of Nietzsche's own mental life, the passage quoted above reveals his own aesthetic, formal appreciation of the sciences. Nietzsche admired the stringency, clarity, and forcefulness of scientific thinking, its relative freedom from prejudice and "Schwärmerei." Insofar as it purported to give true knowledge of the way the world "really" is, Nietzsche regarded science as completely worthless. But as a means of mental discipline, as a means of creating more potent and more sublime illusions, Nietzsche thought very highly of science. Insofar as science attempts to discover "facts" and "explain" the world, it is pernicious. Yet as a means of destroying our fossilized preconceptions about the world and revealing to us new creative possibilities, science is invaluable[29].

Nietzsche deftly uncovered the paradox latent in the attitude held by eighteenth century scientists and their spiritual heirs, the positivists of the nineteenth century, that science "explains" the world and makes it more understandable[30]. What the natural scientist does, according to Nietzsche,

---

[27] See Henri Ellenberger, op. cit.

[28] GA XVI, 93.

[29] Cf. Nachlass Herbst 1887, 9 [60]; KGW VIII 2, 28—32. Nachlass Herbst 1887, 9 [48]; KGW VIII 2, 23, GA XVI, 93.

[30] Few scientists today would still maintain that it is their task to "explain" the world, but rather, to 'describe" it. See Ernest Nagel, op. cit., pp. 26—28.

is render the familiar objects of our experience far less familiar and understandable in his attempt to "explain" them, i. e. the scientist achieves the
opposite of what he intends[31].

> Die Entwicklung der Wissenschaft löst das „Bekannte" immer mehr in ein
> Unbekanntes auf: sie will aber gerade das Umgekehrte und geht von dem
> Instinkt aus, das Unbekannte auf das Bekannte zurückzuführen.[32]

The reader need only ask himself whether a visual, tactile examination of
an object such as a table or chair is more understandable, or an "explanation" or description of the object in terms of atoms, light waves, electromagnetic fields, etc. When the scientist attempts to explain the concrete,
factual world of the naive realist in scientific terms, its concreteness and
facticity seem to slip through his fingers. Pressed to its ultimate conclusion, this means nothing other than that science, in its search for facts,
for stable and concrete knowledge about the world, shows both to be
futile attempts.

> In Summa bereitet die Wissenschaft eine souveräne Unwissenheit vor, ein
> Gefühl, dass „Erkennen" gar nicht vorkommt, dass es eine Art Hochmuth
> war, davon zu träumen, mehr noch, daß wir nicht den geringsten Begriff
> übrig behalten, um auch nur „Erkennen" als eine Möglichkeit gelten zu
> lassen — daß „Erkennen" selbst eine widerspruchsvolle Vorstellung ist. Wir
> übersetzen eine uralte Mythologie und Eitelkeit des Menschen in die harte
> Thatsache: so wenig Ding an sich, so wenig ist „Erkenntnis an sich" noch
> erlaubt als Begriff. Die Verführung durch Zahl und Logik . . .[33]

We have seen that Nietzsche regards knowledge, in the traditional, correspondential sense, as being "about" or "corresponding to" a stable,
factual world, to be completely untenable[34]. The traditional, Western mode
of thinking which we outlined earlier is a perspectival interpretation
which has become fossilized and has outlived its usefulness, and which
now acts as a dead weight which keeps man from developing his power
and creativity in new directions and toward new goals. But science, when
freed from the constraining prejudice that its task is to deliver factual
knowledge which correctly corresponds to factual states of affairs, can be
used as a means of disciplining and directing our creative powers, and
instead of gleaning knowledge from a supposedly stable world of facts,
can be used to impose new and higher forms upon our world. Nietzsche

---

[31] See Heller, p. 57f.
[32] Nachlass Sommer 1886—Herbst 1887, 5 [14]; KGW VIII 1, 193.
[33] Ibid. See Chapter III.
[34] Cf. H. Baier, "Nietzsche als Wissenschaftskritiker," *Zeitschrift für philosophische Forschung* XX/1 (1966), pp. 130—143.

is not interested in the content of science, but rather in its form and creative potential.

> Wir haben die Welt, welche Werth hat, geschaffen! Dies erkennend erkennen wir auch, dass die Verehrung der Wahrheit schon die Folge einer Illusion ist — und dass man mehr als sie die bildende, vereinfachende, gestaltende, erdichtende Kraft zu schätzen hat . . .[35]

Knowledge, as Nietzsche redefines and re-evaluates it, is not analytical, discursive, explanatory. Neither does it refer or correspond to some onto-logical realm of facts and stable objects. Rather, knowledge is regarded as a synthetic, creative, poetic[36] *process*, which imposes its freely created forms upon that chaotic, ambiguous reality of which it is an essential part.

V. The Transformation of Thinking

We have already characterized that mode of thought peculiar to our intellectual tradition as analytical, disjunctive, discursive and rational. We have further characterized it as regarding truth as the correspondence of thought and thing and employing language in a metaphysical (i. e. truth functional) manner. If we use this characterization as a reference point, we may characterize Nietzsche's own thinking (as well as his redefinition of what authentic thinking is) as synthetic, non-rational, and aesthetic, and which further regards truth as functional and language as metaphorical (i. e. non-truth-functional). Knowledge, in the only sense which Nietzsche regards as meaningful, is not gotten by sifting through the myriad occur-rences and "facts" of the world. It is not gained by analyzing "things" or discovering universally applicable "laws of nature" or "categories of the understanding." If the reader will allow a spatial metaphor, we might claim that within the dominant Western cognitive paradigm, knowledge (or more precisely, the data upon which we claim to base our knowledge) flows from a source external to ourselves, i. e. from outside of ourselves to within. According to Nietzsche, this scheme is completely backward, because knowledge — indeed, the characteristics of the world in its entirety — proceeds outward from us. What we claim to know about the world or concerning objects is properly a creation of our own, projected "outward" and not gleaned from a careful examination of "things." Ultimately, as we shall see, even the objects in the world and the world itself are as much our interpretations as our more obviously subjective interpretations "of" them.

---

[35] Nachlass Frühjahr 1884, 25 [505]; KGW VII 2, 142.
[36] In the sense of the Greek *poiesis*, "to make."

... der Mensch findet zuletzt in den Dingen nichts wieder als was er selbst in sie hineingesteckt hat: das Wiederfinden heisst sich Wissenschaft, das Hineinstecken — Kunst, Religion, Liebe, Stolz ... .[37]

We have already dealt with Nietzsche's flux ontology at sufficient length that it should by now be fairly obvious that knowledge, in the traditional sense of stable, objective, correspondential knowledge, is on such a basis quite impossible. We cannot obtain any knowledge at all of a world which is constantly changing, constantly becoming. The fact remains, however, that to all appearances we do have knowledge of one sort or another, and the question arises, where did we get it[38]? Nietzsche's answer to this question is that we did not "get" our knowledge at all, but rather, spontaneously created it and projected it into the world. The process which carries out this task of creation and projection is authentic thinking[39].

Man, with his intense longing for a stable world, a world which is predictable, which can be "counted on," has created a world which is commensurate with this desire, has constructed a world in which he can exist. But man has also mistakenly assumed that, because he has created a world like this for himself, this represents the "real" world, the only possible world. Nietzsche attempts to overcome this narrow, constraining, and decadent perspective and open up new horizons for man's creative capabilities.

Dass der Werth der Welt in unserer Interpretation liegt (— dass vielleicht irgendwo noch andere Interpretationen möglich sind als bloss menschliche —)

---

[37] Nachlass Herbst 1885—Herbst 1886, 2 [174]; KGW VIII 1, 152.

[38] One attempt to answer this question, which is quite typical of our dominant cognitive paradigm is sketched by H. W. Walsh, *Metaphysics* (New York, 1963), p. 27: "One line of argument to which Platonists appealed in defence of their theory of Forms was known as the 'argument from the sciences.' It ran roughly as follows: knowledge is possible, as the existence of geometry and arithmetic shows. Knowledge cannot be had unless there are stable entities to be known. The things we know through the senses do not fulfill this requirement ... and we must in consequence recognize the existence of entities of a different sort; inaccessible to the senses but open to the intellect, which are the true objects of scientific knowledge ..." There is an obvious parallel between Nietzsche's view that the world is an unknowable flux, and the similar view of the Platonists viz., that "knowledge" is not derived "from" the world. But there is a vast difference between Nietzsche's answer to the question of where our knowledge comes from, and that of the Platonists. To construe Nietzsche's philosophy simply as "umgekehrter Platonismus" has a certain degree of validity, but to insist that Nietzsche's views amount to no more than this is to be ignorant of his epistemology. Cf. Chapter II.

[39] All thinking has this creative function, although ordinarily it is carried out within an inauthentic, deficient mode which remains unaware of its truly creative function, naively assuming that it encounters a world "ready made." Cf. Heidegger, Nietzsche I, pp. 11—254, 495—589.

dass die bisherigen Interpretationen perspectivische Schätzungen sind, vermöge deren wir uns im Leben, das heisse im Willen zur Macht, zum Wachsthum der Macht erhalten, dass jede Erhöhung des Menschen die Überwindung
engerer Interpretationen mit sich bringt, dass jede erreichte Verstärkung und
Machterweiterung neue Perspektiven aufthut und an neue Horizonte glauben
heisst — dies geht durch meine Schriften. Die Welt, die uns angeht, ist falsch
d. h. ist kein Thatbestand, sondern eine Ausdichtung und Rundung über einer
mageren Summe von Beobachtungen; sie ist „im Flusse", als etwas Werden-
des, als eine sich immer neu verschiebende Falschheit, die sich niemals der
Wahrheit nähert: denn — es giebt keine „Wahrheit".[40]

When Nietzsche speaks of thinking, of knowing, it is consistently in terms
of "Schaffen," "Schöpfen," "Sinn-hineinlegen," "Zurechtmachen," etc.
Nietzsche's notion of what thinking and knowing ultimately are is much
closer to free and spontaneous artistic creation, than to a rational analysis
of facts and objects. This should not be misconstrued to mean that Nietzsche is advocating some sort of shallow relativism, or a mindless sort of
pseudo-artistic "Schwärmerei." Neither is he exhorting us to retreat from
"reality" into a make-believe realm of our own fashioning. The creative
function of authentic thinking is to be taken quite literally, and not merely
as a subjective interpretation of something already present. In order to
clarify this still ambiguous point, let us isolate the two main currents
which Nietzsche synthesized within his own mode of thought, i. e. his
own cognitive paradigm, to produce a model of intellectual activity which
was both rigorous, exacting, and disciplined, but at the same time freely
creative, spontaneous, and aesthetic.

VI. The Sources of the Transformation of Thinking

We have been contrasting two modes of thought which we shall iden-
tify as the rational mode and the aesthetic mode. The resemblance here to
the Apollonian and Dionysian outlooks elaborated in *Die Geburt der Tragödie* is not at all gratuitous. Nietzsche began his professional career as a
classical philologist and made some minor but nevertheless significant
contributions to this field before devoting himself entirely to philosophy[41].
Classical philology is, of course, an exacting and rigorous discipline with
a very strict internal methodology and procedure. It is a demanding and
exacting science: the philologist is not free to interpret a text in any way
he pleases, but is bound to explicate as objectively and impartially as

[40] Nachlass Herbst 1885—Herbst 1886, 2 [108]; KGW VIII 1, 112.
[41] Cf. Martin Vogel, *Apollinisch und Dionysisch* (Regensburg, 1966), especially Chapter I,
  "Nietzsche als Philologe."

possible what is written. Nietzsche greatly admired the intellectual strength, the dispassionate discipline and formality of philology, as well as the other exact sciences. Nevertheless, there came upon him a growing awareness (which is easily traceable in his earlier works) that such exact sciences are ultimately sterile: they analyze, compartmentalize, label, and criticize, but they do not create or produce anything original. They are purely formal, and depend upon other sources for their content. This disenchantment with classical philology is apparent in *Die Geburt der Tragödie*, which was heavily criticized at the time of its publication as entirely too imaginative and too unscholarly (no footnotes!) to be considered good philology, as good philology was understood at that time. Yet even in this early work, we notice the attempt at a synthesis (which nevertheless was not fully carried out) between the clarity and precision of formal discipline (the "Apollonian") and the formlessness and ambiguity of pure, exuberant creativity (the "Dionysian"). The carrying-out of this synthesis in Nietzsche's mature thought was the genesis of the will to power.

From boyhood on, Nietzsche was intensely interested in the arts, particularly music — the Dionysian art form *par excellence*[43]. Yet Nietzsche is not simply a dilettante, giving voice to his own infatuation with the beautiful. Nietzsche elevates art — both as artistic creativity and energy, and as aesthetic contemplation — to the status of a world principle by incorporating it within the mature notion of the will to power. In early works such as *Die dionysische Weltanschauung*, *Die Geburt des tragischen Gedankens*[44] et al., artistic creativity is rooted in the turbulent, fertile flux of the Dionysian element. Nonetheless, the overflowing creative vitality of "the Dionysian" is a formless chaos without the imposition of order, form, and harmony. The imposition of form upon the chaos of creative energy becomes (in *Die Geburt der Tragödie*) tragedy. Tragedy is the paradigmatic synthesis of the Apollonian and Dionysian elements.

In the early works mentioned above, Nietzsche still maintained the dichotomy between these two poles of existence, the Dionysian and the

---

[42] See Chapter V, footnote 10.

[43] See Karl Schlechta and Anni Anders, *Friedrich Nietzsche: Von den verborgenen Anfängen seines Philosophierens* (Stuttgart and Bad Cannstatt, 1962). See also Frederick Love, *Young Nietzsche* (Chapel Hill, N.C., 1963).

[44] *Die dionysische Weltanschauung*, KGW III 2, 43—69; *Die Geburt des tragischen Gedankens*, KGW III 2, 71—91.

[45] This is an inadequate characterization of the knowing process which still implies many of the traditional epistemological and ontological distinctions which Nietzsche seeks to overcome. Nevertheless, our investigation must proceed somewhat further before the groundwork can be laid for an adequate characterization. This will be done in the next chapter. Cf. GA XII, 150f.

Apollonian (i. e. nature and culture, matter and spirit, *nomos* and *physis*). As the concept of the will to power matured, however, these two poles were forged together into a unitary principle which was both the surging chaos of creative vitality and the urge to impose order, form, and harmony upon this chaos: the will to power. The heart and core of Nietzsche's theory of knowledge is noticeable here in its earliest form, i. e. the creative imposition of form and order upon an ambiguous, chaotic reality.

In the early works mentioned above the creative power of the mind is not fully explored. As will be recalled from Chapter IV, Nietzsche felt that the classical Greeks had constructed for themselves a world of timeless beauty and harmony as a refuge from the tragic and intolerable reality which was the world. In *Die Geburt der Tragödie*, this ideal world is regarded as an illusion, a comforting and sublime illusion, but an illusion nonetheless. As the notion of the will to power matured, however, and the traditional distinctions between true and false, appearance and reality, etc. were dissolved within it, that perspective from which the ideal world of the classical Greeks might be called "illusory" was also dissolved. As Nietzsche became increasingly aware of the epistemological importance of the will to power, he came to the conclusion that the only world which can even concern us is the one which we have constructed for ourselves. This is the "real world" — indeed, the only world. The world itself (sic) has no character, has no meaning, has no significance other than that which man imposes upon it. Man creates his own world, and the manner in which this is carried out might best be characterized at this point as an artistic process of creation.

VII. Creative Thinking and Will to Power

We have seen that, on the basis of Nietzsche's flux ontology, knowledge cannot be something which is derived "from" the world. Rather, it is something imposed upon the chaos of power-quanta which gives that chaos whatever meaning and character it has (somewhat analogous, I would think, to the process whereby a potter may impose any form he chooses upon a formless lump of clay). Nietzsche implies that before we can even "perceive" any sort of world at all, we must have already created for ourselves a form, an interpretative scheme of some sort, which is imposed upon or projected into the flux of power-quanta. "Bevor 'gedacht' wird, muss schon 'gedichtet' worden sein . . . ."[46]

---

[46] Nachlass Herbst 1887, 10 [159]; KGW VIII 2, 276.

In his attempt to combine the opposed forms of thought mentioned earlier, i. e. the rational and the aesthetic, the activity of thinking becomes a "formal" activity for Nietzsche. One must not be misled here into construing the word "formal" in the traditional sense[47]. Nietzsche often makes reference to the formgiving capacity of the understanding, but what he means is essentially different from, for example, the empty, logical categories of Kant[48]. "Formal" does not imply a lack of content for Nietzsche. On the contrary,

> Man ist um den Preis Künstler, dass man das, was alle Nichtkünstler „Form"
> nennen, als Inhalt, als „die Sache selbst" empfindet. Damit gehört man freilich
> in eine verkehrte Welt: denn nunmehr wird einem der Inhalt zu etwas bloss
> Formalen, — unser Leben eingerechnet.[49]

Formal should be understood here in that sense which was established in Chapter V, as being a characteristic of the creative, synthetic mode of thought which was contrasted with the traditional mode of Western thought at the beginning of the present chapter. It would be quite misleading to insist that Nietzsche intended to work out an epistemology of subjective forms or cognitive categories according to which the data of the "external world" are assimilated and rendered meaningful. Nietzsche makes frequent use of terms such as "Gestalten," "Gestalten-durchsetzen," "Bilden," in addition to "Form" or "Formen-auferlegen," and for purposes of convenience, let us designate this productive, synthetic, creative mode of cognition as *formal*.

If Nietzsche had regarded the cognitive process as primarily a matter of bestowing meaning or intelligibility upon a chaos of sense impressions or giving shape to an amorphous material element, he would have to be regarded as still firmly within the Western metaphysical context. But to fully appreciate the radical nature of this formal aspect of Nietzsche's theory of knowledge, the reader must also understand it as involving the abandonment (or destruction) of the traditional epistemological categories such as matter and form, knower and known, truth as correspondence, etc. Formal, in the sense in which it is here intended, does not imply that there is a world already present, upon which we project cognitive forms. *Rather, the world itself is identical with those forms which we freely and spontaneously create.* The artistic analogies which we have had recourse to can be as misleading as they can be illuminating. If we visualize an artist bestowing

---

[47] With regard to "formal" see Chapter V.
[48] Nachlass Ende 1886—Frühjahr 1887, 7 [4]; KGW VIII 1, 267—278.
[49] Nachlass November 1887—März 1888, 11 [3]; KGW VIII 2, 251f.

form upon an amorphous lump of matter, we nevertheless regard the matter as being something distinct from and independent of the artist. For Nietzsche, however, the artist, his activity, and his creation are not separate entities (although our cognitive paradigm forces us to regard them as such).

> Die seiende Welt ist eine Erdichtung — es giebt nur eine werdende Welt. — So könnte es sein! Aber setzt die Erdichtung nicht den Dichter als seiend voraus? — Vielleicht ist die erdichtete andere Welt erst eine Ursache davon, dass der Dichter sich für seiend hält und gegenüberstellt . . .[50]

Art or artistic activity does not even require an artist (in the sense of an agent or subject) for Nietzsche:

> Das Kunstwerk, wo es ohne Künstler erscheint z. B. als Leib, als Organisation (preussisches Offiziercorps, Jesuitenorden). In wiefern der Künstler nur eine Vorstufe ist. Was bedeutet das „Subjekt" —?[51]

The will to power itself is an aesthetic, artistically creative force, and thus all activity, being rooted in the fundamental reality of the will to power, shares this aspect. Art, viewed as an exclusively human activity, is only a weak and derivative aspect of this underlying force. As long as we regard art (meaning the whole realm of creative, synthetic, aesthetic activity) as something which man does, we are missing Nietzsche's point[52]. Reality itself has a distinctly aesthetic character, and Nietzsche thus can regard "Die Welt als ein sich selbst gebärendes Kunstwerk . . . ."[53]

VIII. Conclusion

In the preceding chapters we have already seen, in a number of various applications, Nietzsche's abolition of all distinctions which separate action and actor. Our tendency to understand the world in terms of subject and object, matter and form, etc. is simply inherent to our particular cognitive paradigm. It is a perspectival falsification intended to make a chaotic world predictable, manageable, and enable creatures such as ourselves to survive in it. Distinctions like these, while having a certain pragmatic justification,

---

[50] Nachlass Frühjahr 1884, 25 [116]; KGW VII 2, 40.

[51] Nachlass Herbst 1885—Herbst 1886, 2 [114]; KGW VIII 1, 116f.

[52] It might be more true to Nietzsche's intent to say that art does man, rather than conversely. Cf. *Wahrheit und Lüge*, KGW III 2, 377: ". . . nur dadurch, dass der Mensch sich als Subjekt, und zwar als künstlerisch schaffendes Subjekt vergisst, lebt er mit einiger Ruhe, Sicherheit, und Consequenz . . ."

[53] Nachlass Herbst 1885—Herbst 1886, 2 [114]; KGW VIII 1, 117.

have no claim to being representative of the way the world "really" is, and the notion which Nietzsche opposes to this conventional world-view — viz. the abolition of all such perspectivally false distinctions which claim to be statically, referentially true — should be regarded as more "true" only in the sense of truth established in Chapter II (i. e. indicative of a greater degree of will to power).

There is no ultimate difference between an actor, his activity, and that upon which he acts. Thus, if we regard thinking (or any other form of cognition which we might care to distinguish such as perceiving or imagining) as an activity, this activity is identical with its object, and it is in the light of this identification that we must understand the formal character of Nietzsche's epistemology[54]. If we were to characterize the traditional Western mode of thinking as being *of* or *about* things, then thinking, for Nietzsche, is *thinking the things themselves*.

> Die Entstehung der „Dinge" ist ganz und gar das Werk der Vorstellenden, Denkenden, Wollenden, Erfindenden. Der Begriff „Ding" selbst ebenso als alle Eigenschaften. — Selbst „das Subjekt" ist ein solches Geschaffenes, ein „Ding", wie alle Andern: eine Vereinfachung, um die Kraft, welche setzt, erfindet, denkt, als solche zu bezeichnen . . .[55]

We have characterized this formal, creative aspect of the will to power as artistic. Normally, however, we regard artistic activity as presupposing some material substrate which serves as the "substance" upon which the form created by the artist is imposed. Again, this is a perspectival falsification which Nietzsche strives to overcome, even though he does refer, in places, to the creative, formal aspect of the will to power *as if* there were some independent reality upon which this creative activity is exercised. But this is due simply to the fact that ordinary language is constitutive of the traditional cognitive paradigm and forces one into this mode of expression, and not an inconsistency on Nietzsche's part. Nietzsche's frequent use of expressions such as "Schein," "Täuschung," "Illusion," etc. might also lead to the mistaken conclusion that there is some independent reality *about which* we are deceived, mistaken, and so on. This is yet another example of how the propositions of ordinary language beg those very epistemological questions to which Nietzsche is addressing himself: Nietzsche's destruction of the correspondence theory which such propositions presuppose does not answer such begged questions — it dissolves them.

---

[54] "Gedanken sind Handlungen . . ." Nachlass Herbst 1885—Frühjahr 1886, 1 [16]; KGW VIII 1, 10. Cf. Nachlass Ende 1886—Frühjahr 1887, 7 [1]; KGW VIII 1, 257f.
[55] Nachlass Herbst 1885—Herbst 1886, 2 [152]; KGW VIII 1, 139.

Nietzsche uses artists and aesthetic productivity as a metaphor, as an illustration of the formal, creative function of the will to power. Scholars and scientists, for example, analyze and scrutinize that which is already present (sic), whereas an artist freely creates something novel.

> Das philosophische Objektiv-Blicken kann somit ein Zeichen von Willens- und Kraft-Armuth sein. Denn die Kraft organisirt das Nähere und Nächste; die „Erkennenden", welche nur fest-stellen wollen, was ist, sind solche, die nichts festsetzen können, wie es sein soll.
> Die Künstler eine Zwischenart: sie setzen wenigstens ein Gleichniss von dem fest, was sein soll — sie sind produktiv, insofern sie wirklich verändern und umformen; nicht, wie die Erkennenden, welche Alles lassen, wie es ist.[56]

Nietzsche is not asserting that any and all artists display this powerfully creative energy. Rather, the artist represents a higher degree of will to power in that he does create and produce, as opposed to simply attempting to discover truth and facts conceived as having been always already present. The conventional artist, as a creative force, is but a few steps closer to realizing that radically creative potential which is the will to power. What we normally regard as artistic creativity is but a weak derivative of a much more fundamental, aesthetic-creative energy, but is nevertheless a closer approximation of the will to power *qua* cognition than the conventional objective-realistic mode of thinking.

> ... der Künstler-Philosoph ... höherer Begriff der Kunst. Ob der Mensch sich so fern stellen kann von den anderen Menschen, um an ihnen zu gestalten? (Vorübungen: 1) der Sich-selbst-Gestaltende, der Einsiedler 2) der bisherige Künstler, als der kleine Vollender, an einem Stoffe ...[57]

Since Nietzsche identifies subject and object, actor and act, etc., we see that the presupposition of an independent, external reality upon which we exercise our creative powers is indicative of a relatively weak degree of will to power. In the "higher conception of art" mentioned above, we catch a glimpse of what Nietzsche is attempting to express, viz. the will to power as a radically free and creative principle which, rather than moving the furniture of the world around into new arrangements, creates it. Artistic creativity and the objects of its creation are identical. This is what Nietzsche means when he says,

> Man ist um den Preis Künstler, dass man das, was alle Nichtkünstler „Form" nennen, als Inhalt, als „die Sache selbst" empfindet. Damit gehört man freilich

---

[56] Nachlass Herbst 1887, 9 [60]; KGW VIII 2, 30f.
[57] Nachlass Herbst 1885—Herbst 1886, 2 [66]; KGW VIII 1, 87.

in eine verkehrte Welt: denn nunmehr wird einem der Inhalt zu etwas bloß
Formalen, — unser Leben eingerechnet.[58]

The creative potency of thinking (*qua* will to power) produces, brings
forth its own contents. The perspectival illusion that there must be a
material or substantial substrate to support the artistically created form,
becomes a mere formality itself and, as such, utterly superfluous.

> Dem Dasein eine ästhetische Bedeutung geben, unseren Geschmack an ihm
> mehren, ist Grundbedingung aller Leidenschaft der Erkenntnis. ... Erken-
> nenwollen und Irrenwollen sind Ebbe und Flut. Herrscht eines absolut, so
> geht der Mensch zugrunde, und zugleich die Fähigkeit.[59]

---

[58] Nachlass November 1887—März 1888, 11 [3]; KGW VIII 2, 251f.
[59] GA XII, 48f.

CHAPTER SEVEN

KNOWLEDGE AS POWER

I. Nietzsche's Revaluation of Cognition

In the last chapter we examined the *modus operandi* of Nietzsche's will to power as a cognitive principle and as constitutive of a new cognitive paradigm. Thinking, for Nietzsche, is a creative process which is responsible for and identical with its contents. It remains to be seen how this creative mode of thinking must be viewed as an integral function of the will to power *qua* ontological model or, to put it into traditional terminology, how Nietzsche's epistemology relates to his ontology.

In the last chapter, we saw that Nietzsche presents us with a radically new notion of what thinking and its correlate, knowledge, are. But more than this, he gives us a radically new notion of what thinking and knowledge *are for*. Traditionally, knowledge has been regarded as being of or about a relatively stable world order. The more complete our knowledge, it was thought, the better able we would be to understand, explain, and predict the phenomena of our experience. For Nietzsche, of course, there is absolutely no stable order, no facts, no unchanging frame of reference to ground either a correspondence theory of truth, or a truth-functional language. Rather than being descriptive or explanatory in nature, knowledge, for Nietzsche, is prescriptive and constructive: it is an instrument of power.

> Die Erkenntniss arbeitet als Werkzeug der Macht. So liegt es auf der Hand, dass sie wächst mit jedem mehr von Macht . . . das Mass des Erkennenwollens hängt ab von dem Mass des Wachsens des Willens zur Macht der Art: eine Art ergreift so viel Realität, um über sie Herr zu werden, um sie in Dienst zu nehmen[1].

Knowledge is not an end in itself, and may perhaps be better described as a means to an end, that end being an enhancement or increase in will to power. We do not gain knowledge purely for the intellectual pleasure of intuiting the unchanging nature of reality or eternal verities, and Nietz-

---

[1] Nachlass Frühjahr 1888, 14 [122]; KGW VIII 3, 94.

sche criticizes this traditional intellectual approach as "artistisch" (as opposed to "aesthetisch"), which means for him ". . . sich vor das Leben hinsetzen." [2] Knowledge is not the result of observation for Nietzsche: we are not patrons in an epistemological movie house. Reality and our knowledge with regard to it are *processes* in which we are actively engaged, not separate realms of being which we passively observe and comment upon.

Nietzsche's approach to the problem of knowledge might tentatively be regarded as an instrumentalist or pragmatic approach, although when one realizes the ontological implications of the will to power, one also realizes that Nietzsche's epistemology is far more radical than the traditional categories of instrumentalism or pragmatism. Indeed, knowledge for its own sake is, for Nietzsche, the most futile sort of non-goal. Knowing is that process by means of which we construct and control reality: it is purely active and creative i. e. *the cognitive act is an act of creation*[3].

It cannot be stressed heavily enough that, for Nietzsche, knowledge is not something we derive, but something we do — not something we acquire, but something we create. Thus we see that, for Nietzsche, knowledge is power, and in the most radical and literal sense, but we must not do Nietzsche the disservice of giving this statement the traditional Baconian interpretation. Nietzsche means far more than merely, that by having knowledge of the world and its contents, we can use this knowledge to explain and predict phenomena which, in turn, will enable us to better understand and explain these phenomena and utilize them for our own advantage. Such a view still perpetuates all the inconsistencies of the traditional cognitive paradigm viz., the subject-object distinction (in all its various guises), the notion that there is a "real" world apart from us which it is our task to know and dominate. Such a view is incapable of accommodating the knowledge-power equation as Nietzsche exposes it.

> So lange du noch die Sterne fühlst als ein „Über-dir", fehlt dir noch der Blick des Erkennenden[4].

II. Preliminary Interpretations of Nietzsche's "Creative Cognition"

In Chapter I, a sketch was given of the will to power as an ontological principle (i. e., will to power *qua* being). In subsequent chapters, the will

---

[2] Nachlass Ende 1886—Frühjahr 1887, 7 [3]; KGW VIII 1, 264.
[3] Cf. Z II 2, "Auf den glückseeligen Inseln": "Auch im Erkennen fühle ich nur meines Willens Zeuge- und Werde-Lust; und wenn Unschuld in meiner Erkenntniss ist, so geschieht diess, weil Wille zur Zeugung in ihr ist." KGW VI 1, 107. Cf. also MR II 119: ". . . Erleben ist ein Erdichten." KGW V 1, 112.
[4] JGB 71; KGW VI 2, 86.

to power as a cognitive principle was explored, with the result that Nietzsche's equation of knowledge and power was exposed. We must now explore in greater depth the actual relationship between will to power as *knowing* and will to power as *being*. More specifically, we must ask what the relationship is between "der Wille" and "das Gewollte."

We cannot use the common, everyday human experience of willing to clarify this relationship because Nietzsche denies to this psychological sort of willing all but the most provisional, perspectival sort of validity[5]. What Nietzsche means by the *will* to power is not the everyday, psychological sort of will (e. g. I shall, I want, I demand, etc.). Like all our other psychological apparatus, this psychological will is itself only a derivative of the more fundamental will to power. We have also seen that Nietzsche denies the validity of the subject-object relationship (as well as the myriad perspectival falsifications which presuppose it). Thus, it would seem that we are not allowed to understand this in terms of a human subject possessed of a will, by means of which he alters the objects in his world and changes them around to suit himself by means of his creative, powerful will. Trees do not go flying through the air merely because I want them to.

If we attempt to explicate the notion of the creative will within the context of everyday, human, personal existence, we find that Nietzsche denies, in effect, all of the traditional categories and presuppositions upon which such a model must rest.

> Es giebt weder „Geist", noch Vernunft, noch Denken, noch Bewusstsein, noch Seele, noch Wille, noch Wahrheit: alles Fiktionen, die unbrauchbar sind. Es handelt sich nicht um „Subjekt und Objekt" sondern um eine bestimmte Thierart, welche nur unter einer gewissen relativen Richtigkeit, vor allem Regelmässigkeit ihrer Wahrnehmungen (so dass die Erfahrung capitalisiren kann) gedeiht . . .[6]

In the absence of the subject-object relationship and its derivative, the cause-effect relationship, no matter what ontological status the human individual has and no matter what kind of will he might possess, we simply cannot say that this will causes or otherwise brings about any changes in objects apart from the individual himself. Granted that ordinary language forces us to employ terms like these, these very terms are

---

[5] Nachlass Juni—Juli 1885, 38 [8]; KGW VII 3, 334ff.
  Nachlass Frühjahr 1888, 14 [219]; KGW VIII 3, 186.
  Nachlass Frühjahr 1888, 14 [122]; KGW VIII 3, 93ff.
  Nachlass Herbst 1887, 9 [98]; KGW VIII 2, 278f.
  Nachlass November 1887—März 1888, 11 [73]; KGW VIII 2, 278f.
  Nachlass November 1887—März 1888, 11 [74]; KGW VIII 2, 279.
[6] Nachlass Frühjahr 1888, 14 [122]; KGW VIII 3, 93f.

themselves perspectival falsifications and are meaningless outside of that
cognitive paradigm of which they are a part[7]. Thus we have seen at least
one way *not* to regard the epistemological function of the will to power.

Notwithstanding these linguistic difficulties, we might be tempted to
regard the epistemological function of the will to power as some type of
radical subjectivism or idealism[8]. In the absence of a cause-effect relationship, we cannot very well maintain that we, as willing subjects, bring about
or cause some substantial change in those objects effected and/or affected
by our will. Nevertheless, we might possibly regard the mind as being
capable of interpreting or reinterpreting its cognitional objects pretty much
as it pleases, or as being able to form whatever perspective it thinks will
be of use, and do all this without necessitating a physical rearrangement
of things in the world. In other words, we might be able to interpret
objects or shift the perspectives we have upon them "as if" a causal connection were involved without requiring a "real" causal relationship. A
view like this would regard causality simply as a cognitive category and
would not need to demand an extra-mental ontological status for this
relationship. Nietzsche often reminds us that, after all, we possess nothing
more than interpretations of anything[9]. We might conveniently reconcile
all this with Nietzsche's notion that the cognitive function of the will is
a perspectival "overpowering" of things within the context of some sort
of subjectivism or idealism. Moreover, the fact that Nietzsche has but a
single criterion for truth, i. e. "die Steigerung des Machtgefühls" would
appear to reinforce this subjectivist interpretation. It should be pointed
out that Nietzsche does not say "Steigerung der Macht," which could be
interpreted as involving some causal, forceful rearrangement of objects in
the world. Rather, he refers to "die Steigerung des Macht*gefühls*" (my
emphasis), and it is difficult to imagine how one could get any more
subjective than that.

We now have a second alternative. We could conceivably interpret the
creative-cognitive function of the will to power in terms of a radical
subjectivism.

... die fingirte Welt von Subjekt, Substanz, „Vernunft" usw. ist nöthig —:
eine ordnende, vereinfachende, fälschende, künstlich-trennende Macht ist in

[7] See Chapter V.
[8] Naturally, Nietzsche also denies this. "'Es ist alles subjektiv' sagt ihr: aber schon
das ist Auslegung, das 'Subjekt' ist nichts Gegebenes, sondern etwas Hinzu-Erdich-
tetes, Dahinter-Gestecktes. — Ist es zuletzt nöthig, den Interpreten noch hinter die
Interpretationen zu setzen? Schon das ist Dichtung, Hypothese."
Nachlass Ende 1886—Frühjahr 1887, 7 [60]; KGW VIII 1, 323.
[9] JGB 22; KGW VI 2, 31.

uns. „Wahrheit" — Wille, Herr zu werden über das Vielerlei der Sensationen.
die Phänomene aufreihen auf bestimmte Kategorien
— hierbei gehen wir vom Glauben an das „An sich" der Dinge aus (wir
nehmen die Phänomene als wirklich) . . .[10]

This, of course, sounds distinctly Kantian, and there a number of passages
in the *Nachlass* of the 1880's which might be cited (out of context) in
support of this sort of subjectivism[11]. If this actually were Nietzsche's
epistemological position — which it most decidedly is not — we might
justifiably maintain that a) Nietzsche was not particularly original; b) that
Nietzsche was simply another figure within the mainstream of nineteenth
century German idealist metaphysics; or c) that Kant, Fichte, Hegel,
Schelling, Schopenhauer, et al. made much the same point, and made it
better. But even if it sometimes appears that Nietzsche takes this direction,
and that this is what he intends with his perspectivism, we must not do
him the disservice of citing only those particular passages which happen
to favor our interpretation.

While the two alternative interpretations of the epistemological function of the will to power ("mind over matter," and subjective idealism) may
have a superficial degree of validity on the basis of the texts I have cited,
they do not authentically come to grips with the utter radicality of Nietzsche's thinking. Nietzsche's epistemological position *would* be something
like the two alternative positions I have given above *if he were operating
within the traditional cognitive paradigm, which he is not!* Nietzsche's theory of
knowledge is not a revision of the dominant cognitive paradigm of our
tradition — it is constitutive of a new and radically different cognitive
paradigm. Unless one realizes this, one cannot help but fail to adequately
understand Nietzsche's epistemology. Interpretations of Nietzsche's theory
of knowledge such as the two given above might seem tempting and
convenient, but they are useless: such interpretations are firmly within the
traditional cognitive paradigm and, for that very reason, unaware of their
own presuppositions. Such interpretative schemes regard their own perspectival falsifications as objective truths, and are therefore incapable of
discovering their own epistemological point of departure.

Some of the presuppositions upon which the characterizations of
Nietzsche's epistemology given above rest is that the subject-object relationship is objectively valid i. e., that every deed requires a doer, that every
effect presupposes a cause, that every interpretation requires an interpreter,

---

[10] Nachlass Herbst 1887, 9 [89]; KGW VIII 2, 46.
[11] See Vaihinger, loc. cit., for an exhaustive list of relevant passages (all referring, naturally, to GA).

and so on, all of which rest upon a metaphysical i. e. truth-functional linguistic paradigm. Now, it is one thing to deny the relationship of, e. g., causality in the everyday sense in which we are inclined to think of it. If this is done, causality becomes simply a subjective cognitive category, a manner of thinking. We, the thinker (it might be argued), necessarily think of occurrences as having been caused, and we are capable of thinking in this manner in the full awareness that this habit of thought is not necessarily descriptive of an ontologically separate state of affairs. Nevertheless, this manner of thinking still presupposes the thinker-thought dichotomy. No matter how we wish to juggle our data or categories about, we still experience immense difficulty in trying to conceive an interpretation without an interpreter, a feeling without a feeler, or a thought without a thinker. Our apparent inability to think except in such terms is indicative of nothing more than this very inability[12]. Nietzsche frequently reminds us that such ways of thinking are traps into which our very language leads us. Ordinary language contains an implicit metaphysics which necessarily and inexorably leads our thought in certain, predetermined directions toward foregone conclusions. If we wish to arrive at a position more fundamental than that upon which ordinary language rests, if we wish to express something other than the foregone conclusions which our cognitive-linguistic paradigm contains, we certainly cannot do this in ordinary language.

> Grundlösung:
> wir glauben an die Vernunft: diese aber ist die Philosophie der grauen Begriffe, die Sprache ist auf die aller naivsten Vorurtheile hin gebaut
> nun lesen wir Disharmonien und Probleme in die Dinge hinein, weil wir nur in der sprachlichen Form denken — somit die „ewige Wahrheit" der „Vernunft" glauben (z. B. Subjekt Prädikat usw.)
> wir hören auf zu denken, wenn wir es nicht in dem sprachlichen Zwange thun wollen, wir langen gerade noch bei dem Zweifel an, hier eine Grenze als Grenze zu sehn.
> Das vernünftige Denken ist ein Interpretiren nach einem Schema, welches wir nicht abwerfen können.[13]

> Die Forderung einer adäquaten Ausdrucksweise ist unsinnig: es liegt im Wesen einer Sprache, eines Ausdrucksmittels, eine bloße Relation auszudrükken . . . Der Begriff „Wahrheit" ist widersinnig . . . das ganze Reich von „wahr" „falsch" bezieht sich nur auf Relationen zwischen Wesen, nicht auf das „An sich" . . . Unsinn: es giebt kein „Wesen an sich", die Relationen constituiren erst Wesen, so wenig es eine „Erkenntnis an sich" geben kann . . .[14]

---

[12] Nachlass Herbst 1887, 9 [93]; KGW VIII 2, 97 f.
[13] Nachlass Sommer 1886—Herbst 1887, 5 [22]; KGW VIII 1, 197 f.
[14] Nachlass Frühjahr 1888, 14 [122]; KGW VIII 3, 95.

If we could grasp the will to power without somehow positing a subject or agent back of every activity, we could conceivably satisfy Nietzsche's negative conditions (i. e., what the will to power in its epistemological application is *not*) and gain a more fundamental point of departure. Consider the following passage:

> Man darf nicht fragen: „wer interpretirt denn?" sondern das Interpretiren selbst, als eine Form des Willens zur Macht, hat Dasein (aber nicht als ein „Sein", sondern als ein Prozess, ein Werden) als ein Affekt.[15]

If we sufficiently grasp the radical intent of this passage, we thereby dispense with the need or possibility of any sort of perduring ego-substance as the substrate upon which any and all action (whether intellectual or physical) must ultimately rest. What this leads to is an *identity* between what we have heretofore designated as the perceiving subject and the objects of his perception. We may no longer regard this identity as arising out of some radical type of subjectivism: it is not an identity in the sense that everything exists only insofar as it exists in someone's mind. What Nietzsche means is that mind, consciousness, thinking, ego, etc. are themselves not anything different from the world, but aspects of it, and without any special ontological or cognitive status. The traditional cognitive paradigm assumes that the mind is somehow prior to objects, which it subsequently discovers in the world, and then "reads off" the meaning which they bear (or which the mind, perhaps, attributes to them). But this is simply another of the perhaps useful, but ultimately erroneous perspectives which Nietzsche strives to overcome.

Let me repeat the new position at which we have arrived, which will enable us to harmonize Nietzsche's otherwise paradoxical assertions: the "mind" and all the cognitive faculties which it entails, is not something distinct from the "world" (i. e., the will to power). It exists alongside things, and has no special status with regard to them. Everything, Nietzsche tells us again and again, is will to power. Thus, physical objects must be as much aspects or manifestations of will to power as apparently immaterial things such as thought, mind, affect, etc. We must think of mind as something fundamentally identical with the sum total of its operations and relationships (and not as a separate and distinct "thinking substance") because all of these are various aspects of the will to power in different relationships to one another, and viewing one another from different perspectives[16].

---

[15] Nachlass Herbst 1885—Herbst 1886, 2 [151]; KGW VIII 1, 138.
[16] See Chapter I.

Martin Heidegger, in his Nietzsche lectures, attributes great significance to the following passage[17]:

> ... nicht „erkennen", sondern schematisiren, dem Chaos so viel Regularität und Formen auferlegen, als es unserem praktischen Bedürfnis genug thut ...[18]

At first glance, Nietzsche would seem to be implying that the chaos is something "out there," the mind's task being to synthesize and categorize it into intelligibility à la Kant. Heidegger, however, cautions against taking the traditional mind-matter, subject-object approach and observes that we must not think of "Chaos" and "Erkenntniss" as fundamentally different things, but rather, as aspects of the same reality — the will to power[19]. It is, I think, obvious that we do not first experience a chaos, which we then subsequently and deliberately render intelligible: we always already exist in a world characterized by some degree of intelligibility and order. We must think of "knowing" (i. e. "Erkenntnis") and "Chaos" as both being aspects (or affects) of the dynamically creative and active will to power. The individual mind (or "Erkenntnis") is not the doer or the thinker: it is not the interpreter, but is itself an interpretation of and by the more fundamental will to power. Thus, it is no longer a question for Nietzsche of my willing, my interpretation, my perspective: I am myself an interpretation, am a perspective, and do not will, but rather, am willed[20].

> Man darf nicht fragen: „wer interpretirt denn?" sondern das Interpretiren selbst, als eine Form des Willens zur Macht, hat Dasein (aber nicht als ein „Sein", sondern als ein Prozess, ein Werden) als ein Affekt.[21]
>
> Die Entstehung der „Dinge" ist ganz und gar das Werk der Vorstellenden, Denkenden, Wollenden, Erfindenden. Der Begriff „Ding" selbst ebenso als alle Eigenschaften. — Selbst „das Subjekt" ist ein solches Geschaffenes, ein „Ding", wie alle Andern: eine Vereinfachung, um die Kraft, welche setzt, erfindet, denkt, als solche zu bezeichnen, im Unterschiede von allem einzelnen Setzen, Erfinden, Denken selbst. Also das Vermögen im Unterschiede von allem Einzelnen bezeichnet: im Grunde das Thun in Hinsicht auf alles noch zu erwartende Thun (Thun und die Wahrscheinlichkeit ähnlichen Thuns) zusammengefasst.[22]

---

[17] Heidegger, *Nietzsche* I, p. 555ff.
[18] Nachlass Frühjahr 1888, 14 [152]; KGW VIII 3, 125.
[19] Heidegger, *Nietzsche* I, pp. 556—557.
[20] Cf. Z III 5: 2 "Von der verkleinernden Tugend": "Einige von ihnen wollen, aber die Meisten werden nur gewollt." KGW VI 1, 209.
[21] Nachlass Herbst 1885—Herbst 1886, 2 [151]; KGW VIII 1, 138.
[22] Nachlass Herbst 1885—Herbst 1886, 2 [152]; KGW VIII 1, 139.

III. The Revaluation of the Thinking Subject

Up to this point I have been characterizing the cognitive function of the will to power as basically that creative, world-constituting ability by virtue of which the individual constructs his own reality. This is, however, something of an oversimplification which nevertheless was necessary in order to bring our investigation to this point. To maintain that the individual constructs his own reality is not incorrect within the guidelines thus far established. Yet it is incorrect if explicated on the basis of a traditional philosophical anthropology (i. e. within the traditional cognitive paradigm).

Let us view man for a moment in the traditional manner: man is a union of a material body and an immaterial (and immortal) soul. He possesses a mind which is the seat of his consciousness and whose primary function is to think. By means of his mind and its inherent faculties, man becomes aware of the objects in the world around him, and this information is digested and reflected upon by the mind according to innate logical or cognitive categories. This enables man to relate properly to his environment and to have true knowledge of it, so long as his ideas are accurate copies of the objects which they represent. Nietzsche rejects such a view outright.

> Es giebt weder „Geist", noch Vernunft, noch Denken, noch Bewusstsein, noch Seele, noch Wille, noch Wahrheit: alles Fiktionen, die unbrauchbar sind.[23]

Nietzsche rejects not only the cognitive or psychological functions which we have traditionally attributed to the mind (*qua* thinking substance), but also rejects the whole notion of consciousness or intellect or the "thinking I" which we posit back of these functions as the agent responsible for them.

> ... durch das Denken wird das Ich gesetzt; aber bisher glaubte man wie das Volk, im „ich denke" liege etwas von Unmittelbar-Gewissem, und dieses „Ich" sei die gegebene Ursache des Denkens, nach deren Analogie wir alle sonstigen ursächlichen Verhältnisse verstünden. Wie sehr gewohnt und unentbehrlich jetzt jene Fiktion auch sein mag, — Das allein beweist noch nichts gegen ihre Erdichtetheit: es kann ein Glaube Lebensbedingung und trotzdem falsch sein.[24]

The paradox with which we seem to be faced is this: if we accept the preliminary formulation of the epistemological function of the will to power (i. e., the active creation and structuring of reality according to the

---

[23] Nachlass Frühjahr 1888, 2 [122]; KGW VIII 3, 93f.
[24] Nachlass Juni—Juli 1885, 38 [3]; KGW VII 3, 325f.

"formal" character of the will to power *qua* thinking), we have no one left to carry out this project. If mind, soul, thought, things, facts, will, etc. are negated, if they are not somehow actually existing entities or psychological structures, then it would seem that Nietzsche has himself negated the very basis on which the will to power — as creative cognition — could function.

In order to resolve this apparent paradox, we must return to that preliminary characterization of the will to power as an ontological model given in Chapter I. As stated there, for Nietzsche all that is, is quite simply (or quite complexly) will to power — and nothing else. Everything which exists is constituted out of what Nietzsche calls power-quanta ("Machtquanten"), which might be regarded as individual instances of the will to power. These power-quanta may group together to form those power-constellations which are subsequently perspectively interpreted as persons, objects, etc. Each of these power-constellations is concerned exclusively with increasing that power *which it is* and the control or domination of other power-constellations which it encounters. This might take place in innumerable ways. For example, if everything is will to power, that particular power-constellation which we call an amoeba or a plant exercises its drive to increase its own power by assimilating surrounding, weaker power-constellations in the form of nourishment. This naturally increases the strength or power of the individual organism (i. e. power-constellation) and enhances the quality of its "life." Within the human perspectival scheme, that power-constellation which we call a person may discharge this fundamental drive in a vastly greater number of ways, since it represents, comparatively speaking, a much greater quantity of power. Certainly a human person may exercise physical control and domination over his surroundings, and assimilates nourishment. But he may also exercise what we might call, for want of more adequate language, cognitional control over other "Machtconstellationen." We might say that that power-constellation which we call a person creatively interprets the other power-constellations with which he comes into contact, and relates to them from whatever perspective will most efficaciously enhance or increase his will to power, and enable him to utilize or otherwise dominate foreign power-constellations. Since we cannot meaningfully talk about absolute truth or unchanging knowledge, there can exist any number of perfectly valid "truths" for any particular power-constellation, the sole criterion being the relative increase or decrease of power. This is what Nietzsche means by "perspectivism."

Our preliminary description of the epistemological function of the will to power is further complicated by the fact that Nietzsche does not allow us to think of the human individual in the traditional terms of ego, subject, cogito, etc. For Nietzsche, the human individual is not a unified, substantial, homogeneous entity at all, and he allows to terms such as "I" or "self" only the most provisional, perspectival sort of validity. The human individual is a power-constellation, comprised of a number of individual and mutually antagonistic power-quanta, and the self-identity or unity which the human power-constellation displays is of the most tenuous, provisional sort. The unity which any power-constellation has might be regarded as analogous to the unity displayed by a political federation, made up of distinct individuals who have found their way together for a common purpose (viz. to increase their power). This loosely-knit federation of power-quanta might be demonstrated in a human person by pointing out the large number of opposed drives and urges which we all have within us, and which are constantly at war with one another, but which are nevertheless united in some fashion and able to join forces and work together toward a common goal. Even this, however, should be regarded only as an analogy and an over-simplification.

> Der Mensch als eine Vielheit von „Willen zur Macht": jeder mit einer Vielheit von Ausdrucksmitteln und Formen. Die einzelnen angeblichen „Leidenschaften": (z. B. der Mensch ist grausam) sind nur fiktive Einheiten, insofern das, was von den verschiedenen Grundtrieben her als gleichartig ins Bewusstsein tritt, synthetisch zu einem „Wesen'" oder „Vermögen', zu einer Leidenschaft zusammengedichtet wird. Ebenso also wie die „Seele" selber ein Ausdruck für alle Phänomene des Bewusstseins ist: den wir aber als Ursache aller dieser Phänomene auslegen (das „Selbstbewußtsein" ist fiktiv!)[25].

What we are accustomed to regarding as a unity is, according to Nietzsche, a rather complex plurality, and that unity or individuality which we attribute to a "human individual" is but another of our perspectival falsifications[26]. We are not even allowed to think of the human power-constellation as a discrete and independent entity, not even in a relative sense overagainst all other power-constellations:

> Der Mensch eine Atomgruppe, vollständig in seinen Bewegungen abhängig von allen Kräften, Verteilungen und Veränderungen des Alls — und andererseits wie jedes Atom unberechenbar . . .[27]

[25] GA XIII, 70.
[26] Nachlass Herbst 1885—Herbst 1886, 2 [91]; KGW VIII 1, 104.
[27] GA XII, 303.

Such a view of man or the "human individual" naturally demands a thorough re-examination of what we mean by such expressions as "I feel," "I will," "I think," etc.[28].

We ordinarily regard knowing as being intrinsically connected with the cognitive processes of a unitary thinking substance such as mind or intellect. But Nietzsche denies the reality of any such unitary thinking substance. We have been operating, up to this point, on the assumption that knowledge (or the objects of knowledge) is constructed through the cognitive activities of a thinking individual. We have seen, however, that for Nietzsche there is ultimately no such thing as a thinking individual, and that what we are accustomed to labeling a "human individual" is actually a plurality — a complex of power-quanta.

> Es kommt darauf an, die Einheit richtig zu bezeichnen, in der Denken, Wollen, und Fühlen und alle Affekte zusammengefaßt sind: ersichtlich ist der Intellekt nur ein Werkzeug, aber in wessen Händen? Sicherlich der Affekte: und diese sind eine Vielheit, hinter der es nicht nöthig ist, eine Einheit anzusetzen: es genügt, sie als eine Regentenschaft zu fassen[29].

Nietzsche no longer allows us to regard thinking as the activity of a unified mind or intellect. Can we, then, still regard man as a "thinking being" in any sense whatever? What is the fundamental meaning of "thinking" for Nietzsche? If man is a complex of power-quanta, viz. urges, drives,

---

[28] The reader familiar with psychoanalysis and dynamic psychiatry will immediately recognize many of the themes with which we are dealing here. Nietzsche was truly a pioneer in the exploration of the mind, and many of the leading themes of psychoanalysis either originated with Nietzsche, or were given their first adequate formulation by him. It is tempting here to give a long list of quotations from Freud, Jung, Adler, et al. in order to demonstrate the astounding corroboration which Nietzsche's "model" of the human psyche has found: it has proven itself to be a supremely useful interpretation. The notion that the ego-functions such as rational, conscious thought were actually functions of a much more fundamental, unconscious and irrational dynamism is only one of Nietzsche's original contributions. Nietzsche was the first to formulate and describe the mechanism of repression, sublimination, and even the concept of the "id" (das Es) originates with Nietzsche. Nietzsche's model of the psyche, i. e. a system of "dynamic quanta" or drives and urges which may collide or merge with one another, which may transfer energy from one to another, has thus shown itself to be a supremely useful interpretation. I mention this not as evidence for the "correctness" of Nietzsche's views in this regard, but for their utility, which is the only criterion in which he is interested. Henri Ellenberger gives a highly informative account of Nietzsche's influence upon dynamic psychology and, as his references are exhaustive, I refer the reader to him. See Henri Ellenberger, *The Discovery of the Unconscious* (New York, 1970), pp. 271—278.

[29] GA XIII, 245f. Cf. Sigmund Freud, *The Ego and the Id* in *The Standard Edition of the Complete Psychological Works of Sigmund Freud*, trans. and ed. by James Strachey et al. (London, 1959), Vol. XIX, pp. 12—66.

instincts, affects, etc., how do these disparate and antagonistic elements combine to produce that activity we call thinking?

> Gesetzt, dass nichts Anderes als real „gegeben" ist als unsre Welt der Begierden und Leidenschaften, daß wir zu keiner anderen „Realität" hinab oder hinauf können als gerade zur Realität unsrer Triebe — denn Denken ist nur ein Verhalten dieser Triebe zu einander . . .[30]

Or again:

> Die Gedanken sind Zeichen von einem Spiel und Kampf der Affekte: sie hängen immer mit ihren verborgenen Wurzeln zusammen[31].

> Alles, was ins Bewusstsein tritt, ist das letzte Glied einer Kette, ein Abschluss. Dass ein Gedanke unmittelbar Ursache eines anderen Gedankens wäre, ist nur scheinbar. Das eigentliche verknüpfte Geschehen spielt sich ab unterhalb unseres Bewusstseins: die auftretenden Reihen und Nacheinander von Gefühlen, Gedanken, usw. sind Symptome des eigentlichen Geschehens! — Unter jedem Gedanken steckt ein Affekt. Jeder Gedanke, jedes Gefühl, jeder Wille ist nicht geboren aus einem bestimmten Triebe, sondern er ist ein Gesamtzustand, eine ganze Oberfläche des ganzen Bewusstseins und resultiert aus der augenblicklichen Machtfeststellung aller der uns konstituirenden Triebe, — also des eben herrschenden Triebes sowohl, als der ihm gehorchenden oder widerstrebenden. Der nächste Gedanke ist ein Zeichen davon, wie sich die gesamte Machtlage inzwischen verschoben hat.
> „Wille" — eine falsche Verdinglichkeit.[32]

Thinking, or any other "psychic" process for that matter, is the result of an infinitely more complicated situation than has traditionally been held to be the case. It is a consequence, a symptom, of that inner tension produced by the mutually antagonistic power-quanta which comprise a person, i. e., the drive of each quantum to increase its own power at the expense of other quanta. Only by looking at the whole (i. e., the power-constellation) rather than the parts (i. e., the quanta) are we able to simplify and falsify this internal tension into what appears to be a unified and deliberate intellectual activity[33]. Obviously, with this notion of what lies

---

[30] JGB 36; KGW VI 2, 50.
[31] GA XIII 65.
[32] Ibid.
[33] To clarify this somewhat, I offer the following analogy: decision-making is a common, everyday activity which is familiar to everyone. It usually appears to be a fairly clear-cut, not overly complex intellectual activity, and we generally pride ourselves upon our ability to make sound, rational decisions. Yet from the perspective of dynamic psychology, what appears to be a clear-cut, rational decision may actually be the product of a whole host of unconscious, irrational elements, e. g. likes and dislikes, prejudice, desire for peer approval, neurosis, etc. What subsequently appears to be a rational, univocal decision may, in fact, be the result of a tense power-struggle between mutually antagonistic, irrational elements which are sublimated and

at the basis of the psychic processes, it makes little sense to posit an ego
or a subject as the agent responsible for the activity of thinking. Since,
according to Nietzsche, our mental activities are the result of the tensions
and struggles between a number of power-quanta, there remains nothing
which would justify talking about a unified "self."

> Die Annahme des Einen Subjekts ist vielleicht nicht nothwendig; vielleicht
> ist es ebensogut erlaubt, eine Vielheit von Subjekten anzunehmen, deren
> Zusammenspiel und Kampf unserem Denken und überhaupt unserem Bewusst-
> sein zu Grunde liegt? Eine Art Aristokratie von „Zellen", in denen die Herr-
> schaft ruht? Gewiss von pares, welche mit einander an's Regieren gewöhnt
> sind und zu befehlen verstehen?
> Meine Hypothesen:
> das Subjekt als Vielheit . . .[34]

In the absence of an ego or a self, usages such as "I think," "I do," "I
wish," etc. lose their significance: there is no "I" to think, do, wish, or
anything else. Self-interest, in the traditional sense, can no longer be
accepted as the motive for anything:

> Das „Ich" (welches mit der einheitlichen Verwaltung unseres Wesens nicht
> eins ist!) ist ja nur eine begriffliche Synthese — es giebt gar kein Handeln
> aus „Egoismus"[35].

It might be objected here that even if that aggregate which we call a human
individual does not ultimately constitute a "self," at least the individual
quanta which go to make up this aggregate function on the basis of some
sort of self-identity or self-assertion, since their sole drive is to increase
or enhance *their own* will to power. Phrased somewhat differently, we might
say that the "selfhood" or unity of a human "individual" is the sum of
all the lesser "selves" which collectively make up the human aggregate.
But Nietzsche also denies this possibility:

> Keine Subjekt-„Atome". Die Sphäre eines Subjektes beständig wachsend
> oder sich vermindernd — der Mittelpunkt des Systems sich beständig ver-
> schiebend —; im Falle es die angeeignete Masse nicht organisiren kann, zer-
> fällt es in 2. Andererseits kann es sich ein schwächeres Subjekt, ohne es zu
> vernichten, zu seinem Funktionär umbilden und bis zu einem gewissen Grad
> mit ihm zusammen eine neue Einheit bilden. Keine „Substanz", vielmehr
> Etwas, das an sich nach Verstärkung strebt; und das sich nur indirekt „erhal-
> ten" will (es will sich überbieten —)[36]

rationalized until we are not even aware of their existence. See Sigmund Freud, *The
Psychopathology of Everyday Life* in the *Standard Edition*, Vol. VI.
[34] Nachlass August—September 1885, 40 [42]; KGW VII 3, 382.
[35] Nachlass Herbst 1885—Frühjahr 1886, KGW VIII 1, 28.
[36] Nachlass Herbst 1887, 9 [98]; KGW VIII 2, 55f.

Even the power-quanta themselves are not to be thought of as indivisible, ultimate entities (such as the word ἄτομ implies): as Nietzsche says in the passage cited above, the power-quanta may merge themselves to form a single greater quantum, or disintegrate into lesser quanta. There is nothing within such a system of power-quanta which we could designate as a "self" or an "individual" in any univocal sense. "Dass der Mensch eine Vielheit von Kräften ist, welche in einer Rangordnung stehen ... Der Begriff 'Individuum' ist falsch."[37]

This naturally serves only to sharpen the paradox which was mentioned at the beginning of this chapter. If we wish to characterize Nietzsche's theory of knowledge as being grounded in the subjective creation of reality on the part of the thinking individual, we have, it would seem, no one to carry out this project. Nietzsche denies the ultimate reality of the ego[38], of subjects[39], of the unity of consciousness[40], and even the logical "laws" which our paradigmatic system of rational intellection presupposes[41]. It would therefore seem that Nietzsche denies those very things which any theory of knowledge necessarily presupposes, and that we — together with Nietzsche — have painted ourselves into an epistemological corner.

With regard to consciousness, mind, ego, thinking, etc., let us attempt the following reconciliation: if we regard all the psychological apparatus which we appear to possess as creations or projections of that power-constellation called man, we could without any great difficulty harmonize this "power ontology" with the previously elaborated epistemological function of the will to power. "Schafft sich nicht ewig der Mensch eine fingirte Welt, weil er eine bessere Welt haben will als die Realität?" Nietzsche asks[42]. To this I would add that perhaps even man's traditional concept of his own identity is as much a perspectival falsification as anything else in his "fictitious world."[43]

---

[37] GA XIII, 169f.
[38] Nachlass Herbst 1885—Frühjahr 1886, 1 [87]; KGW VIII 1, 28.
Nachlass Herbst 1887, 9 [108]; KGW VIII 2, 131.
[39] Nachlass Herbst 1885—Herbst 1886, 2 [87]- KGW VIII 1, 102f.
Nachlass Herbst 1887, 10 [19]; KGW VIII 2, 131.
[40] Nachlass August—September 1885, 40 [42]; KGW VII 3, 382.
Nachlass Frühjahr 1888, 15 [90]; KGW VIII 3, 252ff.
[41] Nachlass Sommer 1886—Frühjahr 1887, 6 [11]; KGW VIII 1, 243.
Nachlass Herbst 1887, 6 [91]; KGW VIII 2, 47ff.
Nachlass Herbst 1887, 9 [97]; KGW VIII 2, 53f.
Nachlass Herbst 1887, 9 [144]; KGW VIII 2, 81f.
[42] Nachlass Frühjahr 1888, 14 [168]; KGW VIII 3, 441.
[43] "NB. 'Bewusstsein' — in wie fern die vorgestellte Vorstellung, der vorgestellte Wille, das vorgestellte Gefühl (das uns allein bekannte) ganz oberflächlich ist! 'Erscheinung' auch unsere innere Welt!" Nachlass Sommer—Herbst 1884, 26 [49]; KGW

Certainly Nietzsche denies to consciousness, mind, ego, thinking, etc. that sort of substantial existence which has been traditionally attributed to them. But is he really claiming that they are "mere illusions" which do not really "exist" in any manner at all? I think not. If we accept the notion that man is fundamentally an aggregate or complex of power-quanta, whose existential tendency is to increase his "own" power, and if this power is regarded as creative and productive, then it is certainly conceivable that mind, thinking, ego, etc. are perspectival falsifications of and by this power-constellation which are efficacious in increasing its power and domination of other power complexes.

It is a truism today in psychology that man is a vastly more complex creature than has traditionally been believed, and that the human psyche is far from being a happy and harmonious unity. Nietzsche frequently reminds us that our way of looking at the world involves a very great deal of oversimplification and falsification, and perhaps man's concept of himself is a prime example of this. All the drives, urges, instincts, affects, which together constitute a person must be held in some sort of equilibrium if the power-constellation is to maintain its integrity. A construct such as "ego" or "self" is, for this reason, of greatest value in yoking together the disparate elements of the human aggregate and giving their combined energies a common direction. "Der Mensch hat ... eine Fülle gegensätzlicher Triebe und Impulse in sich gross gezüchtet: vermöge dieser Synthesis ist er der Herr der Erde."[44] The notions of ego or individuality, even though they are "perspectival errors", are indispensable as unifiers of man's innate complexity. Without such a unifying perspective, the mutually antagonistic power-quanta which constitute man would destroy the artificial unity of the whole. Thus, the task of "ego" or "mind" becomes " ... in Eins zu dichten und zusammen zu tragen, was Bruchstück ist am Menschen und Räthsel und grauser Zufall ..."[45] Man is not a unity, but unless he regards himself as one, he cripples or destroys himself. Thus, individuality or selfhood, while not corresponding to any sort of substantial entities, are nevertheless among our most useful and most necessary errors. And while assertions about the ego or the self may not be true in the correspondence sense, we might nonetheless claim some

VII 2, 159. "Wir meinen, unser bewusster Intellekt sei die Ursache aller zweckmässigen Einrichtungen in uns. Das ist grundfalsch. Nichts ist oberflächlicher als das ganze Setzen von 'Zwecken' und 'Mitteln' durch das Bewusstsein: es ist ein Apparat der Vereinfachung (wie das Wort-reden usw.), ein Mittel der Verständigung, practicabel, nichts mehr — ohne Absicht auf Durchdringung mit Erkenntniss." Nachlass Sommer bis Herbst 1884, 26 [52]; KGW VII 2, 159.
[44] Nachlass Sommer—Herbst 1884, 27 [59]; KGW VII 2, 289.
[45] Z III 12:3; KGW VI 1, 244.

sort of "truth" for them in Nietzsche's sense, since constructs such as these
serve to increase the collective power of all the separate quanta which
constitute man by binding them together and giving them a common
orientation. In the last analysis, that unity or individuality which man
attributes to himself is a means to an end, that end being, as always with
Nietzsche, the increase of will to power[46].

Man is not an indivisible self, not a substantial entity, not a univocal
something, but a plurality of power-quanta which is essentially fluid and
ambiguous. Man's self-identity is nothing more than a perspectival falsification which serves as a means of increasing the power of the collective
power-quanta. If this is the case, however, are we still justified in regarding man as a "thinking being?" If man has no univocal "an sich" nature,
what accounts for the provisional, perspectival nature he does have? Nietzsche's answer to this question of what constitutes "nature" or essence is
entirely consistent with his flux ontology of power-quanta: *it is precisely*
the tension-relationship of the dynamic quanta of power to one another which con-
stitutes their "essence."[47]

> Das Ich ist nicht die Stellung eines Wesens zu mehreren (Triebe, Gedanken,
> usw.), sondern das ego ist eine Mehrheit von personenartigen Kräften, von
> denen bald diese, bald jene im Vordergrund steht als ego und nach den anderen
> wie ein Subjekt nach einer einflußreichen und bestimmenden Außenwelt hin-
> sieht. Der Subjektpunkt springt herum, wahrscheinlich empfinden wir die
> Grade der Kräfte und Triebe wie Nähe und Ferne, und legen uns wie eine
> Landschaft und Ebene aus, was in Wahrheit eine Vielheit von Quantitäts-
> graden ist[48].

---

[46] Karl Jaspers gives a succinct formula which casts a good deal of light on the fundamental significance of this creative self-deception: man as his own creator. Jaspers, however, restricts this formula to the area of morality. This is certainly valid, but to
maintain that man is his own creator in only this sense, that he projects those values
which dominate and regulate his social milieu, is to miss the fundamental point. See
Jaspers, p. 139 ff.

[47] "Wir haben Einheiten nöthig, um rechnen zu können: deshalb ist nicht anzunehmen,
dass es solche Einheiten giebt. Wir haben den Begriff der Einheit entlehnt von
unserem "Ich"-begriff, — unserem ältesten Glaubensartikel. Wenn wir uns nicht für
Einheiten hielten, hätten wir nie den Begriff "Ding" gebildet. Jetzt, ziemlich spät,
sind wir reichlich davon überzeugt, dass unsere Conception des Ich-Begriffs nichts
für eine reale Einheit verbürgt ... Eliminiren wir diese Zuthaten: so bleiben keine
Dinge übrig, sondern dynamische Quanta, in einem Spannungsverhältniss zu allen
anderen dynamischen Quanten: deren Wesen in ihrem Verhältnis zu allen anderen
Quanten besteht, in ihrem "Wirken" auf dieselben — der Wille zur Macht nicht ein
Sein, nicht ein Werden, sondern ein Pathos ist die elementarste Thatsache, aus der sich
erst ein Werden, ein Wirken ergiebt ..." Nachlass Frühjahr 1888, 14 [79]; KGW
VIII 3, 50 f. See Müller-Lauter, op. cit., pp. 10—33. See also the same author's
"Nietzsches Lehre vom Willen zur Macht," *Nietzsche-Studien* III/1974, pp. 1—60.

[48] GA XI, 235. See Müller-Lauter, opera cit. (above, note 47).

According to Nietzsche, man is not an indivisible, substantial self which, as an agent, carries out the activity of thinking. Rather, thinking, as well as all the rest of our "psychic" functions, is a simplification and interpretation of that tension existing between the mutually antagonistic power-quanta which constitute the human aggregate. Terms such as "ego," "subject," "self," etc. cannot be consistently regarded as corresponding to substantial entities: they are signs, metaphors, conceptual syntheses which have a great utility in organizing and giving direction to the human aggregate, and this is their justification. With this in mind, we must now explicate with greater radicality the characterization of creative cognition or authentic thinking which was given in the last chapter.

IV. Thought and Thinking as Perspectival Falsifications

In Chapter VI, the activity of thinking was characterized as a synthetic, creative, aesthetic function which actively interpreted and constructed the *Lebenswelt*. This was the preliminary characterization given to the will to power as a principle of cognition. This preliminary characterization is not inaccurate but, as it was carried out largely in terms of the traditional cognitive paradigm and could be misconstrued as sharing the assumptions of that paradigm, must not be regarded as representative of Nietzsche's ultimate position. This preliminary characterization itself rests upon a more fundamental perspectival falsification, viz. the "artificial" construction and synthesis of that activity which we have designated as *thinking*. Our preliminary characterization of authentic thinking or creative cognition appears to be meaningful in terms of the traditional, paradigmatic sense of thinking. But we must now realize that Nietzsche's intent is far more radical than any sort of subjective idealism: that activity which we call *thinking* or *cognizing* not only perspectivally falsifies — *it is itself a perspectival falsification*.

The activity of thinking itself rests upon a twofold falsification: a) as characterized in Chapter VI, thinking interprets, simplifies, constructs, and otherwise "falsifies" the "external world;" b) however, the thinking activity itself is a simplification and falsification of the tensions existing between the power-quanta which comprise the human aggregate, i. e. the "Spannungsverhältnis" existing between the power-quanta themselves is simplified and falsified into that activity we call thinking. Thinking not only constructs — it is itself constructed[49].

49 Nachlass November 1887—März 1888, 11 [145]; KGW VIII 2, 309 f.
   Nachlass Sommer—Herbst 1884, 26 [114]; KGW VII 2, 178 f.
   Nachlass Sommer—Herbst 1884, 26 [92]; KGW VII 2, 171 f.

We might say well and good to all this. But our very language forces us to ask a further question: allowing that all the above is the case, who is doing all of this? Who is interpreting, falsifying, synthesizing, constructing, etc.? If we grant that thinking rests upon a twofold falsification, who is the falsifier? Couched as they are within the language of the traditional cognitive paradigm — which implicitly assumes a distinct metaphysics and logic — questions such as these beg a much larger question. In other words, questions such as these already presuppose a specific answer, an answer which is useless for our purposes since it remains merely on the surface of our problematic, without penetrating to its roots. For example, the question "who falsifies?" already presupposes that "someone falsifies" which, in turn, presupposes the separability of actor from act (i. e. the subject-object distinction), which distinction must be abandoned if one is to authentically grasp Nietzsche's cognitive paradigm.

Ego, self, as well as conscious, rational, reflective thought already exist on a fairly complex level of perspectival falsification, and it is not the ego or the self which is the primordial falsifier: both are already falsifications.

> Das „Ich" (welches mit der einheitlichen Verwaltung unseres Wesens nicht eins ist!) ist ja nur eine begriffliche Synthesis — also giebt es gar kein Handeln aus „Egoismus."[50]

The ego, the "thinking I", is not the unitary agent responsible for all our cognitive activities, but is itself posited or created through a more fundamental *thinking*[51]. Conversely, this creative thinking which constructs the "I" is not the activity of some more fundamental thinking agent[52]. Nor is this falsifying, creative, thinking to be thought of as conscious, rational, or deliberate[53]. "Das Denken ist noch nicht das innere Geschehen selber, sondern ebenfalls eine Zeichensprache für den Machtausgleich von

---

[50] Nachlass Herbst 1885—Frühjahr 1886, 1 [87]; KGW VIII, 1, 28.

[51] "... durch das Denken wird das Ich gesetzt ..." Nachlass Juni—Juli 1885, 38 [3]; KGW VII 3, 325.

[52] GA XVI, 71 f.

[53] "Das bewusste Denken ... ist die unkräftigste und deshalb auch die verhältnissmässig mildeste und ruhigste Art des Denkens ..." FW 333; KGW V 2, 239. At first glance, this characterization of conscious thought as impotent would seem to thoroughly undermine the notion of "creative cognition" which was sketched in the last chapter. But when Nietzsche criticizes consciousness, calls it impotent or without effect, what he is really criticizing is reflective, second-order *self*-consciousness, which artifically introduces a distinction between myself and that stream of lived experience *which I am*. That negatively-differentiated sort of egoistical consciousness (to which we normally restrict ourselves) functions on the basis of a false distinction which it has introduced into the nature of things, and Nietzsche seems to think that

Affekten[54]." Thinking is an epiphenomenon of that fundamental tension of opposites existing between the power-quanta which comprise an "individual". It is a superficial interpretation and simplification of that turbulent state of tension and mutual aggression and urge to dominate which is, for Nietzsche, the fundamental reality of the will to power. Ego, self, consciousness, etc. are like the proverbial iceberg, of which we see only a small fraction above the surface of the water, while the greater part of its bulk is hidden from view beneath the surface.

Thus we see that our preliminary characterization of thinking as a process of perspectival falsification and construction of the lived world was not inaccurate, but should not be regarded as Nietzsche's (nor our) last word on the subject. The thinking "I" or self, as well as the activity of thinking itself are no less perspectival falsifications. All these components of the cognitive process are simplifications and falsifications of that turbulent, dynamic drive for increased power which is the world, which is ourselves, which is — the will to power.

V. Conclusion

The purpose of this chapter has not so much been to answer the question "What is Nietzsche's theory of knowledge?" as it has been to throw the problematic with which we are here concerned into proper focus. On the basis of the traditional cognitive paradigm, we cannot adequately grasp the utter radicality of Nietzsche's intent, because he explicitly denies those elements of the cognitional process which a traditional theory of knowledge necessarily presupposes.

In the preceding chapter, an initial characterization of the will to power as a way of knowing was given, to the effect that the thinking, cognizing individual actively constructs, simplifies, interprets, i. e. perspectivelly falsifies his world for his own advantage. As we saw, however, Nietzsche denies the reality of ego, will, thinking, etc. in that sense in which we ordinarily speak of them, with the result that if we accept the preliminary characterization given in Chapter VI, we have no one left

---

this makes it more difficult to act potently and efficaciously. I am reminded of the old saw about the centipede who, after reflecting upon how it was that he could manage 100 legs, found that he was now incapable of doing that very thing. Cf. John T. Wilcox, *Truth and Value in Nietzsche* (Ann Arbor, 1974), pp. 172—180.

[54] GA XIII, 69. "Der Intellekt ist das Werkzeug unserer Triebe und nichts mehr, er wird nie frei. Er schärft sich im Kampf der verschiedenen Triebe, und verfeinert die Tätigkeit jedes einzelnen Triebes dadurch." GA XI, 200.

who could carry out this process of creative falsification. This initial characterization is not inaccurate, but the deeper context in terms of which it is to be understood remains to be adequately clarified. It *is* inaccurate, however, if we regard this creatively interpretative mode of cognition in terms of the traditional cognitive paradigm, and two examples were given of how *not* to understand this preliminary characterization[55]. Traditional epistemology is incapable of exposing its own ground, and is certainly incapable of adequately grasping the radical nature of the will to power as a principle of cognition, i. e. Nietzsche's new cognitive paradigm. In order to achieve an authentic understanding and supply the proper context for the understanding of our preliminary characterization, it was necessary to further clarify what is involved in this characterization.

Thinking (or knowing, or cognizing) rests upon a twofold falsification: a) the activity of thinking perspectivally falsifies its world; b) not only the "object" of thought, but the activity of thinking and the agent to which we attribute this activity are themselves simplifications and falsifications of the power-play of those dynamic quanta which collectively comprise the human aggregate[56]. We do not think, strictly speaking, but rather, are thought[57].

The greatest difficulty in grasping all of this is no doubt a linguistic one: the language which we are forced to use (for we have no other) already assumes those things which Nietzsche is calling into question. If we accept that knowing, cognizing, etc. in addition to all other "psychic" activities are simplifications and falsifications of a more fundamental interpretative process, we are still tempted to inquire about who it is, ultimately, who is doing the interpreting, falsifying, etc. But this begs the question and — if one does not follow Nietzsche's shift into a new cognitive paradigm — makes his answer appear unintelligible. Nietzsche's answer to this begged question, paradoxical as it might appear, is that "no one" is doing the interpreting.

> Man darf nicht fragen: „wer interpretirt denn?" sondern das Interpretiren selbst, als eine Form des Willens zur Macht, hat Dasein (aber nicht als ein „Sein", sondern als ein Prozeß, ein Werden) als ein Affekt.[58]

---

[55] Viz. a) that the psychological will structures its world in the sense of a "mind over matter" sort of physical causality; b) in terms of a radical subjectivism or idealism.

[56] "Zweifache Fälschung, von den Sinnen her und vom Geiste her, um eine Welt des Seienden zu erhalten, des Verharrenden, Gleichwerthigen usw. ... Werden als Erfinden Wollen Selbstverneinen, Sich-Selbst-Überwinden: kein Subjekt, sondern ein Thun, Setzen, schöpferisch, keine 'Ursachen und Wirkungen'." Nachlass Ende 1886—Frühjahr 1887, 7 [54]; KGW VIII 1, 320f.

[57] Nachlass Juni—Juli 1885, 38 [3]; KGW VII 3, 325.

[58] Nachlass Herbst 1885—1886, 2 [151]; KGW VIII 1, 138.

Mind, will, consciousness, thought, etc. are not to be regarded as irreducible factors within the cognitive process, since they themselves are signs and metaphors, simplifications and interpretations of that turbulent and enigmatic power-struggle existing between the quanta of the will to power.

> Es kommt darauf an, die Einheit richtig zu bezeichnen, in der Denken, Wollen und Fühlen und alle Affekte zusammengefaßt sind: ersichtlich ist der Intellekt nur ein Werkzeug, aber in wessen Händen? Sicherlich der Affekte: und diese sind eine Vielheit, hinter der es nicht nöthig ist eine Einheit anzusetzen: es genügt, sie als eine Regentschaft zu fassen[59].

We may certainly let our preliminary characterization of the epistemological function of the will to power stand, but with this proviso: thinker, thinking, and the objects of thought are all interpretations, simplifications, signs and metaphors for the primordial power-play existing between the quanta of the will to power. Ultimately there are neither thinkers, thoughts, nor objects of thought as traditionally conceived. Yet we must not make the mistake of thinking that Nietzsche is enjoining us to cease thinking in terms of such entities and activities. Indeed, that would scarcely be possible. There are, after all, necessary "errors."

The ego and its activities are instruments, perhaps necessary "errors," which enable the human aggregate to organize, direct, and thereby increase its will to power. This is for Nietzsche the highest — indeed, the only — justification. In the same light, we should view the preliminary characterization of Chapter VI not as the final form of Nietzsche's theory of knowledge, but as working hypothesis which serves to overcome the traditional limits placed upon human cognition by our dominant paradigm, and thereby liberate man to more actively and potently enhance and increase that which he ultimately is. And that, for Nietzsche, is the will to power — and nothing else.

---

[59] GA XIII, 245f. Cf. GA XI, 200 (above, note 54).

CHAPTER EIGHT

THE CONSTRUCTION OF REALITY

In this chapter we shall attempt to synthesize all that has previously been said, and demonstrate the world-creating function of the will to power in the radical and fundamental sense in which Nietzsche intended it. This constructive, creative, formative character of the will to power has, of course, been often mentioned. However, in the course of our preliminary investigation, we were, for the most part, forced to remain within the limits of the traditional cognitive paradigm and employ its language. This means that our discussion of Nietzsche's theory of knowledge was carried out in terms of concepts and categories which themselves, according to Nietzsche, are nothing more than conventions and useful fictions. In order to gain an authentic understanding not only of these perspectival inter-pretations and falsifications, but of the process of interpreting and falsify-ing as such, we must now conclude our discussion on the most fundamental level, the level of the will to power as being itself, and in terms of that radical dynamism which characterizes it.

I. The Ontology of Power

All objects and phenomena are, for Nietzsche, reducible to will to power in various configurations and at various levels of power. Arthur Danto refers to this reduction of everything to will to power as Nietzsche's "methodological monism," which is apparently meant to be taken pejoratively[1]. Nonetheless, we pointed out in Chapter I that Nietzsche's "methodological monism" is anything but an attempt at a simplistic world-view, or a world-view which attempts to make things easy for itself by explaining away the complexity and ambiguity of the world. Even though a catch-phrase such as "methodological monism" may sound attractively simple, the net effect of Nietzsche's "reductionism" is to create a world-view which is vastly more complex, enigmatic, paradoxical, and defiant of traditional philosophical categories than any-

[1] Danto, pp. 216—218.

thing attempted by his predecessors. Our task is now to demonstrate how the process of human cognition in all its various ramifications is rooted in the fundamental reality of the will to power and its ceaseless drive for ever more power. This task was begun in the last chapter, which focused upon the individual knower as a complex of power-quanta, and will be completed in this chapter, not in terms of any predetermined categories — cognitive or otherwise — but solely on the basis of the will to power as Nietzsche characterizes it.

In the first chapter we saw that Nietesche's answer to the question "What is there"? is will to power — and nothing else. A brief synopsis of some of the points made in the first chapter will be helpful at this point. The will to power is all that exists, but must not be thought of in terms of a homogeneous, self-identical world stuff. The will to power, according to Nietzsche, is not a unitary substance or "Weltgeist" which smoothly exfoliates according to its own internal principles[2]. The will to power, viewed *in toto* is comprised of discrete quanta which might be regarded as specific instances or particular cases of the will to power[3]. These power-quanta are not inviolate, ultimate entities i. e., they should not be confused with the elementary particles of physics, but may merge to form a new, single quantum, or may be split into separate quanta[4].

> . . . es giebt keine dauerhaften letzten Einheiten, keine Atome, keine Monaden: auch hier ist „das Seiende" erst von uns hineingelegt, (aus praktischen, nützlichen perspektivischen Gründen) . . .[5]

> Daß die letzten kleinsten „Individuen" nicht in dem Sinn eines „metaphysischen Individuums" und Atoms verständlich sind, dass ihre Machtsphäre fortwährend sich verschiebt — das ist zuallererst sichtbar . . .[6]

And while Nietzsche cautions against regarding the quanta of will to power as ultimate entities, he equally cautions against regarding the will to power as an all-embracing collective entity: ". . . es giebt keinen Willen: es giebt Willens-Punktationen, die beständig ihre Macht mehren oder verlieren . . .[7]" There are no "laws of nature" or mechanical principles which

---

[2] Nachlass Juni—Juli 1885, 38 [12]; KGW VII 3, 338f.
[3] Nachlass Frühjahr 1888, 14 [184]; KGW VIII 3, 162f.
  Nachlass Frühjahr 1888, 14 [79]; KGW VIII 3, 49ff.
  See W. Müller-Lauter, "Nietzsches Lehre vom Willen zur Macht," *Nietzsche-Studien* III/1974, pp. 1—60. Müller-Lauter sometimes expresses a preference for the rendering, "*die* Willen zur Macht."
[4] Nachlass Herbst 1887, 9 [98]; KGW VIII 2, 55.
[5] Nachlass November 1887—März 1888, 11 [73]; KGW VIII 2, 278.
[6] Nachlass November 1887—März 1888, 11 [111]; KGW VIII 2, 294.
[7] Nachlass November 1887—März 1888, 11 [73]; KGW VIII 2, 278f.

heteronomously govern the interactions of the power-quanta. Indeed, the power-quanta themselves are not even to be thought of as individual entities which might act according to some external principle, or as agents which perform an activity:

> Der Wille zur Accumulation von Kraft als spezifisch für das Phänomen des Lebens, für Ernährung, Zeugung, Vererbung ... nicht bloss Constanz der Energie: sondern Maximal-Ökonomie des Verbrauchs: so dass das Stärker-werden-wollen von jedem Kraftcentrum aus die einzige Realität ist, — nicht Selbstbewahrung, sondern Aneignung, Herr-werden, Mehr-werden-, Stärker-werden-wollen. ... wenn etwas so und nicht anders geschieht, so ist darin kein „Princip", kein „Gesetz", keine „Ordnung".
> Kraft-Quanta, deren Wesen darin besteht, auf alle anderen Kraft-Quanta Macht auszuüben ...[8]

The quanta of the will to power are not entities which possess or exercise this will: they are themselves the will to increase and accumulate more power; they are themselves identical with their activity.

In the absence of any fixed, ultimate entities and unchanging laws governing their activities, it is an extremely precarious undertaking to give the will to power any characterization at all. Still, according to Nietzsche's model, the will to power is fluid and dynamic — it is constantly in a state of change or becoming. Yet our linguistic paradigm is simply incapable of expressing in any adequate fashion this ambiguous and chaotic flux of power-quanta, of which Nietzsche frequently reminds us. Nevertheless, insofar as it can be characterized at all, Nietzsche characterizes the will to power as a vast (though finite) number of power-quanta which are ceaselessly striving for more power. Obviously Nietzsche discards the traditional metaphysical notion of a continuously present world of static being. But even the apparently antithetical concept of a world of constant becoming (as with Heraclitus) is not adequate to express that enigmatic chaos of power-quanta which, for Nietzsche, is the case.

> ... der Wille zur Macht nicht ein Sein, nicht ein Werden, sondern ein Pathos ist die elementarste Thatsache, aus der sich erst ein Werden, ein Wirken ergiebt ...[9]

Even though the quanta of the will to power *are* simply will to ever more power — and nothing else — we must refrain from thinking that Nietzsche is characterizing reality simply as an atomistic system of identical power-quanta which are discrete and each one of which is opposed to all

[8] Nachlass Frühjahr 1888, 14 [81]; KGW VIII 3, 53.
[9] Nachlass Frühjahr 1888, 14 [79]; KGW VIII 3, 51.

the rest. The quanta of the will to power may arrange themselves in myriad combinations or, as Nietzsche usually refers to such combinations, "Macht-konstellationen."

> Meine Vorstellung ist, dass jeder spezifische Körper darnach strebt, über den ganzen Raum Herr zu werden und seine Kraft auszudehnen (— sein Wille zur Macht:) und Alles das zurückzustossen, was seiner Ausdehnung wider-strebt. Aber er stösst fortwährend auf gleiche Bestrebungen anderer Körper und endet, sich mit denen zu arrangiren („vereinigen"), welche ihm verwandt genug sind: — so conspiriren sie dann zusammen zur Macht. Und der Prozess geht weiter . . .[10]

Such an arrangement or constellation of power-quanta does not constitute a new, substantial entity. Each power quantum *is* simply the will to increased power, and this fundamental characteristic is not compromised by entering into such an arrangement. Rather, a particular quantum may better increase its own power by entering into a power complex with other quanta, similar to the old saw about there being strength in numbers. All the power-quanta in such a constellation remain fundamentally antagonistic toward one another, but by combining their energies collectively, might more effica-ciously increase their individual power. Such a power group is not necessarily a unified, homogeneous thing, and the apparent unity which it might display is only of a provisional sort, akin to a political federation[11]. What the power-quanta in such a configuration have in common is the drive to dominate all the others and increase their own power, respectively, at the expense of the others in the group. Where the quanta comprising a power-constellation are relatively equal in degree of power, a tense equilibrium ("Spannungsverhältnis") would exist, this tension being the motive force which impels the collective to increase and enhance its power[12]. Of course, this is only one possible scenario. One power-quantum (or sub-constellation within a larger collective power-group) might achieve some sort of hegemony over the others, for example, and the list of possible

---

[10] Nachlass Frühjahr 1888, 14 [186]; KGW VIII 3, 165f.
[11] Nachlass Herbst 1885—Herbst 1886, 2 [87]; KGW VIII 1, 102: "Alle Einheit ist nur als Organisation und Zusammenspiel Einheit: nicht anders als wie ein menschliches Gemeinwesen eine Einheit ist: also Gegensatz der atomistischen Anarchie; somit ein Herrschafts-Gebilde, das Eins bedeutet, aber nicht eins ist." Cf. Müller-Lauter, p. 33: "Nietzsches Rede von der Vielheit der Willen zur Macht geht nicht von fixen Ein-heiten aus."
[12] Cf. Müller-Lauter, p. 22: "Das Spannungsverhältnis der dynamischen Quanten zu-einander macht ihr 'Wesen' aus. Sie bestehen nicht erst für sich, um dann in ein Verhältnis zu geraten. Sie sind nur in der (unaufhörlich wechselnden) Bezogenheit aller auf alle. Die Spannung innerhalb des Beziehungsfeldes resultiert aus dem Gegeneinander der Quanten."

permutations might easily be extended[13]. Let us regard a human being as a rather complex power-constellation for the moment, made up not only of individual cells, organs, etc. but possessing a consciousness and psyche which comprise a number of dissimilar and often antagonistic affects.

> Was *gemeinsam* ist: die herrschenden Triebe wollen auch als höchste Werth-Instanzen überhaupt, ja als schöpferische und regierende Gestalten betrachtet werden. Es versteht sich, dass diese Triebe sich gegenseitig entweder anfeinden oder unterwerfen (synthetisch auch wohl binden) oder in der Herrschaft wechseln. Ihr tiefer Antagonismus ist aber so gross, dass wo sie alle Befriedigung wollen, ein Mensch von tiefer Mittelmässigkeit zu denken ist.[14]

Let this example serve as a model for the general structure and internal order of a power-constellation.

No matter what type of collective power-group the power-quanta enter into, Nietzsche emphasizes that each quantum remains that primordial will to increase its own power, and at the expense of other power-quanta. Within a power-constellation, this will to increase power might be held in check by the equal and opposed drives of the other component quanta, and the will to power of the whole directed "outward" toward other power-groups, so that it might appear that, relative to "external" power-groups, the component quanta of a "Machtkonstellation" do not encroach upon one another. Yet within the collective, each quantum would readily dominate and control the whole if it could, if a disruption of the equilibrium of the whole were to occur. The point here is that the will to dominate, assimilate, control — the will to power — is the primordial characteristic of all that exists. Whether individually or in combination, the quanta of the will to power *are* this fundamental urge, and are continuously locked in combat with one another for more power. The motive energy back of all phenomena is this struggle of the quanta of will to power to increase and enhance their own power; the ever-changing phenomena of the world around us are ultimately the result (i. e., an interpretation) of the mutal aggression of power-quanta and -constellations, and shifts or realignments of power-centers[15]. Reconciling the power-quanta to one another, within Nietzsche's model, would be tantamount to negating reality.

---

[13] The similarity to the various types of government (or personality types) which these various types of power configuration display is not at all gratuitous. Cf. Nachlass Frühjahr 1888, 14 [81]; KGW VIII 3, 53: "Der Wille zur Accumulation von Kraft als spezifisch für das Phänomen des Lebens, für Ernährung, Zeugung, Vererbung, für Gesellschaft, Staat, Sitte, Autorität ... sollten wir diesen Willen nicht als bewegende Ursache auch in der Chemie annehmen dürfen? und in der kosmischen Ordnung?"
[14] Nachlass Ende 1886—Frühjahr 1887, 7 [3]; KGW VIII 1, 265. Cf. note 13, above.
[15] Cf. Müller-Lauter, p. 30.

Der Grad von Widerstand und der Grad von Übermacht — darum handelt
⟨es⟩ sich bei allem Geschehen: wenn wir, zu unserem Hausgebrauch der
Berechnung, das in Formeln von „Gesetzen" auszudrücken wissen, um so
besser für uns! Aber wir haben damit keine „Moralität" in die Welt gelegt,
dass wir sie ⟨als⟩ gehorsam fingiren —
Ein Machtquantum ist durch die Wirkung, die es übt und der es widersteht,
bezeichnet. Es fehlt die Adiaphorie: die an sich denkbar wäre. Es ist essentiell
ein Wille zur Vergewaltigung und sich gegen Vergewaltigung zu wehren.
Nicht Selbsterhaltung: jedes Atom wirkt in das ganze Sein hinaus, — es ist
weggedacht, wenn man diese Strahlung von Machtwillen wegdenkt. Deshalb
nenne ich es ein Quantum „Wille zur Macht": damit ist der Charakter ausgedrückt, der aus der mechanischen Ordnung nicht weggedacht werden kann,
ohne sie selbst wegzudenken.[16]

We must not be misled into thinking that Nietzsche attempts to establish
a mechanistic world-view based on power-quanta and the various combinations into which these quanta may enter. In fact, in the *Nachlass* fragment
of which a portion was just quoted, Nietzsche criticizes the physicists of
his day precisely for making such an attempt. The internal structure of
the will to power is not rigid and mechanistic, but plastic and fluid. The
terms "Machtquantum" and "Machtkonstellation" are perhaps reminiscent
of mechanistic physics, but Nietzsche also frequently uses the term
"Kraftcentrum" to designate a specific instance of the will to power.
"Kraftcentrum" could, of course, mean either a power-quantum or power-
constellation, but Nietzsche's use of the more inclusive and ambiguous
terms is an indication that he is not attempting to lay down ironclad
mechanistic principles, or attempting to force a rigid, static conceptual
framework upon a dynamic reality.

It is of no great consequence, ultimately, exactly how we think of the
individual cases of the will to power, whether as power-quanta,
constellations, centers, complexes, aggregates, etc. What is of greatest
importance, however, is this: each power-center (quantum, constellation,
whatever) is irreconcilably opposed to every other power-center, and
regardless of what configurations these power-centers may occur in, this
unrelenting will to ever more power is the brute fact of that world which
is the case.

Was ist „passiv"? widerstehen und reagiren. Gehemmt sein in der vorwärts-
greifenden Bewegung: also ein Handeln des Widerstandes und der Reaktion

Was ist „aktiv"? nach Macht ausgreifend . . .[17]

---

[16] Nachlass Frühjahr 1888, 14 [79]; KGW VIII 3, 49f.
[17] Nachlass Sommer 1886—Herbst 1887, 5 [64]; KGW VIII 1, 213.

For Nietzsche, the world *is* this chaotic flux of mutually opposed power-centers, with each power-center acting upon every other power-center. The characteristics which the things in the world have are a function of the degree of will to power which they represent and the relationships which they have to all other quanta. All qualities, all "Wesen," etc. are dynamic and relational. What something "is" is dependent upon how it acts upon other power-centers, and is in turn acted upon by them.

> Die Eigenschaften eines Dings sind Wirkungen auf andere „Dinge": denkt man andere „Dinge" weg, so hat ein Ding keine Eigenschaften d. h. es giebt kein Ding ohne andere Dinge d. h. es giebt kein „Ding an sich".[18]

It should be remembered that the quanta of the will to power are not, strictly speaking, things which act. Rather, they are themselves pure activity. A "thing" could be defined only by the sum total of its relationships, and were one to prescind from these relationships, there would be nothing left[19]. This will undoubtedly be familiar to the reader from our earlier discussion of Nietzsche's rejection of the subject-object, actor-act distinction, and his fundamental identification of a thing with the sum total of its activities[20]. Any attempt to exhaustively define a thing by cataloging all its relationships would naturally be a futile undertaking in such a totally dynamic and ever-changing system, and Nietzsche does not attempt it. This model of what would constitute an adequate definition of a thing serves as a "Grenzbegriff" and not as a methodological tool.

The world is different for each power-center, as it struggles to increase its own will to power and situate itself more advantageously with respect to other power-centers:

> ... jedes Kraftcentrum hat für den ganzen Rest seine Perspektive d. h. seine ganz bestimmte Werthung, seine Aktions-Art, seine Widerstandsart
> Die „scheinbare Welt" reduzirt sich als⟨o⟩ auf eine spezifische Art von Aktion auf die Welt ausgehend von einem Centrum
> Nun giebt es gar keine andere Art Aktion: und die „Welt" ist nur ein Wort für das Gesamtspiel dieser Aktionen

[18] Nachlass Herbst 1885—Herbst 1886, 2 [85]; KGW VIII 1, 102.
[19] Cf. Nachlass Frühjahr 1888, 14 [122]; KGW VIII 3, 95: "Die Forderung einer adäquaten Ausdrucksweise ist unsinnig: es liegt im Wesen einer Sprache, eines Ausdrucksmittels, eine blosse Relation auszudrücken ... Der Begriff 'Wahrheit' ist widersinnig ... das ganze Reich von 'wahr' 'falsch' bezieht sich nur auf Relationen zwischen Wesen, nicht auf das 'An sich' ... Unsinn: es giebt kein 'Wesen an sich', die Relationen constituiren erst Wesen, so wenig es eine 'Erkenntniss an sich' geben kann ..."
[20] Nachlass Frühjahr 1888, 14 [79]; KGW VIII 3, 50: "Es giebt kein Gesetz: jede Macht zieht in jedem Augenblick ihre letzte Consequenz. Gerade, dass es kein mezzo termine giebt, darauf beruht die Berechenbarkeit."

> Die Realität besteht exakt in dieser Partikulär-Aktion und Reaktion jedes
> Einzelnen gegen das Ganze . . .[21]

This is the basis for Nietzsche's perspectivism. A thing or power-center is
not limited to any specific essence or univocal nature: what a thing is, is
determined by its actions and reactions with regard to other power-centers,
and these power-relationships are subject to constant change[22]. A sufficiently
strong power-center could, by situating itself more advantageously toward
other power-centers, become something quite different from what it previously was. Also, a specific power-center may very well be something
different for each and every power-center, which relate to and act upon it
from their own particular lattice of power-relationships. In each case, the
degree of will to power determines what a thing is, and how it relates to
other power-groups or -quanta. There is no a priori nature or essence to
predetermine what a power-center shall be, or in what manner it shall
relate to other power-configurations. For Nietzsche, the world

> . . . ist essentiell Relations-Welt: sie hat, unter Umständen, von jedem Punkt
> aus ihr verschiedenes Gesicht: ihr Sein ist essentiell an jedem Punkte anders:
> sie drückt auf jeden Punkt, es widersteht ihr jeder Punkt — und diese Summi-
> rungen sind in jedem Falle gänzlich incongruent.
> Das Mass von Macht bestimmt, welches Wesen das andre Mass von Macht hat:
> unter welcher Form, Gewalt, Nöthigung es wirkt oder widersteht . . .[23]

It would seem that Nietzsche is describing a purely quantitative world,
since he reduces everything to will to power, and all differences between
things to differences in "das Mass von Macht." Yet this should not be
thought of as a static, dogmatic reduction of everything to quantity in the
mechanistic sense. Descartes' vision of the external world as pure *extensio*,
i. e. his reduction of the physical world to purely quantative characteristics
(or primary qualities) might be regarded as an extreme example of this
sort of mechanistic reductionism, but this is not at all what Nietzsche
intends[24]. Nevertheless, how are we to account for qualitative differences
within a system wherein all differences are reducible to differences in the
quantity (or degree) of will to power?

---

[21] Nachlass Frühjahr 1888, 14 [184]; KGW VIII 3, 163.
[22] Nachlass Herbst 1887, 10 [202]; KGW VIII 2, 246: "Das 'Ding an sich' widersinnig.
    Wenn ich alle Relationen, alle 'Eigenschaften' alle 'Thätigkeiten' eines Dinges weg-
    denke, so bleibt nicht das Ding übrig: weil Dingheit erst von uns hinzufingirt ist, aus
    logischen Bedürfnissen, also zum Zweck der Bezeichnung, der Verständigung . . .
    (zur Bindung jener Vielheit von Relat⟨ionen⟩ Eigenschaften Thätigkeiten)." Cf.
    Nachlass Herbst 1887, 9 [40]; KGW VIII 2, 17.
[23] Nachlass Frühjahr 1888, 14 [93]; KGW VIII 3. 63.
[24] See René Descartes, *Principles of Philosophy*, *Meditations* VI.

Sollten nicht alle Quantitäten Anzeichen von Qualitäten sein? Die grössere
Macht entspricht einem anderen Bewusstsein, Gefühl, Begehren, einem anderen
perspektivischen Blick; Wachsthum selbst ist ein Verlangen, mehr zu sein;
aus einem quale heraus erwächst das Verlangen nach einem Mehr von Quantum; in einer rein quantitativen Welt wäre alles todt, starr, unbewegt. — Die
Reduktion aller Qualitäten auf Quantitäten ist Unsinn: was sich ergiebt, ist
dass eins und das andere beisammen steht, eine Analogie —[25]

The analogy Nietzsche refers to here is this: even though all the phenomena
of the world revolve around quantitative differences in will to power, the
human perspectives views these quantitative differences qualitatively.
We see colors, after all, and not differences in the vibratory frequency of
beams of light.

Die Qualitäten sind unsere unübersteiglichen Schranken; wir können durch
nichts verhindern, bloße Quantitäts-Differenzen als etwas von Quantität
Grundverschiedenes zu empfinden, nämlich als Qualitäten, die nicht mehr
auf einander reduzirbar sind.[26]

The apparent paradox here is essentially that same one faced by a physicist,
who describes the constitution of the world in terms of waves, particles,
fields, mathematical formulae, etc. which bear not the slightest resemblance
to anything in our experience, and are devoid of those qualities which we
observe in the world around us. I should like to point out, however, that
this does not imply that our qualitative perceptions of a "quantitative"
world are incorrect or otherwise mistaken. Quantitaties *are* qualities for us,
and this is simply another of our perspectival interpretations of the world[27].

Unser „Erkennen" beschränkt sich darauf, Quantitäten festzustellen d. h.
aber wir können durch nichts hindern, diese Quantitäts-Differenzen als
Qualitäten zu empfinden. Die Qualität ist eine perspektivische Wahrheit
für uns; kein „an sich".[28]

[25] Nachlass Herbst 1885—Herbst 1886, 2 [157]; KGW VIII 1, 140f.
[26] Nachlass Sommer 1886—Frühjahr 1887, 6 [14]; KGW VIII 1, 244.
[27] I should like to add that our traditional categories of *quantum* and *quale* are not
adequate to express what Nietzsche has in mind when referring to "Machtquanten"
or "das Mass von Macht." It would be unfair to maintain that Nietzsche is simply
applying the category of *quantum* (in the traditional paradigmatic sense) cavalier
fashion to all of reality. I would maintain that "stronger," in the sense in which
Nietzsche uses that term, could and does denote a quality, as well as a quantitative
difference.
[28] Nachlass Sommer 1886—Herbst 1887, 5 [36]; KGW VIII 1, 201. This section continues: "Unsere Sinne haben ein bestimmtes Quantum als Mitte, innerhalb deren sie
funktioniren d. h. wir empfinden gross und klein im Verhältnis zu den Bedingungen
unsrer Existenz. Wenn wir unsere Sinne um das Zehnfache verschärften oder ver-
stumpften, würden wir zu Grunde gehn. D. h. wir empfinden auch Grössenverhält-
nisse in Bezug auf unsre Existenz-Ermöglichung als Qualitäten." Cf. Ornstein,
pp. 16—46.

II. Knowing as a Power Struggle

Hopefully the foregoing discussion will have made clear exactly what Nietzsche means by the quantification of the will to power, and dispel any notion that this reduction of everything to quanta of will to power involves a crude quantitative reduction in the mechanistic sense. Nevertheless, the world in the Nietzschean scheme of things is a system of relationships between power-quanta or power-centers, in which "Das Mass von Macht bestimmt, welches Wesen das andre Mass von Macht hat: unter welcher Form, Gewalt, Nöthigung es wirkt oder Widersteht...[29]" In other words, that quantity of will to power which a "Kraftcentrum" is, determines what the world is like with regard to it. As mentioned earlier, the world literally consists of power-relationships prevailing between various power-centers[30]. The greater the quantity of power which any particular power-center *is*, the more efficaciously it will be able to situate itself relative to other power-centers. Since things, objects, qualities, etc. are perspectival interpretations of power-relationships on the part of a specific "Kraftcentrum," any shift in the degree of power which that power-center is will occasion a change in its power-relationships and its subsequent interpretation of them. This cannot be stressed heavily enough, for it is one of the key concepts of Nietzsche's theory of knowledge. Things, subjects, objects, qualities, activities, etc. are all constituted through the perspectival interpretation of a "Machtverhältnis" on the part of a power-center. If the power of that "Kraftcentrum" changes — whether through growth or decline — its power relationships to and subsequent interpretations of the aforementioned things, objects, qualities, etc. will also change. This occasions a most literal and fundamental change in what the world is (not *appears to be*) for that particular power-center.

> Phänomenal ist also: die Einmischung des Zahlbegriffs, des Subjekt begriffs, des Bewegungsbegriffs: wir haben unser Auge, unsere Psychologie immer noch darin.
> Eliminiren wir diese Zuthaten: so bleiben keine Dinge übrig, sondern dynamische Quanta, in einem Spannungsverhältnis zu allen anderen dynamischen Quanten: deren Wesen in ihrem Verhältniss zu allen anderen Quanten besteht, in ihrem „Wirken" auf dieselben...[31]

The degree or amount of power which any particular "Kraftcentrum" is, is the sole determining factor for the nature of that world which is the case for that power-center. Since power-quanta and their relationships

[29] Nachlass Frühjahr 1888, 14 [93]; KGW VIII 3, 63.
[30] Nachlass Frühjahr 1888, 14 [184]; KGW VIII 3, 162f. Cf. Müller-Lauter, p. 30f.
[31] Nachlass Frühjahr 1888, 14 [79]; KGW VIII 3, 51.

with one another are constantly shifting and changing, the world of any power-center is equally subject to constant change. Within the framework of the will to power, there are no stable states, no facts, no constants, no laws of nature, no absolute entities or principles. Everything is radically dynamic, and all phenomena are constituted out of constantly shifting power states[32].

There are no facts, if by a fact we mean a state of affairs or proposition about a state of affairs which is supposed to be univocally and identically true for all observers.

> Es gibt keine unmittelbaren Thatsachen! Es steht mit Gefühlen und Gedanken ebenso: indem ich mir ihrer bewusst werde, mache ich einen Auszug, eine Vereinfachung, einen Versuch der Gestaltung: das eben ist bewusst werden: ein ganz *aktives* Zurechtmachen.[33]

In place of facts, what we have are interpretations from our own perspective, interpretations whose single aim is to place us into the most advantageous power position with regard to other power-centers. And, as power configurations are constantly realigning themselves (each component quantum in a configuration trying to dominate the other quanta and increase its own power), there are no stable, univocal, or identical states for a statement of fact to be about.

Neither are there laws or principles according to which these power struggles must take place[34]. A law or principle, in the traditionally paradigmatic sense, implies that phenomena must occur in a certain manner, they they take place under some external constraint or necessity. But for Nietzsche, there is no constraint or necessity governing the behavior of power-quanta, nor are there external principles governing their actions. The power-quanta *are* at each instant precisely what they do.

> ... entfernen wir hier die zwei populären Begriffe „Nothwendigkeit" und „Gesetz": das erste legt einen falschen Zwang, das zweite eine falsche Freiheit in die Welt. „Die Dinge" betragen sich nicht regelmässig, nicht nach einer Regel: es giebt keine Dinge (— das ist unsere Fiktion) sie betragen sich ebensowenig unter einem Zwang von Nothwendigkeit. Hier wird nicht gehorcht: denn dass etwas so ist, wie es ist, so stark, so schwach, das ist nicht die Folge

---

[32] Nachlass Sommer 1886—Herbst 1887, 5 [36]; KGW VIII 1, 201.
   Nachlass Sommer 1886—Frühjahr 1887, 6 [14]; KGW VIII 1, 244.
   Nachlass Frühjahr 1888, 14 [184]; KGW VIII 3, 162f.
[33] Nachlass Sommer—Herbst 1884, 26 [114]; KGW VII 2, 177f.
[34] Cf. Nachlass Frühjahr 1884, 25 [427]; KGW VII 2, 121: "Alle unsere mechanischen Gesetze sind aus uns, nicht aus den Dingen! Wir construiren nach ihnen die 'Dinge'. Die Synthese "Ding" stammt von uns: alle Eigenschaften des Dinges von uns. "Wirkung und Ursache" ist eine Verallgemeinerung unseres Gefühls und Urtheils."

eines Gehorchens oder einer Regel oder eines Zwanges ... Es giebt kein Gesetz: jede Macht zieht in jedem Augenblick ihre letzte Consequenz. Gerade, dass es kein mezzo termine giebt, darauf beruht die Berechenbarkeit.[35]

It might be objected that Nietzsche's claim that the quanta of the will to power are constantly striving to increase or enhance their power is nothing other than a thinly-disguised "law of nature" in the best (or worst) post-enlightenment sense. However, it will be remembered that the power-quanta do not, strictly speaking, discharge this activity as an agent performs an act. Nor do they function according to some external principle or necessity. The will to power *is* this struggle, this drive for more power, for growth and domination and, if we press the point, we must conclude that a power-center acts at any given instant according to what it is, and is any any given instant precisely what it does. Activity, essence, and existence are identical for Nietzsche, and the distinctions which we draw between them are purely linguistic (i. e., non-referential) and interpretative. The only law or principle which a quantum of will to power "follows" is the "law" of its own "nature," this nature being something different from any other perspective and constantly undergoing change. Since a law or principle cannot constantly change while remaining a "law" (and certainly not change in the radical and fundamental sense in which Nietzsche views change), we see that the traditional categories of law or principle are inapplicable to the dynamism of the will to power except in a metaphorical, interpretative sense[36].

Our discussion up to this point has been concerned with the quantification of the will to power and the interrelationships of these quanta, i. e. we have been discussing the will to power in terms of its individual instances. Yet, as was indicated in the last chapter, there is nothing ultimate or inviolate about individuality, and Nietzsche regards the concept of individuality itself as simply another of our perspectival vanities. This, however, raises another difficulty with regard to our overall characterization of the will to power.

Nietzsche himself characterizes the will to power as a continual struggle to become more, to become greater and increasingly powerful. Struggle ("Kampf"), of course, is meaningless unless there exists something to

---

[35] Nachlass Frühjahr 1888, 14 [79]; KGW VIII 3, 49f.

[36] Cf. Müller-Lauter, p. 21: "Nietzsche verwirft daher alle Worte, sofern mit ihnen der Anspruch des Begriffes erhoben wird, und gebraucht sie lediglich als 'Zeichen'! Sie sollen auf Sachverhalte nur *hinweisen*. Man muss diesem ihren Hinweisungscharakter folgen, man darf sich nicht auf sie versteifen, man muss das 'Begriffliche' hinter sich lassen, um zu dem zu gelangen, was 'wirklich' vorhanden ist." See Chapter V.

struggle *against*[37]. The necessary opposition is provided by the mutual antagonism of the quanta of the will to power. Expressed somewhat more simply, in order for the will to power to be what Nietzsche says it is, viz. a struggle, there must be things which struggle against one another. The difficulty arises when we attempt to give these struggling entities any positive characterization[38]. The will to power cannot be a uniform, homogeneous totality, because the tension of opposites would then be lacking, which tension is the will to power. On the other hand, Nietzsche does not wish to develop an atomistic-mechanistic world-view in which everything is accounted for by the interactions of identical, though opposed, ultimate entities. The "Machtquanten" may, for Nietzsche, merge, divide, combine, relate, etc. according to their degree of power, and their character, their individuality, is something which may be altered at any instant[39]. Nietzsche's model requires constant struggle, opposition, and competition for his characterization of the will to power. Yet he denies to the strugglers and competitors that inviolate self-identity and self-interest which we would regard as *sine qua non* for the type of struggle mentioned earlier. And yet,

> Alle unsere bewussten Motive sind Oberflächen-Phänomene: hinter ihnen steht der Kampf unserer Triebe und Zustände, der Kampf um die Gewalt.[40]

In the last analysis it would not be completely accurate to regard the quanta of will to power as discrete "individuals" (except in a perspectival, relational sense) acting out of "self-interest." It is not, strictly speaking, an individual power-center (*qua* ultimate entity) which struggles to increase and enhance its own power; rather, it is the will to power *as such* which expresses and discharges itself through what appears to be a particular quantum or configuration of power-centers[41]. The will to power struggles against "itself," and the aggressions and power plays mentioned above

---

[37] Cf. Nachlass Herbst 1887, 9 [151]; KGW VIII 2, 88: "Der Wille zur Macht kann sich nur an Widerständen äussern; er sucht nach dem, was ihm widersteht . . . ."

[38] Cf. Müller-Lauter, p. 15: "Dem genaueren Zusehen zeigt sich nämlich, dass Nietzsche allein jede *als absolut* verstandene Gegensätzlichkeit bestreitet, in der für sich bestehende, in sich beruhende Seiende unvermittelt einander gegenüberstehen sollen. Wohl aber behauptet er eine immanente Gegensätzlichkeit der Weltwirklichkeit . . . . Die wirklichen Gegensätze, die sein Philosophieren zugesteht, sollen einander nicht ausschliessen, sie sollen von einander abgeleitet werden können."

[39] Cf. Nachlass Herbst 1885—Herbst 1886, 2 [87]; KGW VIII 1, 102: "Alle Einheit ist nur als Organisation und Zusammenspiel Einheit: nicht anders als wie ein menschliches Gemeinwesen eine Einheit ist: also Gegensatz der atomistischen Anarchie; somit ein Herrschafts-Gebilde, das Eins bedeutet, aber nicht eins ist." Cf. also Nachlass Herbst 1887, 9 [98]; KGW VIII 2, 55f.

[40] Nachlass Herbst 1885—Frühjahr 1886, 1 [20]; KGW VIII 1, 11.

[41] Nachlass November 1887—März 1888, 11 [74]; KGW VIII 2, 278f.

might be looked upon as arising out of the fundamental tension of opposites, out of the dynamic "Spannungsverhältnis" which characterizes the
will to power as both one and many[42].

> Wie entsteht die perspektivische Sphäre und der Irrthum? Insofern, vermöge
> eines organischen Wesens, sich nicht ein Wesen, sondern der Kampf selber
> erhalten will, wachsen will und sich bewusst sein will.
>
> Das, was wir „Bewusstsein" und „Geist" nennen, ist nur ein Mittel und Werk-
> zeug, vermöge dessen nicht ein Subjekt, sondern ein Kampf sich erhalten
> will.[43]

III. The Constructing of Reality

We must now turn to a consideration of what this primordial tension,
this mutual opposition of power-quanta, has to do with the cognitive
process. In view of the various ways in which this problematic has been
approached in the previous chapters, we may now venture a comprehensive and definitive conclusion as to what knowing ultimately is for
Nietzsche.

The cognitive process is not a means of acquiring "knowledge" but is,
quite simply, a means of gaining power[44]. The world, for Nietzsche, is a
system of power relationships. Each power-center *is* the sum total of its
relationships with other power-centers. From the perspective of any given
power-center, any change or realignment in its sum total of power relationships occasions a corresponding change in the nature of its world (because
world = sum total of power relationships). Each power-center continually
attempts to put itself into the most favorable position with regard to
all other power-centers[45]. This process of setting one's self into the most
favorable (i. e. strongest) position is what Nietzsche refers to as perspectival
interpretation or constructive falsification.

> Erkenntniss: die Ermöglichung der Erfahrung, dadurch dass das wirkliche
> Geschehen, sowohl auf Seiten der einwirkenden Kräfte, als auf Seiten unserer
> gestaltenden, ungeheuer vereinfacht wird: so dass es ähnliche und gleiche
> Dinge zu geben scheint. Erkenntniss ist *Fälschung* des Vielartigen und Unzähl-

---

[42] See Müller-Lauter, pp. 10—33. Cf. GA XVI, 113.

[43] GA XIII, 71.

[44] Knowledge is here to be taken in the traditional, paradigmatic sense of *adequatio intellectu et rei*. See Chapter III.

[45] GA X, 152: "Alles Erkennen ist ein Messen an einem Massstabe. Ohne einen Massstab, d. h. ohne jede Beschränkung, giebt es kein Erkennen. So steht es im Bereiche
der intellektuellen Formen ebenso, wie wenn ich nach dem Werthe des Erkennens
überhaupt frage: ich muss irgendeine Position nehmen, die höher steht oder die
wenigstens fest ist, um als Massstab zu dienen." Cf. GA XII, 241: "Erkennen, das
heisst: alle Dinge zu unserem Besten verstehen."

baren zum Gleichen, Ähnlichen, Abzählbaren. Also ist Leben nur vermöge
eines solchen Fälschungs-Apparates möglich. Denken ist ein fälschendes Umgestalten, Fühlen ist ein fälschendes Umgestalten, Wollen ist ein fälschendes
Umgestalten —: in dem Allen liegt die Kraft der Assimiliaton: welche vor-
aussetzt einen Willen, etwas gleich zu machen.[46]

We must think of each power-center as existing within a complex field of
interlocking power relationships, as acting upon all other power-centers
and being acted upon in turn. If a power-center such as a human being
were to be actively aware of the maze of forces acting upon it, the result
would be an epistemological chaos. Such a power-center therefore directs
the bulk of its energies upon those foreign power-configurations which
have the most immediate bearing upon its power state. This is done by
simplifying and interpreting, i. e. falsifying, the maze of hostile forces
which confronts the power-center in the manner most favorable to the
growth and enhancement of its power.

> Der interpretative Charakter alles Geschehens. Es giebt kein Ereignis an sich.
> Was geschieht, ist eine Gruppe von Erscheinungen ausgelesen und zusammen-
> gefasst von einem interpretirenden Wesen.[47]

Or again:

> Das ganze der organischen Welt ist die Aneinanderfädelung von Wesen mit
> erdichteten kleinen Welten um sich: indem sie ihre Kraft, ihre Begierden,
> ihre Gewohnheiten in den Erfahrungen ausser sich heraus setzen, als ihre
> Aussenwelt. Die Fähigkeit zum Schaffen (Gestalten, Erfinden, Erdichten) ist
> ihre Grundfähigkeit: von sich selber haben sie natürlich ebenfalls nur eine
> solche falsche erdichtete vereinfachte Vorstellung.[48]

We have seen in previous chapters how the cognitive process involves
perspectival falsification, interpretation, simplification, etc. In Chapter I
and the first section of this chapter, we have seen that, for Nietzsche, the
world is a complex maze of power relationships and that, from the perspective of any given power-center, when its system of power relationships
changes, the world in which it exists undergoes a corresponding alteration
of character. The two seemingly divergent positions coalesce at precisely
this point: perspectival falsification, interpretation, etc. is exactly that
activity, characteristic of any power-center, of always seeking to place

---

[46] Nachlass April—Juni 1881, KGW VII 3, 226.
[47] Nachlass Herbst 1885—Frühjahr 1886, 1 [115]; KGW VIII 1, 34. Cf. Nachlass Frühjahr 1884, 25 [116]; KGW VII 2, 40.
[48] Nachlass April—Juni 1885, 34 [247]; KGW VII 3, 223.

itself in the most favorable position of power with regard to all other power-centers.

> Erkennen heisst „sich in Bedingung setzen zu etwas": sich durch etwas bedingt fühlen . . . es ist also unter allen Umständen ein Feststellen Bezeichnen Bewusstmachen von Bedingungen (*nicht* ein Ergründen von Wesen, Dingen, „Ansichs") . . .[49]

The primordial reality of any cognitive act is a "setting oneself into relationship to something else." This activity *is* interpretation, *is* perspectival falsification. It *is* that process which constitutes and characterizes the world relative to any given power-center.

Nietzsche's grounds for asserting this "setting oneself into relationship to something" ("sich in Bedingung setzen zu etwas") to be falsification as well have been sufficiently dealt with in Chapters II and IV and require no further elaboration here. However, this active relational process is also interpretative, synthetic, and creative, and this point must be worked out in greater detail.

An object or thing (or in traditional epistemological language, a phenomenon or "Erscheinung") is constituted within the perspectival sphere of any given power-quantum in the following manner: out of the maze of hostile forces surrounding it, a power-center synthetically binds these stimuli together and bestows (i. e. interprets) upon this artificial synthesis that meaning or significance which best serves to increase or enhance its own power. This, as Vaihinger points out, sounds distinctly Kantian[50]. There is, however, a major difference between Nietzsche and Kant here. For Nietzsche, this perspectival interpretation *is* the object: there is no object apart from the interpretation. The perspectival interpretation is not *of* something or *about* something. Power-quanta and their interrelationships are not "things": things are perspectival interpretations on the part of the power-quanta. For Nietzsche, the activity of perspectival interpretation ("sich in Bedingung setzen zu etwas") and the object are identical: they are "the same thing."

> Ein „Ding an sich" ebenso verkehrt wie ein „Sinn an sich", eine „Bedeutung an sich". Es giebt keinen „Thatbestand an sich", sondern ein Sinn muss immer erst hineingelegt werden, damit es einen Thatbestand geben könne
> Das „was ist das?" ist eine Sinn-Setzung von etwas Anderem aus gesehen. Die „Essenz", die „Wesenheit" ist etwas Perspektivisches und setzt eine Vielheit schon voraus. Zu Grunde liegt immer „was ist das für mich?"[51]

[49] Nachlass Herbst 1885—Herbst 1886, 2 [154]; KGW VIII 1, 140.
[50] Vaihinger, loc. cit.
[51] Nachlass Herbst 1885—Herbst 1886, 2 [149]; KGW VIII 1, 138.

This creative, interpretative "sich in Bedingung setzen zu etwas" is limited or conditioned only by the amount of power which a "Kraftcentrum" represents. A power-center could conceivably mold and structure its world entirely *ad libitum*[52].

> Die „Dingheit" ist erst von uns geschaffen. Die Frage ist, ob es nicht noch viele Art⟨en⟩ geben könnte, eine solche scheinbare Welt zu schaffen — und ob nicht dieses Schaffen, Logisiren, Zurechtmachen, Fälschen die bestgarantirte Realität selbst ist: kurz, ob nicht das, was „Dinge setzt", allein real ist; und ob nicht die „Wirkung der äußeren Welt auf uns" auch nur die Folge solcher wollenden Subjekte ist ... die anderen „Wesen" agiren auf uns; unsere zurechtgemachte Scheinwelt ist eine Zurechtmachung und Überwältigung von deren Aktionen; eine Art Defensiv-Maassregel.[53]

On the basis of Nietzsche's equation of the activity of interpretation with the object of interpretation, we must conclude that the act of cognition (i. e. "sich in Bedingung setzen zu etwas") is entirely creative, and that the world, for any power-center, is a product of its own perspectival activity.

> Schaffen — als Auswählen und Fertig-machen des Gewählten. (Bei jedem Willensakte ist dies das Wesentliche).[54]

Creation here does not mean creation *ex nihilo*. For Nietzsche, a thing, object, quality, etc. is constituted within the sphere of perspectival activity of a power-center. What or how anything is, is a function of this activity and, as we have seen, there can be no thing apart from an interpretative act. Thus the interpretative-cognitive act is entirely creative: not only is this act responsible for its contents — it is also identical with them. The "external world" is not something simply and univocally present, apart from any observer. It is a function of that activity of perspectival interpretation and falsification through which each power-center actively structures and creates its own world.

> Die Umkehrung der Zeit: wir glauben die Aussenwelt als Ursache ihrer Wirkung auf uns, aber wir haben ihre thatsächliche und unbewusst verlaufende Wirkung erst zur Aussenwelt verwandelt: das, als was sie uns gegenüber steht, ist unser Werk, das nun auf uns zurückwirkt. Es braucht Zeit, bevor sie fertig ist: aber diese Zeit ist so klein.[55]

It need scarcely be mentioned that "the world" may be a very different place from the perspectives of different power-centers.

[52] Nachlass Herbst 1885—Herbst 1886, 2 [152]; KGW VIII 1, 139.
[53] Nachlass Herbst 1887, 9 [106]; KGW VIII 2, 60.
[54] GA XVI, 128.
[55] Nachlass Sommer—Herbst 1884, 26 [44]; KGW VII 2, 157.

Nonetheless it might be objected that a power-quantum can do nothing to alter the *quantitative* force of those other quanta which act upon it, except in a mitigated sense by altering its relationship to them. If one were to accept this objection, it would transform Nietzsche's model into nothing more than another version of the traditional realistic notion of a world "out there" over which we exercise only very limited control. If this is the case, is not Nietzsche's notion of the world as a maze of interlocking power-configurations simply another expression of the traditional view of an objective and independent external world, to which our knowledge must correspond?

No, it is not. If the will to power were an *ens metaphysicum*, if the quanta of the will to power were ultimate, inviolate entities, this argument might hold. But these quanta are, strictly speaking, units of activity which are dynamically related to all other units of the same activity, as aspects of the fundamental will to power. Thus, the distinction between subject and object or appearance and reality — which are necessary presuppositions of that traditional cognitive paradigm in which the world is held to be objective and independent of the perceiver, and in which knowledge is conceived as *adequatio* — is inapplicable to Nietzsche's model: such distinctions, as well as that entire cognitive paradigm of which they are a part, are interpretative falsifications carried out within the perspectival sphere of a particular power-configuration, and have validity only within a specific interpretative scheme. Having demonstrated the self-referential inconsistency of this correspondence paradigm, Nietzsche can reject this view as a fiction which is no longer useful. He can therefore claim — and with complete consistency — that there is no external world which acts upon us. The "external world" *is* our activity upon, and interrelationships with, all other power-centers[56]. It could be maintained that "I" am my "external world," since I am identical with my interpretative, creative activity[57]. But we see that in such a statement of identity, the concept "external" becomes superfluous and irrelevant.

[56] Nachlass Herbst 1885—Herbst 1886, 2 [143]; KGW VIII 1, 135.
Nachlass Herbst 1887, 9 [40]; KGW VIII 2, 17.
Nachlass Frühjahr 1888, 14 [79]; KGW VIII 3, 49 ff.
Nachlass Frühjahr 1888, 14 [93]; KGW VIII 3, 62 f.
Nachlass Frühjahr 1888, 14 [122]; KGW VIII 3, 93 ff.
Nachlass Frühjahr 1888, 14 [184]; KGW VIII 3, 162 f.
Nachlass Frühjahr 1888, 14 [184]; KGW VIII 3, 165 f.
[57] Nachlass Juni—Juli 1885, 36 [26]; KGW VII 3, 286.
Nachlass Herbst 1885—Herbst 1886, 2 [83]; KGW VIII 1, 99 ff.
Nachlass Herbst 1885—Herbst 1886, 2 [193]; KGW VIII 1, 160.
Nachlass Herbst 1887, 9 [91]; KGW VIII 2, 47 ff.
Nachlass Frühjahr 1888, 14 [98]; KGW VIII 3, 66 ff.

Within the dynamism of power-quanta, however, if a quantum of inferior strength is confronted by one of superior strength, it cannot arbitrarily negate the superior (and opposing) force. We have already seen in Chapter I what may occur where this power difference is great. Within the sphere of organic life, for example, a superior degree of power represented by, e. g. an animal, may simply overwhelm and engulf an inferior degree of power, e. g. a plant, in the form of nourishment. Where the power differences are not so great, however, we may observe the process of perspectival interpretation as a means of increasing or enhancing one's power by favorably interpreting opposing forces. This is what I referred to in Chapter VII as cognitional control. Let the following examples serve as illustrations of how such cognitional control might take place.

Let us imagine a man locked in a room behind a massive wooden door. Now, the man in question might interpret the door as an obstacle which restricts his freedom. This interpretation transforms the door into a representation of hostile forces, and involves a decrease of the man's will to power. However, he might interpret the door in a positive, power-enhancing manner by regarding it as a friendly barrier which protects him by preventing hostile forces from entering the room and injuring him. In this case, the man would have achieved cognitional control of the door by transforming it into an object which is useful in enhancing and increasing his feeling of power.

Or again: let us imagine a scenario in which the power-centers are one of our primitive paleolithic ancestors, and a sharp stone. Our ancestor might a) totally ignore the stone; b) interpret it in a power-decreasing manner as an injurious object, avoid it, and take care not to tread upon it; or c) give it a positive interpretation by cognitively transforming the stone into a tool or weapon, thereby not only gaining power over the stone itself, but also over hostile animals etc.[58].

These examples, simplistic as they are, do not claim to be anything more than analogies of how the process of constructive falsification, i. e. perspectival interpretation, functions as a means of increasing power through an interpretative restructuring of reality (i. e. one's power relationships). Naturally this interpretative construction of the world is a vastly more fundamental process than any semantic quibbling over whether one's

[58] Probably a better example of such cognitional control is Nietzsche's analysis of the origin of our moral views. The view he puts forth in GM is that those vital values which had initially been regarded as good, were reinterpreted by the weak and impotent (viz. the bad) as evil. At first glance, such a cognitive reinterpretation might appear to be rather minor. Yet I doubt that anyone would seriously question the vast impact this shift has had upon our entire tradition.

glass is half full or half empty. The examples given already presuppose an interpretative sphere of perspectival falsification, and are illustrations of how such a sphere is constituted only in a very limited and analogous sense[59]. Even those psychological activities which we normally regard as responsible for carrying out this perspectival falsification are themselves perspectival falsifications. Knowing, thinking, feeling, etc. are all secondary phenomena, i. e. they are already interpretations of power relationships carried out "internally" by a power-center, from its own perspective. Relating to the "external world" takes place on a much more fundamental level than that of psychic phenomena[60].

Nietzsche's use of the word "Wille," however, might be easily misunderstood in a psychological sense. The will to power is not simply a type of wishing or desiring or demanding, and all of these activities are derivative of a more fundamental "will." The world is not constructed by the will to power merely by desiring or wishing that things should exist in a certain manner:

> „wollen" ist nicht „begehren", streben, verlangen: davon hebt es sich ab durch den Affekt des Commando's
> es giebt kein „wollen", sondern nur ein Etwas-wollen: man muss nicht das Ziel auslösen aus dem Zustand: wie es die Erkenntnisstheoretiker thun. „Wollen", wie sie es verstehn, kommt so wenig vor, wie „Denken": es ist eine reine Fiktion.
> dass Etwas befohlen wird, gehört zum Wollen (: damit ist natürlich nicht gesagt, daß der Wille „effektuirt" wird . . .)
> Jener allgemeine Spannungszustand, vermöge dessen eine Kraft nach Auslösung trachtet — ist kein „Wollen"[61]

The will to power, as creative activity, is intentional in nature: it always wills *something*, and the act of willing and that which is willed are identical. The world-creating will is not a feeble sort of wishing that things might be a certain way, but a potent and creative commanding which makes

---

[59] I would claim that historical examples of such a reinterpretation *cum* restructuring of the world are not lacking. Examples of this would be the radical reinterpretation of the world through Christianity, the Copernican revolution, the rise of dynamic psychology and psychoanalysis, relativity and quantum physics, etc. See Thomas Kuhn, op. cit. Such reinterpretations brought about significant changes in that world which is, for us, the case. In other words, the world became literally a different place as a result of these paradigm shifts: to claim that such reinterpretations amount only to new modes of looking at the same unchanging reality is untenable and an inconsistent position. Cf. Chapter III.

[60] Nachlass Frühjahr 1888, 14 [121]; KGW VIII 3, 92f.: " . . . Dass der Wille zur Macht die primitive Affekt-Form ist, dass alle anderen Affekte nur seine Ausgestaltungen sind . . . ."

[61] Nachlass November 1887—März 1888, 11 [114]; KGW VIII 2, 296.

things to be as they are. Will does not act upon physical objects, matter, intellect, etc. Will acts only upon will, and physical objects, matter, etc. are perspectival interpretations of this interaction[62]. Everything is an interpretation *of* will to power *by* will to power, although we must be careful not to misconstrue this as a subject-object relationship. We might, perhaps, be justified in maintaining that the process of world-constitution is a process of "self-interpretation" by the will to power.

> Man darf nicht fragen: „wer interpretirt denn?" sondern das Interpretiren selbst, als eine Form des Willens zur Macht, hat Dasein (aber nicht als ein „Sein", sondern als ein Prozess, ein Werden) als ein Affekt.[63]

> Die Entstehung der „Dinge" ist ganz und gar das Werk der Vorstellenden, Denkenden, Wollenden, Erfindenden. Der Begriff „Ding" selbst ebenso als alle Eigenschaften. — Selbst „das Subjekt" ist ein solches Geschaffenes, ein „Ding", wie alle Anderen: eine Vereinfachung, um die Kraft, welche setzt, erfindet, denkt, als solche zu bezeichnen, im Unterschiede von allem einzelnen Setzen, Erfinden, Denken selbst. Also das Vermögen im Unterschiede von allem Einzelnen bezeichnet . . .[64]

Nietzsche's mention of the intentionality of the will to power is, I think, simply another way of expressing that fundamental identification of actor with act, of subject with object, which has been emphasized throughout this book. It is on the basis of this fundamental identification that we may conclude our characterization of the will to power as an epistemological principle, which is the core of Nietzsche's theory of knowledge.

We have seen that the will to power is a world-creating principle which constructs the world, always relative to a particular "Kraftcentrum," through active, constructive, perspectival interpretation. Within Nietzsche's model, this activity takes the form of "sich in Bedingung setzen zu etwas" on the part of a particular power-center with regard to all the rest. Furthermore, this activity of perspectival interpretation is always identical with its "contents." There is no ultimate distinction between the two. This perspectival interpretation is carried out by quanta of will to power. These quanta, although they *are* will to power, are all opposed to one another and struggle against one another for more power. This tension of opposites is the fundamental characteristic of the will to power: all dynamic quanta are interrelated with all other quanta, and each seeks to grow more powerful at the expense of all the rest.

[62] JGB 36; KGW VI 2, 50—52.
[63] Nachlass Herbst 1885—Herbst 1886, 2 [151]; KGW VIII 1, 138.
[64] Nachlass Herbst 1885—Herbst 1886, 2 [152]; KGW VIII 1, 139.

The activity of interpretation *is* that process of "sich in Bedingung setzen zu etwas," of actively interrelating which, once again, is the activity of the power-quanta, and the power-quanta *are* that activity. Cognition is interpretation, is a "sich in Bedingung setzen zu etwas," is constructive falsification, and all of these activities *are* will to power. Indeed — knowing *is* power, *is* will to power.

It is hoped that this presentation has enabled the reader to locate our activity of knowing within that dynamism of opposites which is the will to power, and to understand somewhat more adequately what Nietzsche means when he asks,

> — wollt ihr einen Namen für diese Welt? Eine Lösung für alle ihre Räthsel? ein Licht auch für euch, ihr Verborgensten, Stärksten, Unerschrockensten, Mitternächtlichsten! — Diese Welt ist der Wille zur Macht — und nichts ausserdem! Und auch ihr selber seid dieser Wille zur Macht — und nichts ausserdem![65]

---

[65] Nachlass Juni—Juli 1885, 38 [12]; KGW VII 3, 339.

CHAPTER NINE

CONCLUSION

We have now reached the point where we must reflect upon what has been previously said. We must step outside the context of the will to power (insofar as that is even possible at this stage) and attempt to reach some conclusion with regard to the whole. I have been postponing until now a discussion of that final paradox which, throughout this work, has come more and more to the forefront, and which poses itself as the final question: If, as has been abundantly pointed out, there is no truth, if there are no facts, no stable world-order, if our world is nothing less than a matrix of perspectival interpretations and useful fictions, is not everything which Nietzsche says itself nothing more than an interpretation from his perspective?

A question of this nature naturally implies that there is something unsatisfactory about a "mere" interpretation, and can only be asked outside the context which has herein been developed, and I think that these points have been adequately dealt with in the body of this work. Yet if we demand an answer to this begged question, i. e., is what Nietzsche says itself not simply another interpretation?, the only possible answer is — of course!

> Gesetzt, dass auch dies nur Interpretation ist — und ihr werdet eifrig genug sein, dies einzuwenden — nun, um so besser. —[1]

Nietzsche attempts nothing less than to construct a radically new cognitive paradigm, a theory of knowledge which is free from the presuppositions, inconsistencies, and inflexibility of the tradition, a theory of knowledge which is flexible and creative in the most radical sense. Nietzsche's theory of knowledge is not simply another way of looking at the same old world: it represents a cognitive mode in which an entirely new world may be constituted, and do this in a manner entirely free from the traditional presupposition that there must ultimately be a single reality for everyone, which determines and conditions our perceptions. Nietzsche's epistemo-

---

[1] JGB 22; KGW VI 2, 31.

logical *modus operandi* is the notion of perspectival interpretation: the cognitive act is itself regarded as an act of interpretation, which in turn is an act of creation. Of far greater importance, however, is this: while regarding all knowing as perspectival interpretation, *this very position is itself an interpretation*. It is an interpretation which is decisively aware of its interpretative nature, and therein lies one of its chief advantages. Thus, Nietzsche's epistemological position, as I have been characterizing it, not only displays significant advantages over traditional epistemologies, but more importantly, constitutes a radically new and immensely fruitful cognitive paradigm. Nietzsche's theory of knowledge constitutes a self-grounding philosophical position which is subject only to internal verification, which presupposes nothing beyond itself, but which is neither empty nor trivial. How is this possible?

By demonstrating the self-referential inconsistency of the correspondence theory of truth, Nietzsche *a fortiori* demonstrates the untenability and inadequacy of traditional, correspondence-oriented epistemologies. But more than this, by undermining all correspondence criteria, Nietzsche frees himself from the onus of making his views correspond to some static, external reality. Nietzsche does indeed supply an ontological model to support his epistemology — the flux ontology of the will to power. Yet it would be a serious misunderstanding to view this as a claim on Nietzsche's part to have pierced the veil of appearances, and to have had a peep at the ultimate nature of things. Nietzsche not only rejects such a procedure outright — he also rejects that entire cognitive paradigm in which such a proceeding is even thinkable. If Nietzsche, after having denied the possibility of any stable, unchanging, correspondence sort of truth, were nevertheless to claim that his description of the world, i. e. the will to power, were true in a sense of which he has already denied the possibility, then we might justifiably dismiss his views as self-contradictory and incoherent scribblings. But I think that the groundwork has already been laid for answering such a charge.

The will to power as an ontological model is to be properly viewed from the perspective of Nietzsche's epistemology. If this is done, we realize that the will to power is not simply another claim to have discovered once and for all what reality is "really" like, but a model which is very useful in supporting the epistemological claim that there is no stable, perduring world *of* which we have knowledge. As a model, a construct, an hypothesis, Nietzsche's scheme of power-quanta and power-constellations is a considerable aid in grasping what the cognitive act must be like in the absence of fixed truth, stable entities, laws of nature, etc. Naturally, if all knowing is perspectival interpretation, the will to power itself must be such an interpretation, but an interpretation which has great utility in bringing more vividly before the mind, in enabling us to better grasp, that basic epistemological position, viz., that there are only interpretations. It is fundamentally erroneous (or better, a useless interpretation) to construe Nietzsche's flux ontology as a snapshot of ultimate reality. Nietzsche presents this model as a philosophical horizon over against which the doctrine of creative interpretation can be understood.

Does this not mean that after having denied the possibility of any adequate formulation of what the world is like in itself, Nietzsche nevertheless goes ahead and gives us such a formulation? Again, the question is, what status does Nietzsche's characterization of the world as will to power have? Certainly not the status of an unassailable, metaphysical truth. We must view the characterization of the world as will to power *as itself* a creative interpretation which serves to unify and direct the rest of our interpretations, analogous to a working hypothesis in the natural sciences. Its justification lies in how well we can employ it in increasing and enhancing our vital energies and elevating the human condition, not in how "true" or "correct" it is.

What the world might be like in itself is of no ultimate interest. Not only is such a question unanswerable on grounds of that correspondence-paradigm in which the question is framed, but that very context out of which such a question arises is, for Nietzsche, an interpretation which must be cast aside as no longer worth entertaining. The only factor even worth considering is, what is it for me? for us? And here Nietzsche's point is that what the world is, in the only sense in which that statement can be meaningful, is entirely our work, our doing, our responsibility. "There is no specific form or meaning without which we cannot live . . . . How we shall live, and what we shall mean, is up to us to say."[2] The world in and of itself cannot meaningfully be said to have a univocal character, although we (perhaps necessarily) posit one such as the will to power in order to unify and direct our interpretations. Thus, if were to ask Nietzsche, "Is what you say true?", the answer would be, "Of course not, for there is no truth." But insofar as all we have are interpretations which can only be measured according to how well they work in enriching, strengthening, and inspiring life, Nietzsche would undoubtedly assert with equal vigor, that his interpretation was the most useful to date.

We have elaborated Nietzsche's grounds for denying to other philosophical systems that sort of truth which they have been wont to claim for themselves. But Nietzsche does not make an exception for himself, and

[2] Danto, p. 228.

attempt to appropriate that truth, of which he denies the possibility, for himself while denying it to others. Nietzsche's philosophical stature stands revealed to us in all its rigor and honesty when we realize that Nietzsche's reduction of all other modes of philosophizing to interpretations and falsifications applies equally to his own thinking. The will to power *is* an interpretation, *is* a falsification, *is* a sublime illusion, and we need only add that Nietzsche would probably have maintained that it was so far the most efficacious interpretation advanced in enhancing and increasing the vital powers which we are. And this sovereign admission, far from claiming to be a philosophical *non plus ultra* is an open invitation — or better, a challenge — to yet more vigorous and more sublime fictions to elevate and transform the human condition. Even though Nietzsche often seems to be asserting his own doctrines with all the dogmatism of those whom he condemns, this must be understood on the basis of his own criteria, and not condemned out of hand through the application of those very standards which Nietzsche himself has overcome.

There is an obvious circularity present here, as Nietzsche's ontology would seem to presuppose his epistemology, which in turn presupposes his ontology, and so on. But such a charge of circularity is far from being a *coup de grace* to Nietzsche's position and, in the last analysis, is not even an interesting objection. The upshot of such an objection is that, as a closed, circular system, Nietzsche's position must be empty and vacuous. And this can only mean that Nietzsche's epistemology fails to provide a mode of access to the "real world," or fails to provide grounds for a relationship of adequate correspondence. Such a charge is ultimately too superficial to be worthy of refutation, assuming as it does that cognitive statements or philosophical positions must be tested by comparing them to that world which they purport to represent. And this, as I have repeatedly pointed out, is simply a self-referentially inconsistent, self-defeating proposition. Nietzsche's position, however, is quite consistent with itself or, if one prefers, analytically sound. This is what I mean by the self-grounding character of Nietzsche's epistemology: it need not seek beyond itself for a verifying ground in some noumenal and inaccessible reality; neither must it constantly look over its shoulder, so to speak, to ascertain how well its statements correspond to fixed and eternal verities.

There is, however, another attendant difficulty with this self-grounding or analytically circular nature of Nietzsche's position, which might be phrased like this: how can a philosophical position which, in a manner of speaking, is able only to talk about itself tell us anything worth knowing? How can a self-referentially consistent, self-grounding position such as this avoid empty formality, vacuousness, and triviality?

We must view the proposition that all knowing is perspectival interpretation as a formal structure which, in the sense that it is not grounded
in or restricted to any specific interpretative content, is empty. Yet as a
formal cognitive structure, it can constitute *any particular interpretation* out
of itself, and do this without having to grant ultimate or absolute validity
to any specific interpretation. Again, we see that this position has some
significant advantages over traditional epistemologies. Nietzsche's position
can embrace without difficulty the most diverse, the most contradictory
interpretations: it can include interpretations which are mutually exclusive
on the logical-semantic level without having to affirm one and deny the
other; it can include interpretations which — again on the logical-semantic
level — even contradict this position itself. Nietzsche's scheme is capable
of doing this because it does not restrict itself to one particular interpretation for which exclusive "correctness" is claimed and, since no specific
interpretation can claim to be ultimately "correct," the traditional correspondence theory criteria of correctness or incorrectness simply eva-
porate[3]. Individual interpretations are evaluated not according to how
correct they are with respect to some static reality, but according to their
pragmatic utility in a given context of relationships. Pragmatic utility (or
power value, or degree of will to power) is, of course, a perspectival function. This means only that a specific interpretation may work very well
indeed within one context, but not in another. And this, in turn, is only
another indication of Nietzsche's consistency, of his steadfast refusal to
claim absolute validity, value, or correctness for any specific interpretation
— *including his own!* — and his openness to the possibility that any interpretation may have a power-enhancing function within a particular context of relationships. Nietzsche's polemic against that narrow dogmatism
which insists upon the ultimate validity of a particular interpretation
merely because it has proven itself efficacious within a specific context or
from a particular perspective is by this point so familiar as to require no
further comment.

On a practical level we could say that Nietzsche's cognitive paradigm
has the effect of liberating the individual knower from the restrictive belief
that there must ultimately be one correct view of reality, that there exists
a stable and self-identical world apart from his perceptions which determines the nature of those perceptions, and that he is powerless to change

---

[3] The criteria of the correspondence are interpretations, too, but objectionable because
of their inherent narrowness and inflexibility. Nietzsche could not consistently claim
that the correspondence theory was "incorrect," but simply that it represents a "weak"
or useless interpretation, an interpretation which is ignorant of its own interpretative
nature.

his reality in any substantial manner. If the individual knower embraces Nietzsche's position, he must realize that that world which, for him, is the case is entirely his own creation, constituted out of that factical, existential, immanent context of relationships which that knower is, and subject to any reinterpretation or restructuring which that knower is capable of carrying out. But rather than throwing up our hands in despair over the ultimate instability or meaninglessness of the world, we must embrace Nietzsche's position in a positive manner, as a challenge to continually create and recreate a more satisfactory reality for ourselves. Exactly how many or what type of individuals would be capable of embracing this position and using it creatively (rather than passively and uncritically accepting a conventional world view) must remain an open question. Clearly Nietzsche does not address himself to ὃι πολλοι.

Nietzsche's position that the individual knower literally constitutes his reality may at first appear extravagant. Yet this view is no longer as novel as it once might have been. Robert Ornstein (a psychologist who is not alone in this regard) takes the position that an individual's conscious reality is constructed by means of a process of selecting, editing, and interpreting sensory stimuli, and that an individual's conscious reality is quite literally that individual's creation[4]. Thomas Kuhn, in his analysis of scientific revolutions, indicates that a change in the paradigm in terms of which we view the world is constitutive of fundamental changes in that reality which we experience[5]. Kuhn declines to draw the epistemological conclusions which are inherent to his position, but one may (and with considerable justification) maintain that those paradigm shifts (or reinterpretations of the world) brought about by such seminal thinkers as Copernicus, Galileo, Kant, Freud, Einstein, Heisenberg, *inter alia*, constituted literal restructurings of that world which we experience. To assert that such scientific revolutions or paradigm shifts amount only to new ways of looking at the same world is simply an undemonstrable and unverifiable assertion. If we agree with Nietzsche that reality is always identical with our interpretation of reality, and if the mode of interpretation changes, we must agree that reality is also substantially altered in such an event. I hasten to add that it would be methodologically unsound to regard the two positions (or interpretations) which I mention here as somehow constituting evidence for the correctness of Nietzsche's view. Obviously the content of specific interpretations can do nothing to verify a general principle that all knowing is interpreting. But as fruitful and useful applications

---

[4] Ornstein, op. cit.
[5] Kuhn, op. cit.

of a view parallel to Nietzsche's own (and a great many more examples of this sort could be mentioned), I feel that they are highly illuminating and demonstrative of the vast utility of such a view. And such utility, I think, is all that Nietzsche would ultimately claim for his views. In the last analysis we must do more than merely give our theoretical assent to the proposition that all knowing is interpreting. Nietzsche's intent, I think, is that we must *use* this principle to create new and better interpretations for ourselves, and this would then be both the justification and the verification of his position. Nietzsche's cognitive paradigm is practical in its aims, rather than theoretical.

The will to power does not represent a body of logical statements, the truth of which compels our assent. If nothing else, Nietzsche demonstrates the limitations of such an outlook. The will to power represents, rather, an existential directive which is "verified" only through implementation. To put it more simply, Nietzsche is not asking us to believe something, but to do something, and in so doing to overcome what we have hitherto regarded as insuperable human limitations. If we were to press this point, we should have to say that Nietzsche's principle of creative interpretation is not more "true" than other philosophical positions: it works better; it is more useful. We might imagine Nietzsche saying, "If you do not care for the form I give to things, give things your own. Philosophy is a creative business, and the way is always open. Philosophy is a contest of will with will. Insofar as you oppose my philosophy, you illustrate and confirm it."[6]

We might claim for Nietzsche the dubious distinction of being the most misunderstood and exploited philosopher of recent times. A good many — indeed, probably most — of these misunderstandings have arisen because of Nietzsche's mode of expression. Nietzsche does not attempt to give us a logically coherent body of truths to which we can intellectually assent. Obviously Nietzsche's writings are full of overt and usually intentional contradictions. He uses the same words, e. g. truth, will, knowledge, etc. in so many different and contradictory contexts that one is often not sure of how a particular passage is to be understood. But it is ultimately not a question of the truth of falsity of the content of any particular statement, because this very content — insofar as it claims to correspond to some univocal and unchanging reality — is useless. It is not the logical content of Nietzsche's utterances which is ultimately decisive — and it is in full awareness of its implications that I make this statement — but rather, the direction in which they impel us and the stimulus which they give us. This

---

[6] Danto, p. 230.

is the formal nature of Nietzsche's position that all knowing is perspectival interpretation which I have repeatedly referred to. Nietzsche's statements resist any static conceptualization, and intentionally so. He uses his terms not as concepts or logical termini, but as signs ("Zeichen") and metaphors, whose very lack of univocal meaning serves as a stimulus for us to appropriate them and give them a meaning — and thereby increase our will to power.

Naturally this leaves all doors wide open for unfair appropriation of Nietzsche's writings, and one need only consider the rampant exploitation of Nietzsche which occurred earlier in this century to be furnished with an example of this. Such misuse is perhaps the price Nietzsche must pay for his honesty in adhering to his own principle that there are only interpretations.

The problem of textual interpretation becomes particularly acute in a work of this nature, and one must strive to strike a delicate balance between wholesale exploitation of Nietzsche's writings, and the stifling of Nietzsche's spirit by pedantic adherence to the letter. I have attempted to achieve that balance by letting Nietzsche speak for himself as much as possible. It is hoped that, after having paid careful attention to the notes, Nietzsche's music can still be heard.

APPENDIX

I. Editions of Nietzsche's works cited:

KGW: *Nietzsche, Werke.* Kritische Gesamtausgabe, ed. by G. Colli and M. Montinari, ca. 30 Vols. in eight divisions (Berlin, 1967 ff.).

GA: *Nietzsches Werke* ("Gross-Oktav-Ausgabe"), ed. by E. Förster-Nietzsche et al., 2nd ed., 19 Vols. in three divisions with index (Leipzig, 1901—1913).

II. Key to the abbreviations used:

EH: *Ecce Homo*
FW: *Die fröhliche Wissenschaft*
GD: *Götzendämmerung*
GM: *Zur Genealogie der Moral*
JGB: *Jenseits von Gut und Böse*
MAM: *Menschliches, Allzumenschliches* I, II
MR: *Morgenröte*
Z: *Also sprach Zarathustra*

The above is a listing of the texts cited in the body of this work. Since all of Nietzsche's published works are divided into numbered sections (with the exception of Z in which the sections are not numbered), I have given this reference first when citing any of the listed works, followed by the location of the cited material in KGW (e. g., JGB 22; KGW VI 2, 31). This allows the reader to find any particular quotation in any edition or translation of Nietzsche's works, and also the correct division, volume, and page in KGW. All quotations from Nietzsche's writings, unless otherwise specified, are from KGW. The only instance in which this occurs is with those *Nachlass* fragments which were cited from GA because a) they were not yet included in KGW or b) I was unable to discover them in KGW. Thus, the only quotations from GA are *Nachlass* fragments. In all other particulars I have followed the guidelines established by the editors of the *Nietzsche-Studien* for the manner of citing from KGW given in *Nietzsche-Studien* III/1974, pp. 213 ff.

BIBLIOGRAPHY

I. Editions of Nietzsche's Works Cited:

Nietzsches Werke ("Gross-Oktav-Ausgabe"), ed. by Elisabeth Förster-Nietzsche et al., 2nd ed., 19 Vols. in three divisions with index (Leipzig, Alfred Kröner, 1901—1913).

Nietzsche, Werke, Kritische Gesamtausgabe, ed. by Giorgio Colli and Mazzino Montinari, ca. 30 Vols. in eight divisions (Berlin, Walter de Gruyter, 1967ff.).

II. Other Works Cited:

St. Anselm of Canterbury, "Proslogium," in *Proslogium, Monologium, An Appendix in Behalf of the Fool by Gaunilon, and Cur Deus Homo*, trans. by Sidney Norton Dean (La Salle, Ill., Open Court, 1903).

St. Thomas Aquinas, *Truth*, trans. by Robert W. Mulligan, Vol. I (Chicago, Henry Regnery, 1952).

Aristotle, "De Interpretatione," "De Anima," "Metaphysica," in *The Basic Works of Aristotle*, trans. by Richard McKeon (New York, Random House, 1941).

St. Augustine, "The City of God," "Soliloquies," "On the Trinity," in *Basic Writings of Saint Augustine*, ed. with introduction and notes by Whitney J. Oates, 2 Vols. (New York, Random House, 1948).

—, Against the Academics ("Contra Academicos"), trans. by John J. O'Meara (Westminster, Md., Newman Press, 1951).

Baeumler, Alfred, *Nietzsche der Philosoph und Politiker* (Leipzig, Reclam, 1931).

Baier, H., "Nietzsche als Wissenschaftskritiker," *Zeitschrift für philosophische Forschung* XX/1 (1966), pp 130—143.

Becker, Oskar, "Nietzsches Beweise für seine Lehre von der ewigen Wiederkunft," *Blätter für Deutsche Philosophie* IX (1936), pp. 368—387.

Boyle, Joseph M., Jr., "Self-Referential Inconsistency, Inevitable Falsity and Metaphysical Argumentation," *Metaphilosophy* III/1 (January, 1972), pp. 25—42.

Brinton, Crane, *Nietzsche* (New York, Harper and Row, 1965).

Copleston, Frederick, *Friedrich Nietzsche: Philosopher of Culture* (London, Burns Oates and Washbourne, 1942).

Danto, Arthur C., *Nietzsche as Philosopher* (New York, MacMillan, 1965).

Del Negro, Walter, *Die Rolle der Fiktionen in der Erkenntnistheorie Friedrich Nietzsches*, Bausteine zu einer Philosophie des "Als-Ob" Vol. V (München, Rösl, 1923).

Descartes, Rene, "Meditations on First Philosophy," "The Principles of Philosophy," "Objections and Replies to the Objections," *The Philosophical Works of Descartes*, trans. by Elisabeth S. Haldane and G. R. T. Ross, 2 Vols. (Cambridge, Cambridge University Press, 1970).

Diels, Hermann and Kranz, Walter. *Die Fragmente der Vorsokratiker*, 6th edition (Berlin, Weidmann, 1951—1952).

Doney, Willis, ed., "Descartes" *A Collection of Critical Essays* (Garden City, N. Y., Doubleday, 1967).

Ellenberger, Henri F., *The Discovery of the Unconscious: The History and Evolution of Dynamic Psychiatry* (New York. Basic Books, 1970).

Freud, Sigmund, *The Standard Edition of the Complete Psychological Works of Sigmund Freud*, ed. and trans. by James Strachey in collaboration with Anna Freud et al., 24 Vols. (London, Hogarth Press, 1955—1974).

Fink, Eugen, *Nietzsches Philosophie* (Stuttgart, Kohlhammer, 1960).

Gründer, Karlfried, ed., *Der Streit um Nietzsches "Geburt der Tragödie"* (Hildesheim, Olms, 1969).

Grützmacher, Richard H., *Nietzsche* (Leipzig, 1917).

Harris, Errol E., *Nature, Mind, and Modern Science* (London, Allen and Unwin, 1954).

Heftrich, Eckhard, *Nietzsches Philosophie: Identität von Welt und Nichts* (Frankfurt a. M., Klostermann, 1962).

Heidegger, Martin, *Nietzsche*, 2 Vols. (Pfullingen, Neske, 1961).

—, *Sein und Zeit*, 11th ed. (Tübingen, Niemeyer, 1967).

—, *Vom Wesen des Grundes*, 5th ed. (Frankfurt a. M., Klostermann, 1965).

—, *Unterwegs zur Sprache*, 4th ed. (Pfullingen, Neske, 1971).

—, *Vom Wesen der Wahrheit*, 4th ed. (Frankfurt a. M., Klostermann, 1961).

—, *Einführung in die Metaphysik*, 3rd ed. (Tübingen, Niemeyer, 1966).

Heisenberg, Werner, *Physics and Philosophy* (New York, Harper and Row, 1958).

Heller, Erich, *The Disinherited Mind* (Philadelphia, Dufour and Saifer, 1952).

—, "Wittgenstein and Nietzsche" in *The Artist's Journey into the Interior and Other Essays* (New York, Vintage, 1968).

Husserl, Edmund, "Prolegomena zur reinen Logik," *Logische Untersuchungen* Vol. I, 5th. ed. (Tübingen, Niemeyer, 1967).

Jaspers, Karl, *Nietzsche: Einführung in das Verständnis seines Philosophierens* (Berlin, de Gruyter, 1950).

Jung, Carl G., *The Collected Works of C. G. Jung*, ed. by Herbert Read, Michael Fordham, Gerhard Adler, trans. by R. F. C. Hull, Bollingen Series XX, 17 Vols. (New York, Pantheon, 1959 ff.).

Kant, Immanuel, *Immanuel Kants Werke*, ed. by Ernst Cassirer et al. 9 Vols. (Berlin, Bruno Cassirer, 1922).

Kuhn, Thomas S., *The Structure of Scientific Revolutions*, International Encyclopedia of Unified Science II/2 (Chicago, University of Chicago Press, 1962).

Margenau, Henry, *The Nature of Physical Reality* (New York, McGraw-Hill, 1950).

Mencken, H. L., *The Philosophy of Friedrich Nietzsche* (Port Washington, N. Y., Kennikat, 1967).

Mittasch, Alwin, *Friedrich Nietzsche als Naturphilosoph* (Stuttgart, Alfred Kröner, 1952).

More, Paul Elmer, *Nietzsche* (Boston, Houghton-Mifflin, 1912).

Müller-Lauter, Wolfgang, *Nietzsche: Seine Philosophie der Gegensätze und die Gegensätze seiner Philosophie* (Berlin, Walter de Gruyter, 1971).

—, "Nietzsches Lehre vom Willen zur Macht," *Nietzsche-Studien* III/1974, pp. 1—60.

Nagel, Ernest, *The Structure of Science: Problems in the Logic of Scientific Explanation* (New York, Harcourt, Brace, and World, 1961).

Ornstein, Robert E., *The Psychology of Consciousness* (San Francisco, W. H. Freeman, 1972).

Plato, "Republic," "Phaedo," "Philebus," "Statesman," "Theatetus," *The Collected Dialogues of Plato*, ed. by Edith Hamilton and Huntington Cairns, Bollingen Series LXXI (Princeton, Princeton University Press, 1961).

Pöggeler, Otto, "Sein als Ereignis," *Zeitschrift für philosophische Forschung* XIII/4 (1959), pp. 599—632.

Quine, Willard Van Orman, *Word and Object* (Cambridge, Massachusetts Institute of Technology Press, 1960).

—, *Ontological Relativity and Other Essays* (New York, Columbia University Press, 1969).

Reichenbach, Hans, *The Rise of Scientific Philosophy* (Berkeley and Los Angeles, University of California Press, 1963).

Riehl, Alois, *Friedrich Nietzsche, Der Künstler und der Denker* (Stuttgart, Frommann, 1923).

Schlechta, Karl and Anders, Anni, *Friedrich Nietzsche: von den verborgenen Anfängen seines Philosophierens* (Stuttgart-Bad Cannstatt, Frommann, 1962).

Schopenhauer, Arthur, *Schopenhauers Sämmtliche Werke*, ed. by E. Griesbach, 6 Vols. (Leipzig, Reclam, 1890).

Schutz, Alfred, *The Phenomonology of the Social World*, trans. by George Walsh and Frederick Lehnert, with an introduction by Frederick Lehnert (Evanston, Ill., Northwestern University Press, 1967).

Simmel, Georg, *Schopenhauer und Nietzsche* (Leipzig, Duncker und Humblot, 1907).

Urmson, J. O., *Philosophical Analysis: Its Development Between the Two World Wars* (Oxford, Oxford University Press, 1967).

Vaihinger, Hans, *Die Philosophie des 'Als-Ob'* (Berlin, Reuther und Reichard, 1902).

—, *Nietzsche als Philosoph* (Berlin, Reuther und Reichard, 1916).

Vogel, Martin, *Apollinisch und Dionysisch: Geschichte eines genialen Irrtums* (Regensburg, Bosse, 1966).

Walsh, H. W., *Metaphysics* (New York, Harcourt, Brace, and World, 1963).

Wilcox, John T., *Truth and Value in Nietzsche: A Study of his Metaethics and Epistemology*, foreword by Walter Kaufmann (Ann Arbor, University of Michigan Press, 1974).

Wittgenstein, Ludwig, *Tractatus Logico-Philosophicus: The German Text of Ludwig Wittgenstein's "Logisch-philosophische Abhandlung"*, trans. by D. F. Pears and B. F. McGuiness, introduction by Bertrand Russell (London, Routledge and Kegan Paul, 1961).

Windelband, Wilhelm, *Lehrbuch der Geschichte der Philosophie*, 15th ed., ed. by Heinz Heimsoeth (Tübingen, Mohr-Siebeck, 1957).

Woozley, Anthony D., *Theory of Knowledge* (London, Hutchinson, 1949).

III. Additional Works Relating to Nietzsche's Theory of Knowledge:

Bindschedler, Maria, *Nietzsche und die Poetische Lüge* (Berlin, Walter de Gruyter, 1966).

Breazeale, James D., *Towards a Nihilist Epistemology: Hume and Nietzsche* (New Haven, Yale University Press, 1971).

Beub, Bernhard, *Nietzsches Kritik der Praktischen Vernunft* (Stuttgart, Klett, 1970).

Eisler, Rudolf, *Nietzsches Erkenntnistheorie und Metaphysik: Darstellung und Kritik* (Leipzig, Hermann Haacke, 1902).

Flemming, Siegbert, *Nietzsches Metaphysik und ihr Verhältnis zur Erkenntnistheorie und Ethik* (Berlin, Simion, 1914).

Granier, Jean, *Le Problème de la Vérité dans la philosophie de Nietzsche* (Paris, Editions du Seuil, 1966).

Graumann, C. F., *Grundlagen einer Phänomenologie und Psychologie der Perspektivität* (Berlin, Walter de Gruyter, 1960).

Heidegger, Martin, "Nietzsches Wort 'Gott ist tot'" in *Holzwege*, 15th ed. (Frankfurt a. M., Klostermann, 1963), pp. 193—247.

Sallis, John, "Nietzsche's Underworld of Truth," *Philosophy Today*, Vol. XVI, Number 1/4 (Spring, 1972), pp. 12—19.

—, "Nietzsche and the Problem of Knowledge," *Tulane Studies in Philosophy* XVIII (1969), pp. 105—122.

INDEX OF SUBJECTS

In this index I have combined the references for those terms which are English-German cognates (e. g. will, *Wille*); where synonymous terms are not cognates (e. g. truth, *Wahrheit*), I have listed them separately. A term which occurs in a footnote is identified by an "n" after the page on which it appears (e. g. 157n).

INDEX OF NAMES

Walter de Gruyter
Berlin · New York

Monographien und Texte zur Nietzsche-Forschung

Herausgegeben von Mazzino Montinari,
Wolfgang Müller-Lauter und Heinz Wenzel

Groß-Oktav. Ganzleinen

Peter Heller

„Von den ersten und letzten Dingen"

Studien und Kommentar zu einer
Aphorismenreihe von Friedrich Nietzsche

XLII, 512 Seiten. 1972. DM 110,—
ISBN 3 11 003943 5
(Band 1)

Heinz Röttges

Nietzsche und die Dialektik der Aufklärung

Untersuchungen zum Problem einer humanistischen Ethik

VIII, 269 Seiten. 1972. DM 98,—
ISBN 3 11 004018 2
(Band 2)

Richard Frank Krummel

Nietzsche und der deutsche Geist

Ausbreitung und Wirkung des Nietzscheschen Werkes
im deutschen Sprachraum bis zum Todesjahr des Philosophen

Ein Schriftumsverzeichnis der Jahre 1867 bis 1900
XX, 290 Seiten. 1974. DM 112,—
ISBN 3 11 004019 0
(Band 3)

Preisänderungen vorbehalten

Walter de Gruyter
Berlin · New York

Nietzsche · Werke
Kritische Gesamtausgabe

Herausgegeben von Giorgio Colli und Mazzino Montinari
Etwa 30 Bände in 8 Abteilungen. Groß-Oktav. Ganzleinen

Bisher erschienen:

Abteilung III: Band 1 und Band 2

Abteilung IV: Band 1 bis Band 4

Abteilung V

Band 1: Morgenröthe. Nachgelassene Fragmente (Anfang 1880 bis Frühjahr 1881).
IV, 772 Seiten. 1971. DM 78,—; einzeln DM 86,—

Band 2: Idyllen aus Messina. Die fröhliche Wissenschaft. Nachgelassene Fragmente Frühjahr 1881 bis Sommer 1882.
VIII, 587 Seiten. 1973. DM 84,—; einzeln DM 92,—

Abteilung VI

Band 1: Also sprach Zarathustra. Ein Buch für Alle und Keinen (1883 bis 1885)
IV, 410 Seiten. 1968. DM 34,—; einzeln DM 41,—

Band 2: Jenseits von Gut und Böse. Zur Genealogie der Moral. (1886 bis 1887)
IV, 436 Seiten. 1968. DM 36,—; einzeln DM 43,—

Band 3: Der Fall Wagner. Götzen-Dämmerung. Nachgelassene Schriften. (August 1888 bis Anfang 1889): Der Antichrist. Ecce homo. Dionysos-Dithyramben. Nietzsche contra Wagner.
IV, 449 Seiten. 1969. DM 38,—; einzeln DM 45,—

Abteilung VII

Band 1: Nachgelassene Fragmente Juli 1882 bis Winter 1883—84.
VIII, 720 Seiten. 1977. DM 128,—; einzeln DM 138,—

Band 2: Nachgelassene Fragmente Frühjahr bis Herbst 1884.
IV, 323 Seiten. 1974. DM 62,—; einzeln DM 68,—

Band 3: Nachgelassene Fragmente Herbst 1884 bis Herbst 1885.
IV, 472 Seiten. 1974. DM 86,—; einzeln DM 92,—

Abteilung VIII

Band 1: Nachgelassene Fragmente Herbst 1885 bis Herbst 1887.
XII, 368 Seiten. 1974. DM 66,—; einzeln DM 72,—

Band 2: Nachgelassene Fragmente Herbst 1887 bis März 1888.
XII, 478 Seiten. 1970. DM 52,—; einzeln DM 58,—

Band 3: Nachgelassene Fragmente Anfang 1888 bis Anfang Januar 1889.
X, 481 Seiten. 1972. DM 68,—; einzeln DM 74,—

Preisänderungen vorbehalten

Sonderprospekt auf Anforderung vom Verlag